P9-CMX-737

PRINCIPLES OF
INDUSTRIAL THERAPY
FOR THE MENTALLY ILL

BERTRAM J. BLACK, M.S.W.

Professor of Psychiatry (Rehabilitation)
Albert Einstein College of Medicine

Executive Consultant
Altro Health and Rehabilitation Services

Director of Mental Health Rehabilitation Services
Bronx State Hospital, New York

GRUNE & STRATTON
NEW YORK · LONDON

Consulting Editor, Leopold Bellak, M.D.

Library of Congress Catalog Number 73-88017

Printed in the United States of America

(G-B)

To Rose, Bruce, Paul and Anne

PREFACE

This analysis of the principles of industrial therapy for the mentally ill is designed to present the underlying concepts that have governed the development of this rehabilitative approach both in the United States and abroad. It is intended also as an introduction to the variety of programs and methods that now prevail. For the first time it provides an overview of both voluntary and governmental industrial therapy services in the context of the evolution of programs for the rehabilitation of the physically handicapped, as well as those for the treatment and restoration of the mentally ill.

This book has been long in the making. It is based upon more than a quarter century of service as administrator and chief professional officer in agencies treating the mentally ill and emotionally disturbed, and in a center for rehabilitating the physically and mentally handicapped. It incorporates what I have learned as a consultant to both the Rehabilitation Services Administration of the Federal Social and Rehabilitation Services and the National Institute of Mental Health, Health and Mental Health Services Administration, U.S. Department of Health, Education, and Welfare. The gathering of much of the data about industrial therapy in Western Europe was made possible under a grant from the National Institute of Mental Health (MH-1405). The bibliographical research and writing of this book were aided by NIMH project grant MH-2628.

So many professional friends and colleagues have shared in my "on-the-job" education over the years that it would take too much space to thank them individually. I am especially grateful, however, to my co-workers at Altro—the professional staff at Altro Health and Rehabilitation Services; the work supervisors and managers at Altro Workshops; as well as the dedicated, understanding, and highly knowledgeable members of the Altro Board of Directors.

Bertram J. Black

FOREWORD

Mr. Black, in his current position as a professor of psychiatry and rehabilitation, has managed to occupy positions in two very important and profound social movements. Both mental health and rehabilitation are social movements based on humanism, pragmatism, and comprehensiveness. Mr. Black's monograph is comprehensive, not only within the usual parameters, but also in its historical background and thorough review of industrial therapy and rehabilitation based on experiences throughout the world. He has also recorded his experiences, put them in perspective, and produced for us a mental health rehabilitation travelogue that both entertains and educates.

Many important areas are covered. There are intriguing excursions into the economics of work activity. For, in many industrial workshops, the contractor is subsidized, thereby changing the relationship of work to labor economics. One looks forward to a similar review of the role of work in other rehabilitation settings, such as prisons, to broaden this perspective. Overall, the book's international perspective helps us to identify and understand several complex issues.

This book is also relevant to the current issue of "delivery of services and delivery systems." Mr. Black describes suggested models that perhaps should be imported to the United States. Of great interest is the contrast between the American programs that emphasize the mentally ill, while Europeans give equal time to the retarded.

Mr. Black has covered a broad field in depth. The result is a useful and important "state of the art" review of one of man's most important social endeavors.

Bertram S. Brown, M.D.
Deputy Director
National Institute of Mental Health

CONTENTS

CHAPTER I

INTRODUCTION

THE GROWING INTEREST IN INDUSTRIAL THERAPY
FOR THE MENTALLY ILL

Work consumes one third of the daily time of a wage earner; it is thus one of the most important aspects of his life. For one, like the patient in a mental hospital, who has had his work life interrupted, its re-establishment becomes of prime importance in his cure or rehabilitation. To a varying extent work for patients has been used in the treatment of the mentally ill for over a hundred years.

Before the large state hospitals evolved in the late 1800's and after Pinel had removed the chains from his lunatics in the closing years of the previous century, the mentally ill had been housed in small institutions. Their illness was looked upon as a moral failure, and forms of "moral therapy" were much in vogue. Idleness was considered dissonant with godliness. Prayer, good manners, and occupied hands and minds were prescribed by the institution directors, more often clergymen than physicians. In 1812 Dr. Benjamin Rush, who directed one such insane asylum, quoted the poet William Cowper in support of work as moral therapy: "Absence of occupation is not rest; a mind quite vacant is a mind distress'd."[142] He could as easily have quoted another line of Cowper's, "An idler is a watch that wants both hands; as useless if it goes as if it stands."[45] Particularly in New England and on the eastern seaboard, the cradle of American institutional care for the insane, the Calvinistic philosophy prevailed on the virtue of work, both physical and mental. As Alexander Pope had expressed it, "But strength of mind is exercise, not rest."[136]

In time both an increasing patient population and, after the findings of Kraepelin, an increasing shift to a "medical" rather than a "moral" explanation for insanity brought great pressures on the small number of "alienists" available and a deterioration in treatment. Dorothea Dix and her followers had exposed the jailing and maltreatment of the mentally ill, and the efforts of Clifford Beers and his National Committee for Mental Hygiene had brought about the establishment of the state hospital system. Work, if used at all for patients, was tailored to the needs of the hospital— its laundry, its maintenance force, its sewing and upholstery repairs, its farms and gardens, and to a more limited extent, its library and offices. Most patients, because of symptoms and restraints, were not available for much work, and what they did do was considered necessary to the economy of the institution rather than to the therapy of the patients. These state

1

hospitals, with 2000 to 20,000 patients each, were not really hospitals. They were little cities, whose population increased by admissions and declined mainly through deaths. Some form of "self-help" by using patients was necessary, for staffs were never large enough and efficiency almost always at low ebb.

A few forward-looking medical superintendents thought of patients' labor as potential "industrial therapy," but quite a number of cynical or exploitive directors gave but lip service to the concept. In the United States, the term "industrial therapy" came to have a queezy connotation, as with "prison labor." This was not so in Great Britain where, during the late 1920's and early 1930's, a few English mental hospitals did bring simple bench assembly work in on contract with local industry for patients to work on.[26] Rehabilitation was not the goal in those years, however, for there was little expectation that many of the patients would return to their homes. It was rather that repetitive work made patients more manageable and it occupied their time. As William Faulkner expresses it so aptly, ". . . One of the saddest things is that the thing a man can do for eight hours a day, day after day, is work. You can't eat eight hours a day nor drink for eight hours a day nor make love for eight hours—all you can do for eight hours is work."[109] How successful these British programs might have been was never proven, for the Great Depression dried up the sources of work.

The nugget of truth in Faulkner's statement remains. What else than work has the potential of utilizing a patient's time and energies for hours at a time? Since World War II, as the pharmacological revolution has occurred in managing mental patients, interest in industrial therapy has risen again. The time formerly used by patients lodged in restraints, in withdrawal, undergoing immersion baths or electroconvulsive therapy or other management of disturbed behavior has now become available—for what? Psychotherapy, individual and groups, recreational diversions, occupational thrapy, all can occupy but a few hours a week, week after week.

Once the new drugs had demonstrated that the gross symptoms of mental illness could be relieved, therapists began to turn their attention to techniques that could re-establish or increase the functioning capabilities of their patients. From the experiments of Maxwell Jones during World War II with the use of a "therapeutic community" at England's Belmont Hospital have come a number of demonstrations in milieu therapy.[95] In essence, these attempt to recreate within the hospital such living conditions as require the patients to participate in the kinds of activities and decision-making expected of adults in the outside world. It was logical in this context to introduce some work activities into the "therapeutic milieu." Primarily the forms of work used have been either activities relevant to homemaking (cooking, personal sewing) or activities from the hospital's internal maintenance and repair programs.

It was only when it became apparent that many patients could move beyond manageability in the institution and actually be returned to their home communities that "milieu therapy" changed its focus from a technique to "milieu rehabilitation" as a program. The introduction of day hospitals for the treatment of the mentally ill, with their great emphasis on maintaining the patient's abilities in the tasks of daily living, have given impetus to milieu rehabilitation. Among the more interesting examples of day hospital milieu rehabilitation, including industrial therapy as a component, have been those at the Butler Health Center, Providence, Rhode Island, at the Soundview-Throgs Neck Community Mental Health Center, Bronx, New York and at the Mapperly Hospital, Nottingham, England.

The Butler Hospital program uses the physical facilities of what was formerly a private mental institution strongly based in "moral therapy." It provides occupational therapy, arts and crafts, gymnasium, bowling alleys, nature study room, auditorium. For work activities there are a greenhouse, printing, carpentry and jewelry-making shops, a paint shop, work programs on the farm and in-hospital maintenance (including kitchen and cafeteria) and contract work brought in from local industry. The term "milieu rehabilitation" was coined at Butler Hospital.[83]

The Soundview-Throgs Neck Community Mental Health Center is one of the more recently developed comprehensive programs for psychiatric care. Its industrial therapy shop takes in light bench assembly work from local industries. The patients spend part of each day in groups assigned to the "work-for-pay" program.[175] The rest of each day is utilized by a variety of activities including the group dynamics of the therapeutic community.

The Nottingham program is part of a world famous pioneer community mental health service. Industrial therapy, though, is available only for day hospital patients and consists of rather simple bench work contracted from local businesses. The Physician Superintendent, Dr. Duncan Macmillan, sums up the advantages of his work program as embracing both utilization of time of patients as well as incorporating rehabilitation purposes.[27]

THE HOSPITAL—COMMUNITY CONTINUUM

It is the growing recognition that an ever-increasing number of mental patients can cross the bridge back from hospital to community that has given real impetus to the development of industrial therapy. If medication can control the bizarre symptoms, then the right combination of living arrangements, including work activities, should make it possible for the patients to leave the hospitals. At the same time such a combination of medical, domiciliary and work therapeutics should make it possible to retain many mentally ill people in their home communities who would formerly have been sent to state mental hospitals.

The use of a sheltered work environment outside of a hospital as a haven or transition for psychiatric patients was conceived at the end of World War I. The British Ex-Service Mental Welfare Society established Thermega, Ltd., just outside London soon after the war to provide work for "shell-shocked" veterans. Altro Work Shops in New York was serving mentally ill tuberculous patients in the early 1920's. Not until the 1950's, however, did the idea begin to unfold of using sheltered workshops or industrial therapy units as part of the hospital and community mental health developments. Altro Work Shops began to admit dischargees from mental hospitals in 1953, a number of British mental hospitals started industrial therapeutic programs in the middle 1950's and the Dutch and West Germans followed suit. Almost simultaneously the Russian mental hospital programs set up industrial units, and similar programs were reported from Australia to Scandinavia.

In the United States there have been four federal programs that have spurred the development of industrial therapy. The first of these was the Vocational Rehabilitation Act of 1954 which qualified services to the mentally ill among those to other handicapped. Second, the Veterans Administration set up demonstrations using work therapy in certain of its mental hospitals. Third, the Hospital Improvement Grants Program of the National Institute of Mental Health has made funds available to every state hospital for demonstrated improvements, and a number of the hospitals have chosen rehabilitation programs including industrial therapy. Finally, the Comprehensive Community Mental Health Services Act of 1966 provides that rehabilitation services be included as one of the ten recommended for a full program. In a rapidly increasing number of instances, the new mental health centers are defining rehabilitation so as to include some form of industrial therapy.

Occupational to Industrial Therapy?

So much for its development, but just what is industrial therapy? According to the Chief of the Physical Medicine and Rehabilitation Service, Veterans Administration,[101]

> Industrial therapy may be defined as the therapeutic use of hospital maintenance and other related projects for helping the patient in his behavioral and economic adjustment. It has become an accepted physical medicine and rehabilitation modality in psychiatric hospitals. Properly applied, properly managed, and properly supervised, it

offers an extremely useful treatment medium. The activities must be
selected to meet the needs of the individual patient and must provide
an opportunity to obtain acceptance, encouragement, and further
motivation in a true work situation.

His emphasis on selection of activity to meet the patient's need and the
reference to "a true work situation" constitute the clinical essentials of
any industrial therapy program.

In a very real sense, today's industrial therapy programs have grown out
of the occupational therapy services of earlier decades. Formal occupational therapy was introduced into the mental hospitals during World
War I when crafts and skills that had been found valuable in restoring the
physically disabled were adapted to the treatment of the mentally ill. Prior
to this period, sanction had long been given to use of patients in the so-
called hospital industries on the grounds that this was "occupational
therapy." In fact it was a distortion of the theory of moral therapy that
work per se has a remedial effect on mental illness. Occupational therapists
were given responsibility for a wide variety of activity programs in the hospitals. When they accepted these responsibilities, they quickly lost identity
with their professional background. When they resisted movement from
their more traditional role of teaching and supervising arts and crafts used
on prescription of the physician, they were supplanted by an array of
specialized "therapists"—recreational therapist, art, corrective, manual arts,
educational, music, horticultural, library therapists.

In a critique of occupational therapy as practiced in mental hospitals 10
years ago, and the picture is only gradually changing today, Wittkower and
Azima classify the O.T.'s in two groups. The first is interested mainly in
finding some work that will stimulate the patients' interest outside of themselves; the second concentrates on matching program to meet specific
symptom conditions such as social withdrawal, aggressive tendencies, in-
continence of bladder or bowel, etc. Both groups show little evidence of
sufficient understanding of psychiatry or dynamic psychology, and thus
occupational therapists are given low status by the psychiatric staffs.[181]

The evolution of industrial therapy as a rehabilitation procedure and
the introduction of work processes from normal industry broadened the
horizon for occupational therapists. In the Veterans Administration in
this country and in a few of the British mental hospitals, occupational
therapists have embraced industrial therapy and made it their own. In many
of our state institutions the occupational therapists have remained aloof.
Psychiatric nurses and aides have been only too willing to fill in the gap.

At first glance it would seem that a repetitive bench assembly task or
maintenance service offers much less opportunity for matching the activity
to the patient's need. More careful consideration reveals, however, that the

real work situation has a diversity of elements in it, no matter how mundane the work task, that far exceeds the complexity of the arts and crafts situation. There are opportunities for using the group situation dynamically; the skills required are often more complicated than they initially appear; the procedures of production, quality control and supervisory relationships can be modified to meet a range of patient needs, as can motivations and working conditions.

The old, and now frowned upon, uses of hospital industries to put patients to work are all but vanishing from our mental hospitals. This is in part because of changing economic conditions and in part because of changes in the methods of psychiatric treatment. A few years ago the Subcommittee on Tertiary Prevention of the American Public Health Association's Program Area Committee on Mental Health summed up the place of work in a mental hospital as follows[176]:

> For many years in America any patient able to work was expected to do so *in the service of the hospital.* If he was not desocialized to the point where it was considered useless to attempt to make him work or if he was not physically ill, he was expected to perform one of a series of tasks supposed to benefit the hospital. Frequently the work was sheerest drudgery, and often had to be performed under conditions of danger or discomfort, making impossible the obtaining of other workers.
>
> It was often said that these hospitals "could not operate without patient labor." It is unfortunate that in many cases this was a true statement. The hospitals reached an unhappy equilibrium where a great deal of inefficient patient labor was necessary to keep a hospital going, since the hospital had neither adequate equipment nor trained staff for getting essential work done. On the one hand, these were usually the best preserved of the chronic patients, many of whom could have been rehabilitated or discharged from the hospital. In many cases, their usefulness to the hospital, togther with the absence of any source of appreciation and satisfaction for them in the community, was a factor in their continued hospitalization. On the other hand, their labor with inadequate tools was so inefficient that, even at the cost of their maintenance, it was uneconomic. Revulsion over the abuses of this system has led, in some quarters, to a complete about-face, where it is felt that patients should not be forced to work for their keep and should not even be allowed to do so. The potentially beneficial value of work under proper clinical supervision is easily lost from view in this controversy.

Changes in the economy have led gradually to the elimination of hospital industrial work that formerly absorbed substantial numbers of patients, such as sewing rooms (sheets, pillowcases and shifts) and upholstery shops. Also, the use of chemotherapy has, over this past decade, reduced the average length of stay and turned back to the community many patients who formerly became part of the labor pool for hospital industries. The residual load in the hospitals has gotten older, practically a geriatrics population by now, and presents one of the more serious planning problems for future mental health programming. Some of the difficulties to even adequate ·clinical use of hospital industries were illustrated a few years ago in one state hospital's experience. This hospital obtained a research demonstration grant to use its maintenance and service staff as instructors of patients so that the patients could move out of the hospital prepared as housekeeping and building maintenance workers. The demonstration was most effective, and the group of patients included were fairly quickly discharged. The hospital then discovered to its chagrin that its regular staff, now raised to instructor level, were not skilled enough teachers to cope with the next echelon of sicker, more deteriorated patients.

It is therefore obvious why bringing in contract work from outside business and industry is appealing to many hospital administrators. The hospital has the potential work force, and usually has space and available supervision. If simple enough work can be obtained, of the bench assembly type or "gesinter" (this goes into that) variety, an industrial therapy shop can be launched. It is true that the major requirements for an industrial therapy program are simply work to be done, a labor supply of patients, supervision, space and equipment—the deceptively simple elements of any productive business. Industrial therapy, however, is more complex than that, and it is the purpose of this introduction to make the components clear and the issues understandable.

INDUSTRIAL THERAPY DEFINED

Some confusion in the literature results from interchangeable use of such terms as "sheltered workshop," "rehabilitation workshop" and "work-for-pay program" with industrial therapy. In this book the term "industrial therapy" is used in a generic sense to include all of those rehabilitation and resocialization programs for mental patients in which activities of the world of work are utilized, most usually in simulation of a real work situation. A sheltered workshop is a small business, under nonprofit auspices, operated for the purpose of rehabilitating persons who have handicaps or disabilities or for the employment of handicapped people who cannot be expected to compete in the normal labor market. Many sheltered workshops actually serve both purposes. An industrial therapy shop may be a sheltered workshop by this definition, but it may not be.

It is important to point out that the definition of sheltered workshop is different in Europe than in America. There the term is reserved for the second purpose, that of relatively permanent employment of the handicapped. It is understood that industrial therapy (or what is referred to in

France as "ergo-therapy" and in Germany as *beschützende* work) refers to transitional programs through which the patient is expected to move either back into the normal labor market or into an "extended care" sheltered workshop. This latter title uses the terminology of the 1967 amendments to the Federal Vocational Rehabilitation Act. A "rehabilitation workshop" is a less well-defined title, usually used for a sheltered workshop linked with an array of medical and social services as part of a rehabilitation program. Rehabilitation workshops are always "industrial therapy" as the term is used herein.

SOME UNDERLYING CONCEPTS AS TO VALUE

Before describing some of the existing industrial therapy programs for the mentally ill in Europe and in the United States and then examining in detail the structure and organization of industrial therapy, it will be well to discuss some of the underlying concepts that explain its use and value.

The patients for whom industrial therapy programs have been devised are for the most part chronically mentally ill and in state mental hospitals or their equivalents. The majority of these patients are diagnosed as schizophrenic. The tie-lines of these unfortunate people are tenuous at best to the experiences of normal living—family responsibilities, socialization, work habits, etc. The newer treatment approaches of open door hospital, milieu therapy and chemotherapeutics have reduced their grossest symptoms of withdrawal or hyperactivity, have removed most of the dangers to self and others that were characteristics of the earlier "lunatics." The diminution of symptoms, nevertheless, still leaves most of these patients quite handicapped in their abilities to perform as wage earners. In addition to their residual disabilities, which in many cases are very great, a large proportion of the patients come from low educational, cultural and socio-economic levels and have few job skills and frequently, as a result of their illness, a spotty job history.

The traditional approaches of vocational rehabilitation, the procedure of preserving, restoring or developing work abilities for persons who are mentally or physically disabled, in which vocational counseling collaborates with medical and social services, have proven of quite limited value in serving such mental patients. The introduction of industrial therapy has made it possible for vocational rehabilitation to be carried on with greater success, as will be described later. As Dr. Oseas of the Veterans Administration says in summing up an examination of work dilemmas for the recovering psychotic patient,[131]

> The vocational rehabilitation of the psychotic is a difficult undertaking and the techniques for accomplishing it are limited by the incompleteness of our understanding of the real nature of his work

handicaps. Estranged as he is from the world of objects and indifferent to its rewards, concerned with the maintenance of a vulnerable integrity rather than with the development of potentials, lacking the life and work goals toward which a firm personal identity impels, the psychotic is indeed profoundly handicapped. Yet, his survival as a person depends upon his success in finding opportunities for identification, esteem, belonging, and mastery. For him, as for the vast majority of other members of complex industrialized societies, the world of work can potentially provide such opportunities. A carefully structured work setting, with its positive meanings for security to the recovering psychotic, would therefore appear to be a proper starting place for his social restoration.

In another context this author has referred to the psychiatric rehabilitation workshop as providing the three "S's" that mark the role of employment in our culture—salary, status and success.[32] Certainly one of the major means of identifying an individual in our society is by his job. A person is more likely to be defined as an engineer or doctor or clerical worker or factory worker or carpenter or farm hand than as a father, homeowner, tenant or husband. Even housewife, or the more recently preferred title of homemaker, is a designation of type of work. The assignment of a mental patient to a work role is important to his rehabilitation. It is quite significant that in the experience of Altro Work Shops as well as other industrial therapy programs, many patients consider they are "applying for work" and "going to work" rather than entering into rehabilitation.

The importance of work to the ego has been treated at length in the psychological and psychiatric literature. Whether one subscribes to work as an "executant function" of the ego, as does Ives Hendrick, or as a "highly integrated ego activity serving self-preservation," as does Barbara Lantos, it appears to those experienced in rehabilitating the handicapped that the ability to work is often one of the least damaged, or perhaps the last damaged, areas of the ego.[127] For this reason, work would seem to lend itself well as a take-off point for restoration or restructuring of functioning abilities. Such a concept also fits in well with another rehabilitation principle that seems to be as valid for the mentally as for the physically handicapped, that of beginning rehabilitation efforts as close to the onset of the disability as is possible. Industrial therapy as part of the total treatment approach thus becomes imperative.

Two attempts to conceptually explain industrial therapy come from practical psychiatric experience. The first is from Manhattan State Hospital where Drs. Denber and Rajotte ran one of the early modern work therapy units. They say,[47]

Work therapy differs from occupational therapy in that it takes place as part of a total process (therapeutic community), rests upon continuous movement, has a realistic incentive (pay), and presents a goal—rehabilitation for the post-discharge period. Not only does it permit the patient to satisfy inner needs, but it fosters interpersonal relations. . . .

The psychiatric hospital's artificial environment has been recognized long ago, and custodialism is a symptom of this era. The shop (work therapy)* becomes one function of a new environment which now is structured to be neutral, yet warm. It is supportive but does not create dependency. It is permissive but sets limits and boundaries for behavior. It is flexible, yet rigid enough to support the psychotic ego-structure which is in a continuous state of dissolution ⇆ reconstruction. The shop, then, becomes therapeutic because it provides a continuum of these positive factors throughout the day. It is insufficient to use potent drugs, group and individual therapies, music, art and recreational therapies, and then leave the patient "to rest" for the larger part of the day.

The theoretical premise held here is that the schizophrenic ego has lost its boundaries and structure as well as its reality attachments and fixation. The psychotic patient is literally a rowboat adrift in mountainous seas without oars, compass, or food. While the analytic hour or phenothiazine tablet may provide food, it still leaves a patient without direction or ability to move independently. The psychotic patient requires an extraordinary amount of support which varies inversely with the degree of illness. This must be given continuously, all day long by physicians and nurse, and demands the highest and most sincere type of staff.

One of the major difficulties with most treatments is not so much their empiricism but their transitory nature in the eyes of the patient. Work, therefore, offers the patient a fixation point, a daily boundary, and a well-marked path to follow. These parameters must be shifted as the illness becomes less severe and proceeds to resolution.

Since the reality of life is represented by human beings (interpersonal relationships) which have theoretically precipitated the breakdown, the return to reality should optimally take place via inanimate objects. To this end, work becomes therapeutic in that it permits an elementary primitive object fixation which is neutral and non-threatening in a supportive field.

A more psychodynamic interpretation is offered out of the experience of a community-based rehabilitation workshop, Altro Work Shops, Bronx, New York, resulting from work with patients from a mental hospital. They say,[13]

The fact is that all psychiatric disorder involves disturbances in object relationships. . . . All psychiatric therapy in turn has to address itself to the improvement of object relations, be it in terms of perceptual, executive, or libidinal functioning. Originally, only custodial care was made available. Psychological phenomena, as

---

* Parentheses added by author.

we increasingly know, have a homeostatic tendency toward spontaneously achieving some equilibrium again; custodial removal from disturbing stimuli (e.g., burdensome relations to members of the family) permitted some spontaneous improvements to take place.

Modern psychiatry, of course, supplies psychotherapy; also modern psychiatry supplies somatic therapies—shock treatment, lobotomy, and drugs. In spite of these therapies, there is a proportion of patients who still fall short of the improvement necessary to be able to live happily as members of society after all these methods have been judiciously applied. In these instances, the rehabilitation workshop comes into play: it offers restructuring of object relations by providing an environment which allows for trial and error in relearning in an actual life situation (instead of the artificial hothouse conditions of the hospital), but without the immediate dire consequences of error in the real world—where one quickly gets fired from a job or ostracized, etc.

The rehabilitation workshop, then, is an intermediary station between the hospital atmosphere and the real world, and by that definition alone—the finer steps of adjustments it permits—a therapeutic instrument. In addition, the workshop has its staff available to structure the psychological life space, can vary the nature of the task and the nature of the co-workers, and can help the patient to bear conflict in the object relations. . . . The whole atmosphere is one of a reasonably positive transference, with rewards for maturation and with interpretations (which are perceived as mild disapproval very often) for regressive behavior. The whole group structure tends to produce a situation competitive in terms of achievement of "health."

Dr. Leopold Bellak, who developed the conceptual explanation for Altro, likened the workshop setting to that of Arthur Schopenhauer's parable which compared social relations to the problems of some porcupines on a cold winter day. When the porcupines began to freeze, they moved together only to hurt each other with their quills. When they moved apart, they froze. By moving back and forth, freezing and hurting, they finally found the optimum distance so as to provide each other warmth without hurting each other too much.[15] Such is one use of the industrial therapy setting by the patients.

Much can be said of the value of the industrial therapy program for observation of and evaluation of patients. The Manhattan State Hospital report noted that "The shop offers a valuable observation post not available in the ward or in the interview. Here, the patient is seen interacting with others and functioning at the most effective level for a given period of the illness. The work record is a valuable prognostic indicator which sometimes antedates by many days an improvement or recrudescence of symptoms."[48] Such uses of industrial therapy, as well as its usefulness in skill training and as a setting for operant conditioning for teaching new habits of work, will be dealt with more fully in a later chapter.

ECONOMIC VALUE

One characteristic of industrial therapy and of sheltered work infrequently referred to is its economic value. In this computer age of interest in cost benefit analysis and in program planning budgeting (PPB), it is important to at least understand the economic issues. Rehabilitation specialists are fond of pointing out that vocational rehabilitation which results in the return of a handicapped person to wage productivity in the normal labor market is an economic plus for society. They calculate the cost of providing counseling and training and medical services, et al., and match this sum against either the total of future expected earnings of the rehabilitee (as a contribution to the Gross National Product) or his expected income tax payments over his remaining work productive years. The balance is always impressively in favor of the dollar return to society. From an accounting standpoint, many questions could be raised about the adequacy of such measures; many of the costs to the handicapped person and to the community may not have been included in the calculations. Nevertheless, in terms of an individual who has been successfully rehabilitated, there can be little question that the debits will be overcome by credits.

The economic assessment of a program serving the handicapped is much more complex than accounting for the individual. So far as sheltered work for the seriously disabled is concerned, and this seems also to be true of industrial therapy for the mentally ill, at best a bare majority of the patients will make the road back to full economic independence. Even the Altro Work Shops experience, which has as high a success rate for the mentally ill as this writer has come across anywhere, reports 70 per cent successful rehabilitations. Of this proportion a sizeable number are persons who will continue to require social welfare insurance or assistance to supplement their business or industrial earnings. The balance, therefore, for an industrial therapy shop must take into account the failures among the patients as well as the large middle group who require "extended care" and for whom sheltered workshops in the European sense may need to be established.

A beautiful presentation of what is involved in applying cost-benefit analysis to measuring the economic worth of sheltered work and industrial therapy was undertaken by the noted Danish economist Dr. Bent Andersen for the Organisation for Economic Co-operation and Development.[6] Dr. Andersen develops applicable formulae and points out the difficulties of obtaining adequate financial data from the diverse accounting systems now in use. Among the information either not available or "masked" in the bookkeeping are such matters as the following: The actual market price paid for work done in the industrial therapy unit may be undervalued and really include a subsidy to the contractor; or through play upon sympathy may be bringing an overpayment to the real economic value of the work done on the product. Cost of replacement of capital equipment has to take into account whether such equipment is supplied by the prime contractor or supplied by governmental subsidy or donated. If capital equipment has been placed at the disposal of the industrial therapy unit, the cost to society includes the possible yield in alternative investment. These matters are not only pertinent to cost-benefit analysis in order to supply the data for policy-makers and planners who must consider alternative systems of service to the mentally ill; they are also material to business management of the in-dustrial therapy program, and will be so considered in greater detail in a later chapter.

In his report, Dr. Andersen carefully makes the distinction between "economic gains" and "human and social gains." He says,[7]

> It must be emphasized that the cost-benefit analysis is in itself insuf-ficient unless the "unpriced" human gains obtained through em-ployment in MSPE's [Dr. Andersen's reference to sheltered work] are taken into account. If Measures for Substitute Permanent Employment provide an economic gain for the rest of society, this may be offset, or more than offset, by the economic loss or loss of psychological well-being of the unplaceable. And if the cost-benefit analysis shows that there is a loss connected with a Measure for Substitute Permanent Employment, the decision-maker may never-theless decide to establish such an arrangement if he believes that the combined economic and mental gains to the unplaceable are sufficient to offset the economic loss to the rest of society.

It would appear from the earlier discussion in this chapter that there are likely to be sufficient values to the psychiatric treatment program as well as to the individual patients by the introduction of industrial therapy to more than offset any balance sheet deficit. This may be wishful thinking, however, and budget planners of the future may force a rude awakening. It would be well to have this eventuality in mind in setting up an industrial therapy unit and to insure that the information becomes available from which both the economic as well as the human and social gains may be cal-culated. This eventuality will be kept in mind in the chapters that deal with the structure, organization and practices of industrial therapy. But first, the next chapters will describe the array and variety of programs now in operation in Europe and in the United States in relation to their social and psychiatric service settings.

CHAPTER II

EUROPEAN BACKGROUNDS

Industrial Therapy in Western Europe

The British Programs of Industrial Therapy

In the British Isles there are now a number of mental hospitals that carry on industrial therapy programs of some dimension as part of their treatment and aftercare (resettlement) services. A survey completed 5 years ago reported that 60 per cent of the British National Health Service mental hospitals provide industrial therapy; today this must be over 70 per cent. These programs range from small units that take in contract work for a few patients or that make use of the hospital's own service needs to pay working patients to quite complex "small businesses," which fabricate or package on contract for industry or carry on direct manufacture. All of these programs have their origins in two developmental trends—the changes in mental patient care, and the growth of governmental programs for care of the disabled.

During and after World War II, concerted efforts were started toward psychiatric rehabilitation and industrial therapy. Concern for mobilizing all possible manpower in the war effort had led the Ministry of Labour and National Service to introduce in 1941 an Interim Scheme for the Training and Resettlement of the Disabled. Under this scheme there was developed the first center for the industrial rehabilitation of men, located in Egham, Surrey. The Disabled Persons (Employment) Act of 1944 allowed the extension of industrial rehabilitation centers; provided for a national register of handicapped persons; reserved certain occupations and a proportion of all occupations for the disabled; provided for vocational training in government centers, colleges, technical schools or on-the-job and set up a chain of industrial sheltered workshops (Remploy, Ltd.) for the severely disabled.[40] These provisions were carried over into the National Health Service Act of 1946. Rehabilitation, says the Act, shall be regarded as "a continuous process partly in the social and industrial sphere," and calls for close cooperation between the health and industrial services.

During the early years of the National Health Service, most of the work of the governmental programs, industrial rehabilitation units, governmental training centers and Remploy factories involved war casualties. By the 1950s the most frequent disability served had become pulmonary tuberculosis. The discovery of the anti-tuberculosis drugs speeded up the cure and the case rate dropped. By 1960 the mentally disabled had displaced the tuberculous group as the most frequent handicap requiring rehabilitation. In the Industrial Rehabilitation Units, 25 per cent of the applicants consisted of psychotic patients. The advances in chemotherapy for the mentally ill and the shift in treatment emphasis from hospitalization to community care had resulted in pressures for rehabilitative services in England.

The Government Systems

The British government rehabilitation programs are among the most comprehensive in the world. The definition of disability included mental illness and mental handicaps from the inception of the Disabled Persons Act. The specific services were designed, however, to meet the needs of the physically disabled (mainly orthopedic, tuberculous, cardiovascular and neurophysiologic), and there have been difficulties and complications in fitting psychiatric patients into these programs and in using the services to the benefit of the mentally ill. In recent years the Ministry of Labour and the Medical Research Council have cooperated in studies and experiments to clarify these problems. A variety of specially designed efforts in the Waddon I.R.U. and with certain mental hospitals, as described in later pages, has increased the efficacy of rehabilitation of the mentally ill.

Of the three major governmental programs, the Industrial Rehabilitation Units (I.R.U.s), the Government Training Centers and the Remploy Industries, the I.R.U.s are of the greatest interest in industrial therapy for the mentally ill. Since the Disabled Persons Employment Act of 1944, 16 Industrial Rehabilitation Units have been opened, each associated with a Government Training Center. The I.R.U.'s offer a 7- or 8-week course in a variety of workshops. A staff, including occupational supervisors, vocational officer, social worker, doctor, remedial gymnast, and rehabilitation officer, works with the district Disablement Resettlement Officer in evaluating the patient's performance, aids in his development in training and assesses his potential for placement on a job. Each I.R.U. can accommodate up to 100 persons at a time, with turnover from 10 to 14 each week. In the units, realistic production work is subcontracted from local employers, and an environment is developed that simulates factory conditions.

The persons trained and evaluated in the I.R.U. may move out to placement in industry, may be assigned for specialized training in the Government Training Center, may be adjudged too disabled for normal industry and transferred to a Remploy factory or may complete the course or drop out without attaining competence for further work or training. The Ministry of Labour had published in 1962 follow-up figures showing that only a little more than 52 per cent of the cases of "functional psychosis" moved on from completed I.R.U. courses to employment or training.[85] This was far less than the 60 per cent for all disabilities. Some 23 per cent of the mentally ill terminated prematurely as compared with 16 per cent of the total.

The Waddon I.R.U.   The special studies of I.R.U. services to schizophrenic patients, referred to earlier, have been undertaken at the Waddon I.R.U., which is designated as the Ministry of Labour's development unit. A complete, though succinct, description of this I.R.U. and the philosophy of the program are contained in a report prepared by its Rehabilitation Officer, John Crinnion, for the Information Department of the World Federation of Mental Health and released under contract with the National Clearinghouse for Mental Health Information, NIMH.[183]

In brief, the Waddon I.R.U. was serving some 60 persons at the time this writer visited it. The director, having his M.A. in psychology, had particular interest in determining the most effective use of industrial rehabilitation in preparing the disabled person for regular work. After a period of trial and error, he had decided that a ratio of one-third mental and neurological cases is the maximum for insuring best service to these persons. The rest of the load at Waddon was about equally divided between injury cases, mainly orthopedic, and the progressive physical disabilities, e.g., arthritis, circulatory and respiratory. An increase of psychiatric cases beyond one third, believes the director, tends to depress the general performance level in the workshops and reduces incentive.

Production workshops at the Waddon I.R.U. include a section for the assembly of small tools and other items, a machine shop section, a bench fitting section for making metal boxes, jigs and fixtures, an industrial clerical records section and a section for remedial work or upgrading in general clerical and office work. In an Intake Section a series of simple tasks is used in which the supervisor observes how the disabled person performs on dexterity, ability with hand tools, skills, application to work and relationships with fellow workers. In one instance the entrant is given wood and carpentry tools to construct a small ladder; in another, metal pieces for the fabrication of a latch and hinges; in yet another, tiles to be arranged and glued to form a coaster or ash tray. These "work samples" were imaginatively used, and the evaluations from them seemed quite practical and useful. Although English rehabilitation personnel spoke familiarly of the more ornate testing procedures used in the United States, such as the Towers System (see Chapter IV), they seem to prefer relatively simple and direct observation to standardized psychological and psychometric measurements and rating scales. This has been particularly so in assessment of the mentally ill.

Planning and decision-making for individual participants in the I.R.U. are accomplished through "team" meetings attended by Rehabilitation Officer, medical consultant, occupational supervisor, social worker and the Disablement Resettlement Officer. The latter person carries on functions that in this country might be shared between the special placement counselor of a State Employment Service and the rehabilitation counselor from the State Division of Vocational Rehabilitation. It is significant to remember too that the medical officer represents the local or district unit of the Ministry of Health and the National Health Service. This writer was pleasurably impressed with the client-centered approach taken at the team meeting that he attended and with the apparent mutual trust and sharing of information and ideas among those participating.

The Sheltered Workshop—the Remploy System. The Disabled Persons Act of 1944 takes cognizance of the many handicapped persons of some economic value who cannot perform adequately in competitive employment. Because of extremely severe disability or constant need for medical attention or the very slowness of their work capacity or some other handicap, these persons require what the West Germans have so nicely chosen to call "sheltering employment."[20] The Ministry of Labour was empowered to organize a company called the Disabled Persons Employment Corporation, Ltd., better known as Remploy, Ltd.

Remploy, Ltd., has its own board of directors which is appointed by the Minister of Labour and which includes prominent businessmen, labor union officials and persons interested in and experienced in rehabilitation of the disabled. There are now over 90 Remploy factories employing more than 6000 severely disabled persons in England and Scotland. The Act of 1944 provides that the Ministry of Labour grant financial assistance to the company for capital expenses and for subsidizing administrative costs. The aim is to keep this assistance to a minimum in the belief that the best interests of the disabled and the community are served if Remploy, Ltd. can become as nearly as possible self-supporting. Through a manufacturing sponsorship scheme, the Remploy factories secure long-term contracts for the manufacture of goods or performance of services. The number of workers in each factory varies from 25 to about 200. There are some 10 different types of manufacture distributed through a central procurement system to groups of factories engaged in the same processes.

The Remploy workers, with some exceptions, are expected to put in a full 42-hour week. Pay is piece rate or hourly, related to standards of not more than 75 per cent of "normal" industrial production as approved by the trade union. Each factory is allowed to employ up to 15 per cent of its labor force from among the able-bodied to fill key positions essential to efficient operation. The turnover of handicapped workers to regular industry is small but steady, some 200 per year.[41]

The importance of the Remploy system to industrial therapy for the mentally ill is not in the direct services it renders. A very small number of post-psychotic patients are accepted in their factories. The importance is in the set of principles that Remploy, Ltd. has established and the availability of a pattern of sheltered work of which the Ministry of Labour is beginning to permit transposition to special illness categories, including the mentally ill. Two of the industrial therapy programs described in the following pages (Glenside Hospital—I.T.O. Bristol and St. Barnabas—I.T.O. Thames) now have approved Remploy-type sheltered workshops as part of their services.

The Development in the Mental Hospitals

A growing interest of British mental hospitals in "resettlement" of their patients has paralleled the development just described. For a number of years, there has been an increasing trend toward shorter mental hospital stay of patients and greater use of community-based treatment resources. Wing, et al., have pointed out that while in 1930 about 60 per cent of admissions to hospitals in England and Wales remained two years longer, by 1964 the proportion discharged within two years of admission had increased to nearly 90 per cent.[178] Nevertheless, since schizophrenic patients account for 25 per cent of all admissions, there has been a gradual residual accumulation over the years. The Medical Research Council reports that three quarters of the 70 to 80 per cent of present residents of mental hospitals who have been hospitalized for more than two years are schizophrenic. The majority of these are persons under 60 years of age.

Questions as to what to do with this residual population amounting to nearly 50,000 persons with schizophrenia, and twice this number of other psychiatric diagnoses are included, have been raised by British psychiatry since World War II ended; hence, the great interest in Britain in the "transitional" rehabilitation methodologies and resources, including industrial therapy. Impetus to patient turnover in which those with lesser disabilities can more easily return to the community, thus focusing hospital treatment concern on those who remain, came from the Mental Health Acts of 1959 in England and of 1960 in Scotland. These acts provide for entirely informal admission to mental hospitals. A mentally ill patient can receive psychiatric treatment as an outpatient or in a hospital with no more formality than if he had a physical illness.

In general, the underlying theme in industrial therapy in British hospitals seems to be the overcoming of secondary handicaps which may be more disabling to acceptable social functioning than the mental illness itself. Dependence as a result of long institutionalization and the loss of social habits and skills conducive to performance in the work-a-day world are problems secondary to illness, but these may be resolved through industrial therapy.

The Social Psychiatry Research Unit of the Medical Research Council has been engaged in a series of studies that throw light on some of these secondary handicaps and the effect of efforts to deal with them.[179] Experimental observations from the application of such a social and environmental approach as industrial therapy are important to understanding the effect of training for skills, varying modes of supervision, use of money and other incentives, learning ability and other factors of which knowledge is necessary to the design of effective programs. In this regard also, special attention is called to a fine series of studies on employability of schizophrenics, their quality of work and fatigability, undertaken by Dr. William V. Wadsworth and his colleagues at Cheadle Royal Hospital.[169] There are few such studies in the United States. In fairness to the situation in America, however, it should be remembered that most industrial rehabilitation services here are more recent than the British. Furthermore, there is greater diagnostic homogeneity in the British mental patient population exposed to industrial therapy than is true in this country, and therefore, controlled studies may be less easy and of lesser validity when applied to American state hospital patients. This will change as the effects of open door, milieu and chemotherapeutic, and hospital-community programs reduce hospital populations to residual groups more like what has happened in Britain.

Examples of Industrial Therapy in England

The following are reports of personal visits to certain institutions which in this writer's opinion and in the opinion of those with whom he has consulted in English psychiatry have developed the most advanced forms of industrial therapy. They are grouped loosely so that those most closely confined to meeting the inpatient needs of the hospital may be considered first, followed by those that have carried industrial therapy on to a relationship with community psychiatric rehabilitation. The visits described are as of 1964. Changes have been updated through correspondence and by more recent reports of personal visits.

1. *Banstead Hospital (Sutton).*   This hospital an example of industrial therapy serving part of a hospital population.

Banstead Hospital pioneered in 1955 in bringing paid production work into the hospital. An experimental workshop, originally employing 40 women and 20 men, was set up by the Medical Research Council. A large ward, unused because of declining population, approximately 80 by 30 feet in size, was equipped with bench-type tables for the original workshop. At the time of the visit in July 1964, more than one ward area was being used, the women's workrooms being separate from those of the men.

Approximately 60 men were working. They were mostly middle-aged to elderly, and appeared to be typical chronic schizophrenics. Some were obviously hallucinating, but all were working. The major job was packaging modelling clay. The covered clay strips were placed on cardboard and wrapped in cellophane. A group of the men were assembling the clay on a production line basis, each man having three different colored strips. One of these men was described by the work supervisor as the only patient in the room who, in her opinion, has made any recent progress, moving from a catatonic state to active participation in the program. A few of the men were salvaging big paper bags and three men were assembling simple paper boxes, this the final stage of a contract which will no doubt be repeated.

In the women's workrooms there were also about 60 women, two thirds of whom were doing the clay assembly. The other women were sewing up and decorating stuffed toys. In general, the women were more elderly and more decrepit-looking than the men. In both the workshops for men and women, there was a nice atmosphere of calmness and productivity.

During the tea break there was a carryover of meaningful activity, there being little of the lassitude or confusion that one might have expected from the psychiatric characteristics of the workers.

The Deputy Physician Superintendent is in charge of the work program and has supervised it since its inception in 1955. He believes that the industrial therapy has helped to move many patients out of the hospital and back into the community. The hospital population has dropped from 2700 to 1200 over these years. At any one time there are some 200 to 300 patients involved in either the industrial therapy shops or other work programs in the maintenance of the hospital.

The Superintendent described in the early years of this program, the progression of movement of patients first into ordinary hospital work such as floor-scrubbing, laundry, needlework or ward chores, and then into the hospital utility departments such as the laundry or linen room, and finally into the industrial therapy unit which was expected to be a way-station toward discharge from the hospital. It is not clear whether this progression still holds for the remaining hospital population, which is very disabled. They are for the most part old-time, back ward schizophrenics, many with brain damage. They can only do the simplest types of work and at a very slow pace. This latter was certainly borne out from observation.

In an article in *The Lancet* in 1956, the Superintendent had referred to two problems which appeared to be developing from the first year of the industrial therapy experience.[9] The first of these was the question of housing for patients who demonstrated an ability to live out of the hospital while working in a sheltered environment or even while making the transition back to normal industry. Banstead Hospital Management Committee, which carries responsibility for two other hospitals (Downview and Freedown Hospitals), is working, as are other hospitals in the British complex, on the problems of providing hostels and other living arrangements to meet this problem in their catchment areas. The second problem referred to was that satisfactory working arrangements in the hospital factory have tended to hold patients in the hospital. The Superintendent said, "They receive all the benefits of hospital life—full privileges, board and lodging, clothing, television shows, social outings and even summer holidays. They are now able to work under pleasant conditions and receive considerable pocket money. Many could well say to us that they cannot obtain such situations for themselves outside hospital and be reluctant to leave." The Superintendent now says that, in his opinion, the work therapy program belongs out of the hospital. The studies he has conducted as to the effect of his workshop now show that it tends to keep patients in the hospital longer. He is looking forward to the rebuilding of the Banstead Hospital within the decade. He wants it to become a 500-bed hospital with a much better workshop, this to be constructed outside the hospital walls and preferably in closer juxtaposition to the community.

The economic climate in England, particularly the London area, over the past decade has been such that it is an advantage to local industry because of the labor shortages to contract work out to hospital populations. While this condition is still true, these days work is somewhat harder to come by because five mental hospitals in the immediate region of Banstead are competing for it.

The Superintendent himself makes the contacts with local industry and obtains work for his hospital. He does a trial run before deciding to accept a job because he is concerned about the therapeutic value of the work to be done and the ability of his patients to do the work. He has never worried much about pricing or pay rates. He sets the price at what the traffic will bear, figuring average wages up to about 2 pounds per week per patient, and this maximum is apparently limited by the National Assistance regulations. The Superintendent figures a 5 per cent overhead for servicing costs, which he admits by no means covers the real cost to the hospital. His feeling, besides that of other hospital personnel, was that work is quite therapeutic and the pay is a great incentive. This latter belief is in contradiction to Medical Research Council studies that incentives such as money, goal setting and encouragement have little effect. Some people do move out of Banstead Hospital to jobs on the outside.

One value of the work therapy program about which the Superintendent was quite frank is its ability to take care of larger groups of patients with fewer numbers of staff. Without this work to do, the management of patients would be a terrible drain on time and on staff. He believes that the younger patients, particularly, should have a wider range of activity available to them, but this would take staff not now and not likely to be available. Therefore, a workshop can keep patients busy at low staff and overhead costs.

During the writer's visit, the Occupational Therapist Supervisor of the work program told him of meetings between the workshop supervisors of the mental hospitals in the region to try to set up a cooperative arrangement on sources of work and to share work. There had also been overtures from a new profit-making firm which set itself up as a middle man to find work for the hospital workshops at a 20 per cent commission. The Superintendent had hoped that this firm might help to offset the difficulties of obtaining work. In later correspondence with him and with others in England, the writer has learned that there is great dissatisfaction with this middleman commercial approach, and it is the writer's impression that it has closed shop.

A logical question is whether, if England's economic climate changes and there seems to be some tendency toward less of a labor shortage and greater automation, there will be a continuation of contract work for hospital workshops of this sort. All reports in 1968 indicate that there has been no dearth of work for industrial therapy.

2. *Netherne Hospital (Coulsdon South, Surrey).*   This institution an example of industrial therapy serving most of a hospital's population.

The acting Physician Superintendent, Dr. H. E. S. Marshall, was in charge of rehabilitation. The Resettlement Unit had been opened in 1957 by Dr. Douglass Bennett to deal with the problems of patients who have had long hospital stays. Dr. Bennett conceived the idea of bringing industrial work for pay into the hospital from local industries. The first job at Netherne Hospital was one of wiring for Thermega, Ltd., the industrial workshop for the Ex-veterans Welfare Society, and Netherne continues to perform this job.

About 80 per cent of the 1700 patients are long stay, two years or more. The movement out into the community is slow. The hospital has achieved the assignment of all but 326 out of the 1700 patients to work activities. These are divided roughly as follows:

1. Utility activities: These are services within the hospital—maintenance tasks—for which payment cannot be given. At the time of visit, approximately 334 patients were so assigned.

2. Industry: These are sheltered workshops of which there are three grades. To these are assigned approximately 372 patients.

3. Ward work: These are rather mundane duties of a regular nature on the wards. To these 218 are assigned.

4. Supervised group activities, such as grounds clean-up or gardening. To these are assigned approximately 74 women.

5. The department Occupational Therapy Unit: To this are assigned approximately 376 patients, of whom 290 are women. These include

geriatrics group and the Reception or Admission villas. These latter cottages are short stay, usually four weeks, and Dr. Marshall questioned the value of putting patients on such short stay at industrial work.

6. Resettlement (to which approximately 107 are assigned): These people are leaving the hospital daily for work in local industry or trade, work in London, work at the Remploy Industries, or Thermega, or they are assigned to an Industrial Rehabilitation Unit, or a Government Training Center or attending local schools for clerical brushup.

It should be noted that this proportion of patients regularly assigned to job duties is most unusual and is based upon the strong belief by both the Superintendent and Dr. Bennett in the therapeutic value of rehabilitation.

The workshops, or what the Superintendent refers to as the hospital industry, revealed nice, big, light, airy rooms with adequate tables and stock space. The lowest grade patients were folding paper boxes and assembling jumping ropes, both very simple tasks. Occupational therapists supervised them, and while the pace was obviously slow, there was an air of productivity.

The highest grade shop made simple electric harnesses, electronic units and the Thermega cord assembly. It should be noted that the electric work, outside of that for Thermega, was on contract for the Philips Company, one of Europe's largest electronic industries. A few of the patients in the highest grade shop were assembling lamp shades. The middle group was assembling a plastic knife gadget and little metal saws and the like.

The Superintendent believes in a wide variety of work, both for therapeutic value as well as to avoid the danger of collapse of one or more contracts. The impression that this writer gained of the patients was of a relatively wide cross section similar to the range that might be found in any of our large state hospitals. A review of the literature, however, suggests that the illness level among Netherne Hospital patients in the industrial program is somewhat more severe than would ordinarily be recommended for industrial work on the American scene. A random sample analyzed by Bennett, Freudenberg and Catterson in 1960 found 58 per cent of the male patients were severely ill and the remainder were moderately ill; and the corresponding percentages for females were severely ill, 53 per cent and moderately ill, 47 per cent.[17]

The Acting Chief Occupational Therapist, showed the evaluative forms which are used in reports to ward team meetings. These cover the items of capacity and aptitude for work. She has also evolved some very simple evaluation techniques now being tried at intervals but not yet standardized or validated. For example, as a measure of speed, the patient is timed as to the number of rings he can screw on a curtain rod in one minute; as a measure of accuracy, he is asked to count units, the number of which is.

known to the tester; and with regard to judgment, he is asked to decide which of two ribbons is longer.

The Industrial Officer obtains the work on contract from industrial firms in the area. He makes his own trial run in order to set a productivity guide and then negotiates price. The Industrial Officer believes that he sticks to going prices in the community, though the Superintendent suspects the price is set to provide patient wages and little else. The visitor's impression is that the Superintendent's opinion may be accurate since there is much competition between hospital industrial work units in the area of Netherne Hospital. After setting the price, the Industrial Officer works out the wage rates with the occupational therapists. He is not convinced that piece rates are of any value, but it did not seem that he was objecting to piece rates so much as he was to a method the Occupational Therapist was using of averaging out the piece rates in order that all patients get the same hourly rate. A bonus of five or ten per cent is paid as an incentive for good attendance, or a penalty is applied for poor attendance.

A very careful system of work tickets for recording of production is utilized, and certain patients are used for keeping the clerical records and are paid for this work. The maximum pay rates are set at 70 per cent of normal industry by the agreement that the trade unions have with Remploy, Ltd. Pay for the Netherne patients, however, cannot exceed 2 pounds per week because of the National Assistance rules.

Netherne Hospital was not eligible for Ministry of Labour allowances as a sheltered workshop because the work settings are within the hospital walls. The Superintendent hoped for the establishment of a workshop out of the hospital, perhaps in the form of an Industrial Therapy Organization. As a permanent sheltered placement he uses, but is not entirely satisfied with, Thermega, Ltd.

Netherne Hospital has a most interesting employment office control unit. This office keeps a constant record on the movement of patients into the various work units and out into the resettlement jobs in the local community and in London. It provides assistance to the patients in making contact for employment and keeps track of the changes of employment, reasons for work absence, weekly earnings and patient income from pensions, private sources, etc. It supplies a focal point for psychiatric consultants, ward physicians, social workers, Sisters, charge nurses, occupational therapists and others in order that they may have constantly before them the patient's history and experience in industrial therapy.

3. *Cheadle Royal Hospital (Cheadle, Cheshire).* Cheadle Royal an example of a private mental hospital with an industrial therapy program keyed to concern for service to the local community.

The visitor's host was Dr. William Wadsworth, Medical Superintendent. At various times the visit was joined by the financial officer of the hospital, the Chairman of the Industrial Committee of the Management Committee of the hospital, a real estate developer for the British Council of Rehabilitation, an architect for the British Council of Rehabilitation and a regional inspector for the Ministry of Labour.

Cheadle Royal Hospital was originally the psychiatric division of the Manchester Royal Hospital, the general hospital for the city of Manchester, established about 1760. In the mid-eighteen hundreds, the psychiatric division was moved out to Cheadle in the county of Cheshire. Cheadle Royal Hospital is now one of the very few private non-National Health Service hospitals in England.[141] It is a 500-bed hospital on beautiful grounds joining the village of Cheshire. Its buildings, while old, are excellently maintained and beautifully equipped. About 300 of its patients are occupied in industrial therapy and work in special buildings constructed adjoining the hospital. It appears as though the original factory setting was hosptial ward space, but more recent additions to the building constitute one-story, attractively constructed, industrial units.

The greater part of the work is the direct manufacture of paper hats and party favors. A small amount of additional work, including the making of confetti from paper scrap and the packaging of plastic tea sets, has been added on a subcontract basis. Much use is made of jigs and fixtures and the remodeling of working equipment to increase productivity to make the tasks of assembly and production faster and better. The look of the enterprise is that of an up-to-date manufacturing plant. Good use is made of production line, and much time and energy is spent devising and developing electronic devices that make possible faster and more complex production.

The industrial therapy unit at Cheadle Royal Hospital was incorporated as a separate nonprofit membership corporation in June of 1963. It is known as Cheadle Royal (Industries), Ltd. and has powers in addition to those of an ordinary business or the usual American sheltered workshop by providing housing, food and other relief and conducting fund-raising events. The purposes are not limited to serving mental disability alone. The Cheadle Royal (Industries) may have an association membership of 50, and it is governed by a Council of 4 to 12 members to which Dr. Wadsworth and the Chairman of his Industrial Committee belong.

The patient population in the industrial shops seems to be a greater cross section of psychiatric disabilities than was true at Glenside where almost all of the patients appeared to be the chronically disabled schizophrenics. However, the major group at Cheadle Royal is in the schizophrenic categories.

Dr. Wadsworth uses a man trained as an industrial consultant as his factory manager. This manager is paid £ 3000 a year, which is at least £ 1000 a year more than either Glenside Hospital or St. Bernard's is allowed to pay its factory manager under the National Health Service provisions. Pace-setting and cadre positions seem also to be filled by well people from the village. The visitor's impression was that approximately one fourth to one third of the individuals employed are of the nonpatient or expatient categories.

Dr. Wadsworth is not rigid in his opinion about having the workshop on the hospital grounds. In the case of Cheadle Royal, it has turned out to be a convenience. He is interested in developing tie-lines between the hospital and the community around it, and he believes that gradually the industrial setting at Cheadle Royal with its primary purpose of continuing service to patents will become an established and acceptable industry for the village. Dr. Wadsworth sees very great advantages in direct manufacture, especially for hospitals that are not in industrial areas and therefore do not have access to much subcontract work. He is also interested in the findings of research in the industrial therapy of patients and this research being made available to industry.

The visitor was struck by the similarities between the Cheadle Royal (Industries) and Altro Work Shops in New York with regard to the business methods employed. Both are engaged in direct manufacture, both depend upon industrially trained managerial people and both are quite reliant upon an industrial committee of the Board of Managers. The chairman is a dedicated and influential businessman and community leader who is obviously quite willing to devote a great deal of his time to the problems of the industrial unit at Cheadle Royal.

As will be seen as true with Glenside Hospital, part of the factory at Cheadle Royal has been designated by the Ministry of Labour as a "sheltered workshop." There appears to be a very interesting relationship between public and private ventures in the Cheadle Royal organization. The Ministry of Health seems to be anxious to have a private institution continue for its value in demonstration and experimentation. The Ministry of Labour is willing to cooperate in this venture. Dr. Wadsworth's position is slightly anomalous, however, for as a private practitioner, not part of the National Health Service, he may not give treatment directly to patients covered under National Health Service provisions. Nevertheless, he may act as a consultant to National Health Service physicians—that is, psychiatrists—who refer patients to his institution. At its rates, the National Health Service is willing to pay for care of a certain number of patients in Cheadle Royal Hospital.

As is true with some of the other forward-thinking psychiatric administrators in the British Isles, Dr. Wadsworth is concerned about the problem of supplying housing and domiciliary care for patients in their transition to functioning in the world outside the hospital. Cheadle Royal Hospital is located on some of the choicest land on the outskirts of Manchester. The Manchester area has the heaviest population density in the British Isles, if not in the whole of Europe. Therefore, there is interest in the utilization of some of the hospital's beautiful land for a housing development for patients. The British Council on Rehabilitation is handling the setting up of a building corporation in which the profits are to be shared by the hospital and the local county council. Dr. Wadsworth hopes that the building development will house nonpatients as well as patients and their families, geriatric patients and the physically handicapped. The industrial therapy program will then become local industry for residents of this housing development.

Both the Cheadle Royal Hospital industrial therapy program and that of Glenside Hospital in Bristol figure in the film produced by Smith Kline & French Pharmaceutical Laboratories entitled *The Need to Work* in its American distribution. (The title for British and Continental distribution is *The Right to Work.*) Dr. Wadsworth has filmed and taped additional material to the original film, bringing developments in his program up to date. A viewing of this newer material illustrates the interest of Dr. Wadsworth and his staff and Management Committee in gleaning from their experience hints and suggestions of value both to the further development of industrial therapy and greater productivity on the part of patients and a carryover of understanding of the psychiatric patient to regular industry.

4. *Mapperly Hospital (Nottingham).* The pioneer mental health services at Nottingham are world famous and frequently have been visited by psychiatric personnel from the United States. The industrial therapy unit is of more recent origin, however, and is related particularly to the day hospital program.

The visitor was shown through the industrial therapy and occupational therapy units by the Physician Superintendent, Dr. Duncan Macmillan, accompanied by the head male nurse, occupational therapist, director of industrial therapy and the chief occupational therapist.

Dr. Macmillan sketched in the community mental health programs which he heads. He is superintendent of a 500-bed hospital; he is also the medical officer for mental health of the health authority of Nottingham. In this latter capacity he has under his jurisdiction a 160-bed unit in geriatric psychiatry at the general hospital, a day unit for geriatric patients and a day unit for psychiatric patients. The coordination of the various mental health facilities in the Nottingham area makes for a very comprehensive psychiatric service.

Industrial therapy has been developed in the day hospital unit only, though inpatients of the hospital may be assigned to it. Dr. Macmillan preferred to wait until the hospital population had dropped to residual difficult cases before allowing inpatients to make use of the industrial therapy resource.

The major unit for industrial therapy is in a one-story, specially constructed addition to the hospital. Industrial therapy has been in operation at Mapperly Hospital since 1961. Dr. Macmillan did not develop it for the inpatient population because he was afraid it might encourage patients to stay in the hospital and find little incentive for moving out. The opening of the day care program had brought a number of problems including that of providing something for the patients to do during the course of the day. It was decided that for many patients, unless there was an occupational use of their time, day care would become pointless and lead to little therapeutic benefit.

The work done in the industrial day care unit is rather simple bench work. This visitor saw the assembly of paper bags, mostly pasting and gluing; there was a small group of female patients cutting out and finishing garments, and another group working on the trimming of lace and finishing of hats. There was also a group of men who were bundling firewood for heating use by the local shops.

The director of industrial therapy, who had been male nurse and occupational therapist for 30 years and, with the exception of war service, had spent all of it at Mapperly Hospital, had been learning about industrial therapy as the program was developing. He found that the men do not take too well to the simple paper bag assembly, so he was investigating jobs that would be more masculine. While Dr. Macmillan seemed to feel that the best contacts for work come from members of the Management Committee, the industrial therapy director was not so sure that a better variety and at a better price base might not be obtained from a little canvassing among industries in the area. He had learned that overhead costs must be met anyway and that it is not sufficient to assume these will be funded by the hospital or the day care unit whether or not there is work for the patients to do.

Most of the patients are referred from National Health Service general practitioners in the community. Dr. Macmillan has the power of acceptance or refusal. Pay rates seem to be very nominal, as low as 5 shillings a week, payable at the rate of 1 shilling a day, and they cannot go above 1 pound, 19 shillings and elevenpence, the maximum set by the National Assistance Program.

Supervision of patients in the work setting is by the nursing staff.

In a memorandum describing the program, Dr. Macmillan lists certain advantages and disadvantages that are worth repeating.[110] He cites as advantages:

> 1. The work is part of local industry, and the pay is in relation to the amount of effort. The patients, therefore, feel that they are part of the local economic effort.

2. It is the sort of job many people do when actually employed, and for day patients, it provides a similar day pattern to that of employment.

3. There is immediate feedback if the work is not up to standard.

4. It represents another stage in the process of rehabilitation from the ward to occupational therapy and then on to industrial work.

5. It brings local employers into the hospital and demonstrates to them that mental illness is not incompatible with good work.

6. Patients in need of day care will often attend more readily if it is to a worthwhile job.

7. It tides over the period between the end of active treatment and the finding of suitable employment when, without any activity or interest, relapse might result. It is also useful in the event of unemployment in preventing a relapse and possible consquent re-admission to hospital.

8. It is easier for the patient, as well as the staff, to note progress (by increased earnings).

Dr. Macmillan notes as possible disadvantages:

1. Not all people like the repetitive factory-type work.

2. There is the danger that patients might become too settled and contented, not having too much to think about; or too little pressure is put upon them provided they maintain a certain standard. They can also be almost as well off earning the full amount together with National Assistance as in a poorly paid job.

As practical difficulties, Dr. Macmillan lists the following:

1. Industrial work requires a lot of room, both for work and for storage.

2. It needs a higher ratio of staff to patients than normal occupational therapy.

3. There are difficulties in always having sufficient work available, and therefore, at times there is insufficient grading of work.

Dr. Macmillan prefers patients to have had an initial period in the occupational therapy department before being referred to the industrial unit so that time and materials are not wasted there trying to find the right job for the individual patient. He says, "We think that willingness, reasonable neatness and punctuality, as well as the ability to take correction, should be present to a fair degree before commencing industrial work." He looks forward to separating those likely to be able to work outside the hospital within the foreseeable future from those for whom a sheltered workshop atmosphere is the most that seems to be possible.

It struck the visitor that while there are notable differences between the approach taken by Dr. Macmillan in utilizing industrial therapy in the day hospital and either the in-hospital units or the ITO's developed elsewhere, there are also many similarities. On the other hand, Dr. Macmillan's desire to keep the operation a simple one and not to have it become an industrial factory program in its own right is well worth recommending to other settings. The Mapperly experience is worth noting in terms of its relevance to the development of comprehensive mental health service units with day hospital programs in this country.

5. *Glenside Hospital (Bristol) and the Industrial Therapy Organisation, I.T.O. (Bristol), Ltd.*   As a public mental institution concerned with using industrial therapy most adequately as the cornerstone of a community endeavor in rehabilitation of chronic patients, Glenside Hospital is responsible for the most imaginative and perhaps the most comprehensive program in England.

Dr. Donal F. Early, consultant psychiatrist to the hospital, was this visitor's host and guide. He was assisted at various points by the head charge nurse in charge of ward therapy, the chief matron and Vice Chairman of the Management Committee who is also a Labour Member of the City Council. Glenside Hospital was one of the early hospitals in England to incorporate industrial therapy for its patients. Under its earlier name, Fish Ponds Hospital, it opened factory work in 1958 to 14 patients. By December of 1959 this had increased to 385 patients.

Work units are tucked away in rooms all over the hospital. Practically all of the work is of the simple bench job variety such as folding and sealing and gluing plastic sheets and simple boxing. At one point in its history, a good deal of the work was the manufacture of ballpoint pens, but this has since been moved out of the hospital into the Industrial Therapy Organisation. At the time of the visit about 380 patients out of 1200 in the hospital were assigned to work units of this sort. Other patients were on hospital work details such as gardening, etc.

Since its inception in 1958, Dr. Early has developed a variety of industrial work programs for his patients. His was the first of the Industrial Therapy Organisation units of which there are now a number in the British Isles. I.T.O. (Bristol) was formed late in 1959 and early 1960 as a nonprofit factory employing patients from the hospital. Gradually the I.T.O. was opened to accept applicants from all consultant psychiatrists in the Bristol clinical area and from doctors in charge of day hospitals and occupational therapy departments and from medical officers of health.

Dr. Early staunchly believes in industrial work for mental patients. He plans a variety of work units which, when combined with a variety of domiciliary units and with ex-patient clubs and other social activities, offer permutations available for almost any situation required in the rehabilitation or re-establishment of mental patients from hospital back to community.

In brief, the variety of industrial work units available include:

1. Industrial therapy work within the hospital.
2. The Industrial Therapy Organisation (Bristol), Ltd.
3. A "Sheltered Work" program which is a unit of the I.T.O. of Bristol.
4. Individual patients sponsored by manufacturers and assigned to work in real industry.
5. A program of work groups in regular industry. The visitor saw two of these, one being a group of patients working at a hygienic straw company; and the other, a group of patients working at a ladies' shoe manufacturing plant.

Along with these industrial therapy units, Glenside Hospital has a number of domiciliary units available for housing care of patients. These are as follows:

1. The hospital wards.
2. A discharge cottage on the hospital grounds.
3. A hostel run by the local medical authority.
4. A hotel run by the hospital.
5. The County Council houses, something on the order of public housing projects in our country.
6. Foster care with a family.
7. Living arrangements in one's own or family quarters.

Along with the industrial and domiciliary possibilities, there is an ex-patient club, and there are arrangements with various local community centers for them to open their doors to patients from the hospital.

The program at Glenside Hospital began on a shoestring. The first work in the hospital was the assembling of ballpoint fountain pens. The initial suggestion for taking work of this kind into the hospital came from Mr. John P. Turley, a director of Messrs. Tallon, Ltd. It was Mr. Turley's firm that molded the plastic pens and marketed them. Mr. Turley's knowledge and business judgement has aided immeasurably in the development of Glenside's industrial therapy program.

This visitor had the pleasure of meeting with Mr. Turley. He is presently the Honorary Managing Director of I.T.O. (Bristol), Ltd. The growth of the I.T.O. program has been such that the head charge nurse at the hospital retired from that post to become the managing head of the Industrial Therapy Organisation on a full-time basis.

During the tour through the hospital and to the patient groups working in industries, the visitor noticed that nurses supervised the patient workers. Quality control is dependent upon the nursing supervision. Nurses were working cheerfully on box packaging to get "the feel" and to aid patients in meeting production. The assignment of patients to work is really made by the nurses and matrons even though the doctors occasionally review the assignments and changes of assignments. Dr. Early was frank that not all physicians are enthusiastic about industrial therapy, and even at Glenside Hospital there is some opposition from some doctors.

The wage rates paid are in a modified piece-work arrangement which is leveled out so that patients in the hospital get approximately the same rate for similar work.

The Industrial Therapy Organisation is housed in an ancient, parish school building which was vacant between 1950 and 1959 before being renovated for use by the I.T.O. The work atmosphere was good and cheerful. Work tasks during the visit were generally similar to those seen in the hospital industrial therapy units with the exception that the ballpoint pen assembly was much more noticeable in the I.T.O.

The visits to industry to see two patient groups working as "sheltered work" units within industry were extremely interesting. Dr. Early has managed to get the Ministry of Labour to treat the work-in-industry groups as "sheltered workshops." This meant that the Ministry will subsidize 75 per cent of the deficit up to £240 per year per head. Actually one unit of 11 or 12 women in the hygienic straw company cost in wages only about £600 over their earned production. (Note: This is a similar process to our subsidization of below minimum wage levels.) The other unit in the shoe factory actually broke even. At present there are three such units in all, and Dr. Early and Mr. Turley contemplate establishing more. This, they believe, is the real answer to meeting the volume of need for the long-term and chronically ill psychiatric patients. The Ministry of Labour requires a minimum of 10 patients in each sheltered work unit in a regular industry in order to qualify for subsidy.

Another extremely interesting development operated by Glenside Hospital is a car wash not far from the hospital. By choice, the car wash was not fully automated, thus keeping 12 men occupied. It was an interesting experience for this visitor to accompany Dr. Early, have the men work on his car and to listen to conversations between the car owners and the car washers. This seems to be an excellent way of letting the local community get to know the patients in the hospital and of becoming used to them in terms of capacities they have rather than to fear their illness.

The most interesting factor in the visit to Glenside Hospital was the interrelatedness of the various facets of rehabilitation service. Dr. Early serves the hospital nine-elevenths of his time. This allows him two-elevenths time to carry private practice and serve as a medical health officer and as a consultant to the Industrial Therapy Organisation. He seems to have the capacity for great enthusiasm and of carrying a good staff along with him. Under his direction, the hospital has really become a community hospital. Services are always available at Glenside.

In *The Lancet* of October 1, 1960, Dr. Early writes,

> To occupy consistently a third of the patients in a chronic hospital
> is obviously a desirable aim but, it is not an end in itself. Patients

tend to settle down as they have been encouraged to in the past, with a slightly better standard of living, and an "industrial aristocracy" tends to replace the old privileged maintenance department worker. The ultimate aim of discharge may be lost sight of by patients and by staff.

For this reason he has stimulated the establishment of the Industrial Therapy Organisation out of the hospital.

6. *St. Bernard's Hospital (Southall) and the I.T.O. (Thames), Ltd.* Following the lead of the program just described at Glenside Hospital (Bristol) and some of the elements in that of Cheadle Royal Hospital, St. Bernard's Hospital (just outside of London) has developed one of the most interesting and fast growing industrial therapy programs in England.

The host was Dr. C. R. Birnie, Medical Superintendent, who was accompanied by the Psychiatrist-in-Charge of the Workshop Program and Group Therapy, Mr. V. C. McDonnell, Industrial Manager, the head nurse, the financial officer and the chief of records. The hosts and visitor were joined at lunch by the Chairman of the Management Committee of the hospital and by the Executive Director of the National Advisory Council of Industrial Therapy Organisations.

St. Bernard's Hospital has about 2000 patients. Approximately 300 of these have been referred from anywhere in the hospital to the industrial therapy program. What were evidently formerly ward rooms of the hospital were now used as the center of workshop activities. During the visit, the patients were making zippers, stuffing and heat sealing small plastic bags which held medallions for cereal box favors and making wooden drying racks. In one room there was a fully equipped machine shop with lathes, millers, etc., in which was done contract work for industry to within one-thousandth of an inch tolerance. Plans were under way to expand upon a presently small printing operation in order to develop a full clerical shop. The equipment for the various shops has been donated by industry and reconditioned by the staff of the workshop and staff of the hospital.

This visitor was struck by a number of interesting elements in the operation and performance of the work program. The patients are all chronic schizophrenics; yet they appeared to be more productive, both in their motions and their output, than one would have thought possible. Not only were patients being used for production, but they were also being used for quality control. There seemed to be a fine balance of concern for the therapeutic value of jobs. Dr. Birnie, in particular, seemed quite concerned that the work taken have specific value to the treatment plans for the patients.

In this setting, rather than using nurses or occupational therapists for patient supervision, use was made of technically qualified tradesmen. This seemed to add considerably to the training components in the work. This visitor was impressed particularly in the machine shop by the attention given to training. A strong emphasis was evident toward using the work setting as transitional toward rehabilitation. Even though the expected turnover may be very slow, there is very good support for this program from the Ministry of Labour. In fact, the supervisors in the work program have recently been upgraded so that their pay scales are now higher than those for social workers or occupational therapists or nurses in the hospitals.

The key to the development of this program, besides Dr. Birnie's interest, was Mr. McDonnell. He was formerly a Works Manager in regular industry. He had been responsible for obtaining the work done by patients in the hospital, and at various stages and places in the working operation the influence of good business practice was obvious. Mr. McDonnell brought a higher level of work than seen in other hospital settings where the industrial therapy direction had come from professional personnel in the paramedical disciplines or from business people whose backgrounds represent lower managerial levels.

Dr. Birnie is convinced that there must be a next step, that there must be work outside of the hospital to which patients can go after the hospital-based industrial experience. He believes in the development of an industrial therapy organization and Mr. McDonnell had been instrumental in getting I.T.O. (Thames) organized.

Mr. McDonnell, in his capacity as General Manager of the Industrial Therapy Organisation (Thames), took over an old factory building not far from St. Bernard's and rebuilt it. He developed very fine relationships with the building unions and insisted that the contractor include in the building contract the use of some patient labor. This was for the purposes of training as well as for the purposes of providing a transitional outlet for patients to return to the community. At the time of the visit, a good deal of the construction work was under way, and Mr. McDonnell asserted that the use of patient labor, which had been looked upon slightly askance by the building contractor, was now welcomed most heartily. The tradesmen had entered quite well into the pattern of serving as supervisors and instructors to the patients. In more recent correspondence, Mr. McDonnell reported that the plan worked out quite well, the building is completely reconditioned and they have started production. Legally the I.T.O. (Thames) is quite separate from the hospital, though Dr. Birnie serves as psychiatric consultant to the I.T.O. program, and evidently all of the patient population in the new program is coming from St. Bernard's Hospital.

Mr. McDonnell also established a shoe repair shop in the community. He took over an old shoe repair store and placed in it what may be described as "American" type of machinery, mainly for the purposes of repairing soles and heels rather than shoe rebuilding. He staffed the shop with patients. It was a going concern when visited, and looks and performs exactly like any one of the hundreds of shoe repair shops in this country that operate as chain outlets with semi-skilled technicians trained in the use of fairly automatic and sophisticated equipment. It is worth taking note of the effect that such a shop has upon the attitudes of people in the community toward patients in the hospital and toward mental illness. It is the housewives and the working people who come in and out of the shoe store, and since the patients who man it keep changing from time to time as turnover moves them out into the work-a-day world, a greater sympathy arises as to the relative normalcy of functioning of the people behind the counter.

Mr. McDonnell had virtual freedom in setting contract rates and pay rates and in deciding upon the capital outlay that would be made from surpluses from the sale of production. Theoretically, he reported to the psychiatrist in charge and through him to Dr. Birnie. In actuality, he turned to Dr. Birnie for medical advice, but in business matters Dr. Birnie gave him a very free hand. The pay rates to patients are on a graduated scale keyed to their actual production.

On the less positive side, this visitor was not as impressed with the communication between industrial therapy and the psychiatric staff in the hospital as he was in other places in England. Other psychiatric personnel are not quite as enthusiastic about the rehabilitation potential of the industrial therapy program as is Dr. Birnie himself. This may not produce as many problems in St. Bernard's where but 15 per cent of the patients are in the program, but in a place like Netherne Hospital, where roughly 80 per cent of the patients are in some work therapeutic venture, it could be disastrous.

The National Advisory Council of Industrial Therapy Organisations, which has been set up in England through the good offices of the Smith Kline & French Pharmaceutical Laboratories, is much interested in the development of the I.T.O. (Thames) and the work that Mr. McDonnell had done at St. Bernard's. The I.T.O. (Thames) is somewhat different from the other I.T.O.'s in that it represents a more highly developed industrial approach under industrial management and with the use of supervisory personnel from the technical fields. It also works a little more closely with the hospital than is true of some of the others.

Mr. McDonnell has since left the I.T.O. (Thames) to become consultant on rehabilitation programs for the governments of Eire and Northern Ireland. With the assistance of the National Advisory Council of Industrial Therapy Organisations, Mr. McDonnell has been developing industrial therapy and I.T.O. programs for a number of the Irish mental hospitals.

7. *Some Notes about the I.T.O.'s.* The newest development, and perhaps most significant to vocational rehabilitation in community psy-

chiatry, is the appearance of the Industrial Therapy Organisations. This idea began with Dr. Donal Early and Mr. John P. Turley (Glenside Hospital, Bristol) as they faced the problems of the transition of patients from hospital to community. They established in the city of Bristol what we would call a nonprofit business corporation so that patients from the hospital could move out during the day to as nearly a normal working environment as possible.

The first I.T.O. was begun early in 1960 in a renovated, old school building in York Street, St. Phillips Marsh. It is under the control of a board of directors, constituted to have representation from industry, the churches, medicine, civic organizations, public relations and the trade unions. The I.T.O. (Bristol) received initial financial support from the Bishop of Clifton and also from the Transport and General Workers Union. This latter support is of great interest, for publicity during the planning stage had led to charges in the Bristol Trades Council that industrial therapy meant exploitation of labor and possible anti-union activity. After reviewing the program at Glenside Hospital, however, the unions have been strongly supportive.

In structure, principles and practices, the I.T.O. resembles the better community-based sheltered workshops in this country. Local industry agreed that on work contracted for with I.T.O., the price set would be full cost of labor plus 33⅓ per cent for overhead. This addition by no means covers total cost, for the hospital supplies nursing supervision and medical consultation, and social service is provided through assigned health visitors from the county medical officer of health. The agreed upon overhead percentage does prevent a situation, all too prevalent in this country, where the rehabilitation workshop, by charging only labor costs, is actually subsidizing the industrial contractor, thus contributing to unfair competition and invalid labor practices.

In terms of income and expenditures, it is important to note that in the second and third years of its activity, the I.T.O. (Bristol) ran deficits which were made up by the South West Hospital Board, but by the end of its fourth year in January, 1964, the I.T.O. had moved "into the black." The Ministry of Labour quickly saw the value of the I.T.O. as a training center for mental patients and in 1961 acceded to the recommendation that a sheltered workshop (European style—a shop for the long term or permanently disabled) be made part of the factory. Referrals began to come from other hospitals in the area, from medical practitioners, the health and labor authorities, et al., and the I.T.O. opened its doors to other psychiatric patients in addition to those from Glenside Hospital. In turn, I.T.O. (Bristol) has enlarged its scope to include the car wash and the Sheltered Placements in Industry plan, described previously.

During 1965, I.T.O. (Bristol) set up the Industrial Therapy Housing Association (Bristol) Limited. This development was aided by impetus by the Ministry of Labour agreeing to classify as "sheltered workshops" the placements in industry units but requiring that patients participating live outside the hospital. The Transport and General Workers Union assisted in the acquisition of a small hotel as an accommodation for worker patients. Following this, the Association acquired six council houses opposite Glenside Hospital on land previously owned by the Ministry of Health.

Within three years of the opening of I.T.O. (Bristol), four other hospitals opened I.T.O.'s of their own. In the spring of 1964, there were a number of others, and a National Advisory Council of Industrial Therapy Organisations (N.I.T.O.) was formed. Annual meetings have been arranged for the I.T.O.'s and Smith Kline & French Laboratories was gracious in assigning an official of their London offices to serve as Executive Secretary for N.I.T.O. during its formative years.

Each of the I.T.O.'s follows the same general principles as the I.T.O. (Bristol). By agreement it can use the name I.T.O. and a similar coat of arms on its letterhead and literature. Each I.T.O., however, reflects the unique quality of the hospital from which it has originated and the individual differences of the physicians and industrial managers who have nursed it into being. Witness, for example, the differences between I.T.O. (Bristol) and I.T.O. (Thames) as described in the preceding pages.

The I.T.O. pattern of service is worthy of serious attention by mental health planners in the United States. In a number of ways, it represents a more valid and healthier approach to vocational rehabilitation than some of the hospital-based workshops springing up across the country. The CHIRP program of the Brockton Veterans Administration Hospital in Massachusetts (Community Hospital Industrial Rehabilitation Program) has elements in common to I.T.O. but could take note of the I.T.O. job pricing system. The Altro Work Shops, Inc., program of assistance to industrial therapy in mental hospitals in the Bronx, New York, is a form of I.T.O. in reverse, a factory offering service to hospitals, and owes its most recent format of hospital relationships to these visits to I.T.O. (Bristol) and I.T.O. (Thames) as well as to the Cheadle Royal (Industries), Ltd.

The Dutch System of Sheltered Work

On a relatively large scale, The Netherlands has been carrying on rehabilitation for the mentally ill longer than any other European country. "Consultation Bureaux," incorporating many aspects of aftercare, preventive, and social therapies, were opened in the middle 1920's. Soon after World War II when the Social Employment Scheme for Manual Workers was inaugurated in 1949, the new sheltered workshops for the disabled were utilized whenever possible for the mentally handicapped by the hospital aftercare services. Even before this, certain of the mental hospitals had begun to substitute work-for-pay on contract with private firms for conventional occupational therapy.

While a number of the Dutch mental hospitals, all but a very few of which are nongovernmental, have brought work-for-pay into their walls, the most interesting developments of significance to the American scene are in the community sheltered workshops. The Social Employment Scheme for Manual Workers was not limited to handicapped persons. From its inception it was available to all unemployed manual workers who, for reasons including physical or mental handicaps as well as personality factors and socio-economic conditions, were not successful in finding jobs.

> In order to prevent those concerned from losing heart and getting indifferent and in order to make these workers retain or even increase their working capacity, the Minister (of Social Affairs) emphasized the importance of placing these persons at special projects adapted to their physical and mental conditions.[121]

By 1953, the Social Employment Scheme was enlarged to cover nonmanual (white collar) workers.

By 1966, there were 185 sheltered workshops located throughout The Netherlands. Many of these, referred to as Social Workshops, are set up as nonprofit foundations or corporations; some are municipal institutions, and a few, in more sparsely populated areas, are jointly managed by two or more cooperating municipalities. In most instances, The Board of Managers or Trustees is composed of one or more municipal officials and representatives of industry, the employment office and sometimes medicine or public health. State consultants for Complementary Social Provisions (the social security system) are often attached as advisers to the Boards of sheltered workshops.

Within each province, or for groups of provinces, the workshops have formed federations of workshops. These federations and their national association promote cooperation between the workshops, coordinate pricing policies and regulate sales, help to canvass work orders, and otherwise function like trade associations. The Ministry of Social Affairs and Public Health participates in the work of these federations in an advisory capacity.

Services to the Mentally Handicapped

Sheltered work for the feeble-minded in The Netherlands actually predates the Social Employment Scheme by many years. The first such program was opened in Dordrecht in 1920 for aftercare of pupil graduates from a school for mental defectives. A number of other cities followed suit. It is therefore not surprising to find the mentally retarded included without too much question in th Social Workshops of the government-supported program.

By 1961, Dr. A. H. Heering reported to the First Congress of the European League of Societies for the Mentally Handicapped that about 6000 mentally defective persons were working under sheltered conditions.[79] Three fourths of these were covered under the Social Employment Scheme (referred to in Dutch as the G.S.W.—Gemeentelijke Sociale Werkvoorziening). The remainder, whose earning capacity is below one third of normal, have their financial subsidies arranged through the provisions of the Poor Law and under the auspices of the local municipalities. A summary of Social Workshops in The Netherlands[122] lists 17 as specialized for the mentally and intellectually handicapped and one specifically for the epileptic. Nearly 4000 individuals are served in these specialized shops, about half of all the mentally handicapped eligible for coverage under the Social Employment Scheme but more than 75 per cent of those under Poor Law provisions.

During the period of high employment and labor shortage in The Netherlands, between World War II and 1965, almost all of what we would refer to as "high level" mental retardates (the "debiles" in European nomenclature) were employed in regular industry or trades. Since 1965 there has been an economic decline and a period of less than full employment. The handicapped workers already absorbed into industry were among the first laid off and the sheltered workshops are committed to take them back. The government subsidizes each worker fully enough that the workshops can accept them. The mentally retarded in sheltered workshops are of the "imbecile" group and include many persons below levels considered acceptable even to American workshops specializing in service to the feeble-minded. The significance is therefore all the greater that some 4000 of these have achieved more than one third of normal productivity level and that half of these have done so in workshops not specially designed for dealing with their problems. The Dutch are convinced that their very great investment in education and training of the feeble-minded and more recently of the chronic schizophrenic has paid off handsomely. Observing some of the end results, both in terms of individual productivity and of effective social psychiatry, this writer is inclined to concur.

Special Problems of Serving the Mentally Handicapped

Over the past few years there has been an interesting and continuing discussion in professional circles in The Netherlands about the problems of serving the mentally handicapped in the sheltered workshops. While the greatest concern has been with the treatment of the mentally retarded, the experience gained and the changes in viewpoint resulting therefrom are having direct effect as well on the increasing extension of services to the post mentally ill.

The primary issue is best described by Dr. A. H. Heering in his speech to the First Congress of the European League of Societies for the Mentally Handicapped.[79] He stated,

> As regards the admission to "general workshops," that is to say, workshops that have not specially been designed for the mentally handicapped, a certain line of policy has gradually been developed. This line of policy is to the effect that the number of mentally handicapped persons should always be kept comparatively small in proportion to the total number of workers, or the workshop would be in danger of being called a "loony" factory.
>
> It is also of great importance that the said category should be employed in separate groups, although in certain cases exceptions may be made to this rule. And the management should always bear in mind that any plans to place mentally handicapped persons in the same workshop with otherwise handicapped persons should always thoroughly be discussed with the latter group before putting these plans into practice.

Gradually, as larger numbers of the retardates showed capacity for moving up to the G.S.W. standards and as workshop management became more experienced with and comfortable in working with the mentally defective, there has been greater willingness to mix the groups and there has been recognition of gains to be achieved for both. Still, in a special study conference on The Mentally Handicapped Person in the Workshops held in 1963, The Netherlands Society for Social Educational Care (Nederlandse Vereniging voor Social Pedagogische Zorg) concluded indignantly that it is inadmissible for workshops that serve the physically and mentally handicapped in one building but in separate sections to continue to provide separate entrances for the two groups.[123]

The conference was sympathetic to the problems of the small general workshop which tries also to serve the feeble-minded, and it concluded that it is in the larger shops where experimentation should take place in mixing personnel. The conference report also stressed the need for wholesome attitudes on the part of workshop management and the need for careful individual assessment in selection of candidates for workshop placement and in measuring capacities for work.

As is probably already apparent, there is a tendency in The Netherlands to speak of the mentally retarded and the mentally ill as being in the same group, at least as far as industrial therapy is concerned. Both populations are generally considered the responsibility of the psychiatric authorities. Many of the problems of management, training for work, etc., have similarities, particularly as between low grade defectives and "burned out" chronic schizophrenics.

In 1967 a national law enjoined local communities to "promote" the establishment of the Sociale Workshops. The handicapped, too, are urged under the Arbeit Revaladatie Afdeling to apply for and fulfill their "duty" to work. Instead of his workshop earnings serving as a supplement to his disability or sickness pension, the latter becomes supplementation to his earnings in the G.S.W. program. The intent is to supply motivation for the handicapped to enter the workshops.

To help the postmentally ill there has been a push to increase the white collar programs of the G.S.W., or what is referred to by the Dutch as the "head workers program" as distinct from the "hand workers program."[69]

Among the most interesting of the Dutch sheltered work programs because of their revelance to similar programs serving the mentally ill in this country are the Centrale Werkplaats in Veendam, the Dr. Schroeder Van Der Kolk Stichting in The Hague and the Stichting Beileroord in Beilen. The first of these is a small general workshop located in a northern province which is experimenting carefully with introducing the mentally ill. The Dr. Schroeder Van Der Kolk Association is already world famous for its work with the mentally defective and has developed a program just as significant for mixing in the mentally ill. The program at Beilen is illustrative of industrial therapy associated with a rehabilitation-oriented mental hospital having an unusual reputation in family care (foster home services).

1. *Centrale Werkplaats (Veendam, The Netherlands).* This workshop was visited in 1964 and again in 1967.[69] The host was Mr. B. Mijnheer, the Director. During most of the visits Mr. H. Ossel, a regional representative of the Ministry of Social Affairs and Public Health, was also present.

The Centrale Werkplaats serves five municipalities (Gemeentes), including Veendam, in the province of Groningen. It is a generalized workshop serving about 110 people of whom 45 are in the mentally ill and mentally handicapped grouping. In a separate room there was a unit for 15 to 20 mentally handicapped persons, mostly subnormals but with a few schizophrenics. This is for the most part a younger, more volatile group of patients who are found to be too disturbing to the mainly physically handicapped in the rest of the shop.

The Werkplaats was in a specially designed wooden building in which the work space was nicely arranged. Veendam is a small village, and the workshop was pleasantly located within easy access for the people who use it. However, it was already crowded and there are plans in view to rebuild in concrete or brick. At the time of the first visit the Werkplaats served only men; in 1965 a unit of about a dozen handicapped women was added. The new building is planned in an "H" shape with one wing for the physically handicapped and one for the mentally ill and retarded.

Centrale Werkplaats is one of the few sheltered workshop programs in The Netherlands where there is a special interest for the mentally ill. Mr. Mijnheer was trained and has had experience as a male nurse in mental hospitals. He was therefore anxious to introduce such patients into his worker population, and his program was turned to by the officials of the Ministry as a pilot plant in this experience.

Referrals to the workshop come by way of the municipal social affairs committees, mainly the provincial one. Mr. Ossel serves on the Social Affairs Committee for Groningen province, as does Mr. Mijnheer. There is always a medical examination by the consulting physician to the Werkplaats. He is at present a Veendam physician who gives part of his time to the work. By action of the Ministry of Social Affairs and Public Health, there are plans to employ a full-time physician on the Ministry staff who will be shared by three workshops.

It seemed to the visitors that the types of handicapped served in Centrale Werkplaats were mostly what we call the "hidden" ones. There were a few orthopedic cases, but the rest were chest disease, heart, epilepsy, diabetes, asthma, some muscular dystrophy and multiple sclerosis, higher grade subnormals and schizophrenics. One or two of the patients looked oligophrenic.

The work being done was mainly bench-type assembly. A group of patients were working hard assembling corrugated cardboard boxes. There was almost a frenzy in the pace of working. In contrast, work being done in making chairs in another room was at a steady, almost leisurely pace but of good quality. There are plans, in the new building to add more specialized and semi-skilled work.

Mr. Ossel explained that Centrale Werkplaats is typical of the smaller and somewhat less experienced workshops in The Netherlands. There are a number with a larger business production, greater productivity and are somewhat more showy. Some of the workshops make profits, though this depends greatly upon the attitude and the ability of the director and on the kind of patient mix and the rate of turnover of experienced workers. Since Veendam is in an area of very full employment and with a high labor shortage, the Centrale Werkplaats has less productive workers than some of the workshops where there is less labor demand in the community. All of the workshops in The Netherlands have an emphasis on rehabilitation. The aim, if at all possible, is return to industry. Mr. Ossel was frank in stating that the real return to industry amounts to about 5 per cent per year, although seasonal employment does raise this figure to an official rate percentge of 15 to 20. Nonetheless, considering that the country had an acute labor shortage and every possible utilization was made of folk who could be even partially productive and observing the kind of patient personnel used in the workshops, even the 5 per cent figure is impressive.

The method of working together between the assignment committees from the provinces and the local communities and the workshops seems smooth and valid. The workshop director, Mr. Mijnheer in this case, has no veto power on the acceptance of patients. He can discharge a worker, however, after experience with the individual and/or evaluation. Mr. Mijnheer claims never to have discharged anyone without a fair length of trial.

The Ministry of Social Affairs and Public Health subsidizes the deficit of the workshop up to 75 per cent of wages of workers plus an acceptable overhead figure. The method of arriving at wages for workers is a somewhat complicated one. It takes into account five factors: (1) quantity, (2) quality, (3) interest and willingness, (4) behavior (to supervisor and colleagues, whether on time, etc.) and (5) care of materials and tools. Rating scales are used, with ratings up to five points per item. However, Items 1 and 2—that is, quantity and quality—must total 50 per cent of the points out of a possible total of 32. The final score determines the level of wage rate which is then applied in accordance with four difficulty levels for each occupation. The difficulty levels for each task are determined on recommendation of the workshop director. Wage scales are set differentially by the Ministry for each of the regions of the country. The maximum wage possible for an individual in the workshop, for someone who achieves 30 to 32 points on the rating scale, reaches the minimum wage set for work in normal industry. At the time of visit this was 100 florins per week for a 45-hour week. It should be noted that the rating scale procedure has some similarity to that devised by the British industrial rehabilitation units, and, in fact, the Dutch took the British system and modified it to meet their needs.

The government exercises a wage control for each workshop over and above what develops from the individual ratings for workers. Workshop employees are categorized as A workers, those who have not achieved one third of normal production and B workers, those certified to be able to reach or receive 33⅓ per cent of normal level. Workers in category A are paid a lower wage than those in B. The average for any shop in each of the two major categories cannot exceed the median for the scale set by the Ministry. However, in a few instances where the numbers of persons in the workshops are very small, an exception can be allowed. The Ministry can then keep its budget balanced to the median of the scales which it sets. The implication is that workers who reach the 30 to 32 points on the rating scale, and who are therefore earning at the minimum available in normal industry, should move on when jobs are available out of the workshop.

The Ministry of Social Affairs and Public Health has vacillated between a philosophy of wanting integrated workshops serving all categories of handicapped, including mental illness and subnormality, and segregated workshops in which those mentally ill and mentally handicapped are kept out. First there was an insistence upon completely integrated shops, but now, out of the experience at the Centrale Werkplaats, and that of the Dr. Van Der Kolk Stichting in the Hague, and perhaps one or two others, there has been a swing to Mr. Mijnheer's view that some separation is for the good of the patients.

Those, aside from the directors, who supervise the work in the workshops are given a training course of one day every fortnight for 14 weeks. These training programs, set up by the Ministry, are offered at Meppel and Zwolle for the northern provinces and at Utrecht for the southern provinces. There is no training for directors of workshops, and these managers will vary from individuals with business experience to individuals with professional experience in service to handicapped people.

The greatest difficulty in integrating the handicaps appeared to come from the older adolescent-young adult group and particularly those with a certain amount of psychopathy or potential acting out behavior. This is worth noting for its similarity to the problem in integrated workshop settings in our country.

2. *The Dr. Schroeder Van Der Kolk Stichting (The Hague, The Netherlands).* The visitor's host was Dr. N. Speijer, the municipal mental health director of The Hague. Dr. Speijer explained that he has a fully centralized and integrated mental health program for the city of The Hague. It is in seven divisions, as follows:

1. Inpatient service. Reduced now to 200 beds for the whole of the city of 600,000 population.
2. Forecare and aftercare service. Dr. Speijer noted that forecare has become larger and more important than aftercare service.
3. Youth services.
4. Adult, Police and Parole.
5. A department of psychologists.
6. A service especially for governmental employees.
7. A general advisory service.

All psychiatric bed services and emergency services must clear through Dr. Speijer's office. In addition, he is the psychiatric adviser of every cooperating governmental service and is also on the Board of Directors of every sectarian service which receives a subsidy from the city or the national government. The religious subdivisions, faintly reminiscent of New York, are Catholic, Protestant and neutral.

The Dr. Schroeder Van Der Kolk Stichting sheltered workshop program in The Hague is named after one of the early pioneers in modern mental health services. One section of the workshop, serving about 200 people, is for the physically handicapped. The rest of the program, serving some 500 to 600 people, is divided among five buildings. These services are for the mentally handicapped and the mentally ill. As is true with much of the rehabilitation services for the mentally ill in The Netherlands, the mentally retarded and the mentally ill are grouped together. The population of workers is made up of quite seriously mentally handicapped along with quite seriously deteriorated schizophrenics.

The Dr. Van Der Kolk Stichting is a separate corporation which has its own Board of Directors. Important and influential community representatives are on the Board. A great deal of general policy control, however, rests with Dr. Speijer's office, as well as the medical control, since he serves, as noted above, as the medical advisor to the Board. In the months before this writer's visit, the general manager of the Stichting had been ill and unavailable, and Dr. Speijer had also been spending a good deal of time on overall problems of management as well as on medical direction.

Deficits of the workshops are met by the City Council in the form of subsidies on the advice of Dr. Speijer. He has evidently used quite effectively an economic argument with the City Council that the cost of patients in the sheltered workshop is much lower than their cost in institutionalization.

This visitor saw factories representing the various levels of work and of patients. The physical facilities were all excellent. One major installation is in a converted public school building, and another is in a small factory building evidently constructed for the purpose. Equipment was new and maintained in good repair. There was a general atmosphere of productivity and a cheerfulness which left an excellent impression.

The type of work is in four grades in accordance with the amout of skill required. Within each grade there are levels from 1 to 3. Thus, a patient could conceivably move from grade 1, level 1 on up through grade 4, level 3. In actual practice, since many of the patients are low grade subnormals or quite ill schizophrenics, few of them reach grade 4. Almost all, according to Dr. Speijer, do move up to grade 3 even though it may take years for the low grade subnormals.

The example of a grade 1, level 1 job was the assembly of ball point pens. Here the lowest subnormals and obviously deteriorated schizophrenics, were working very slowly putting the various parts of ballpoint pens together. While the level of productivity was very, very low, the visitor was amazed at the complexity of the motions that were possible even here. A higher grade of work was the gluing of corks on bottle tops. In this, a circular table, rotated by the workers, brought the materials to their work position. There was a group sense and camaraderie about the workers though the productivity capacity appeared to be pretty low. In the higher grades, the work skills required increased through a variety of sewing operations up through manufacturing tennis shoes and slippers and even to a rather high grade of semi-skilled electronic assembly.

The visitor was impressed that the jigs and fixtures used were well worked out and the safety precautions were those of normal industry. Dr. Speijer believes only in subcontract work, since this provides for variety. However, he will consider only jobs that have a long flow and vary in complete steps from simple to complex operations. He is fearful of engaging in direct manufacture because of the requirements for a sales organization and the necessity of meeting the demands of a large body of customers. He is also concerned that the tendency might be to sell on the basis of pity or philanthropy rather than on quality and productivity.

There are two supervisors per department—a technician and a nurse. The technicians are trained through the lower grade technical schools for manufacturing processes and then take special training for work in a sheltered workshop. The nurses used are trained in psychiatric service and in work with the mentally deficient.

There is much to learn from the Dutch about their methods of training the subnormals and the seriously disabled schizophrenics. The care and the time spent in teaching simple skills in the industrial process produce amazing results. It was hard for the visitor to imagine some of the patients who were performing rather complex skills doing anything other than the most menial of operations in an American sheltered workshop, even in a shop of high standard. One's timesight would have to be raised in many instances to accept the need for a training period of three or four years.

The Ministry of Social Affairs provides advisers to assist in the organization of the workshop and to aid in various of the business considerations. Capital outlay and construction funds are provided by the City Council upon application by the Board of Directors of the workshop and, it appears, upon approval of the medical adviser.

When it comes to the question of placement of workshop patients into normal industry or, in reverse, the referral of persons from industry who have become ill and who require transitional rehabilitation in the sheltered workshop, there are social workers in each of the large industries in The Netherlands. There is also a staff of social workers in the Ministry of Social Work. These assist in dealing with the family problems, in the problems of public relief, etc. Through the services of the public departments including the municipal mental health program, there is a net of hostels to take care of the living problems of the subnormals and schizophrenics, as well as an arrangement of social clubs for recreation. Patients are taught to manage their transportation through public or private means in the normal manner of workers in industry.

Dr. Speijer has some very interesting concepts on the relationship of illness to work and the methods of increasing the capacity of handicapped persons to perform work, and these carry over into the training methods and teaching methods used on behalf of the patients.[158,159]

3. *The Stichting Beileroord and The Sanatorium Rustoord ('t Beilen, The Netherlands)*.   The visitor's host in 1964 was Dr. R. Zijlstra, the Medical Superintendent; in 1967 it was his successor, Dr. W. Hoekstra.

The Sanatorium is one of three hospitals in the province of Drente. The other two are an 1100-bed Calvinistic hospital and a 500-bed hospital under the auspices of the Dutch Reformed Church. These latter two are the more traditional mental hospitals, having no more than the usual emphasis upon rehabilitation and nothing special in the way of work activities.

The Stichting Beileroord serves three provinces, those of Groningen, Drente and Freisling, which are the three most northern of The Netherlands. Rustoord is the rehabilitation institution for mental patients from these provinces. It is operated by a Board of Directors made up of officials from the three provinces, although it has independent powers in the making of policy and in the handling of finance. Deficits of the hospital are made up by the provincial governments, and these governments also underwrite any building programs. The hospital and work activity programs serve approximately 500 patients. About 160 are in the hospital and the remainder are in about 160 foster family homes. As a matter of fact, the program in Beilen is internationally famous for its work in family foster care of the mentally ill. Intake referrals and decisions for placement in foster homes are made by provincial social psychiatric units which are staffed primarily by psychiatric social workers.

All the patients in the hospital and in the foster homes are in some sort of work activity during the day. There are interruptions for treatment, but it appears that these are kept to a minimum during regular working hours.

The hospital is a beautiful, new two-story building, well equipped and in attractive colors. It serves people in the 16 to 65 year old age range. There is some carry-over of deteriorated, aged schizophrenics from earlier years, but the hospital does not accept the elderly now. Children are not served in this institution although the older adolescent and young adults with psychopathic tendencies are taken.

The sanatorium provides nurses' training. Young nurse cadets work hard at housekeeping tasks and at work supervision as well as in studies. There is a 3-year course leading to a diploma in psychiatric nursing. This visitor's opinion is that the degree granted is somewhat between what in this country would be a full-fledged ward attendant and a registered nurse. There is quite a turnover of the young women, for, according to the Superintendent, they make good candidates for marriage. The older adolescent-young adult patients are difficult for the young women nurses to manage. It is possible that some of this may be overcome by the introduc-

tion of more male nurses, though with the shortage of labor in The Netherlands, these would be hard to come by.

During the trip through the hospital, this visitor was impressed by the
staff and by their enthusiasm and their care of patients. A head matron,
for example, was doing a wonderfully imaginative job with older chronic
schizophrenic women. The staff appears to be quite psychoanalytically
oriented. There is a lot of use of psychotherapy, both individual and
group treatment, as well as utilization of chemotherapy. The shock treatments, insulin and ECT are infrequently used.

In the work activities there is a good deal of use of hospital occupations.
These include the trades of carpentry, painting, plumbing, etc., and there
is a fairly complete farm where wheat and vegetables are harvested. There
is a large and well-equipped greenhouse for flowers. Everywhere there are
flowers, all year around.

The activities building, designed specifically for the Stichting, is in the
shape of a dodecahedron in which all of the interior walls of the ten
peripheral rooms are of glass. The central core has private interviewing
rooms on the first floor and a second story, completely of glass, from
which the supervisor can see every one of the ten workrooms.

In each of the workrooms patients were occupied in activities ranging
from occupational therapy to subcontract work. Among the latter were the
assembly of clothespins, the weaving of raffia rugs and mats, the repair
and binding of school books and the making of stuffed dolls. The book-
binding and repair work is on contract with the local school system; the
other work is on subcontracts with local industry.

The quality of work being done was of the highest caliber. A care and
meticulousness was involved which can only be described as within the
Dutch character. It would be hard to imagine patients in an American
mental hospital performing at this level of quality without extremely careful screening, and there was no evidence that patients used were other than
a cross section of the patient population.

The emphasis in the work activity is on return to productivity. Payment
to the patients is limited to a maximum of about 3 florins per week per
patient. This is mostly looked upon as pocket money and is paid to all
patients on activity whether they are doing productive work or not. It
appears that the next move of the patient after treatment in this setting
would be either into sheltered work programs in the provinces or back to
normal industry.

Some Comments on the Dutch Programs

1. Although at first glance The Netherlands does not appear to have developed as many different industrial therapy programs for the mentally ill

as have the British, in proportion to population there is probably greater coverage in The Netherlands. At least two important trends have led to a country-wide program with great potential in modern social psychiatry: one being the more rapid movement towards community-based treatment of the mentally ill in place of hospitalization; the other being the economic pressure in a labor shortage to use all available manpower.

The number and percentage of mentally handicapped workers in the sheltered workshops is growing. In 1966, about 17 per cent of all workers in the social workshops were of that category. Over 60 per cent of the workshops serving a general handicapped population had ten or more per cent mentally ill in their worker load. Workshops are having increasingly successful experiences in cooperating with mental hospital directors.

> They are in the process of reaching out to a growing number of hospitals and they believe that the ideas for cooperation are by no means exhausted. They are encouraging the transfer of workers who are ready from the workshops on hospital grounds to the workshop in the community where the hospital is located and then to the community in which the worker wishes to live.[69]

While the British do not seem to have taken much cognizance of the Dutch programs in developing industrial therapy, the Dutch are well aware of the British programs. Other countries of Western Europe, and also some behind the Iron Curtain, have watched the growth of the Dutch services with interest and have borrowed ideas and experience.

2. The Dutch services have demonstrated that it is possible to raise the level of productive capacity of severely handicapped mental retardates and of the mentally ill far above commonly accepted standards in the United States and elsewhere in the world. Those who critically consider the Dutch experience can hardly be satisfied that in this country all is being done that can be done in behalf of the handicapped. This is so even though one may argue that the cost of training is actually greater than the economic return in productivity or that it is not easy to reproduce the dedication to supplying each individual his "right to work" which is almost a religious hallmark of the Dutch.

3. It should be noted that the cost of supporting a chain of sheltered workshops is great. Governmental payments cover 75 per cent of the payroll in most of the workshops, and there are matching grants for administrative overhead and long-term loans or outright grants for capital construction or supply of tools and equipment. The major economic argument in support of this outlay is that the total cost per individual is usually less than, and never more than, the cost of maintaining the "patients" and "pupils" in an institutional custodial program. It has been estimated by

Dr. Heering that the G.S.W. program cost about $2600 per handicapped worker in 1967.

4. The emphasis upon industrial work has had the effect of introducing three principles of great importance to industrial therapy.

    a. The kind of work, in addition to being therapeutic in a medical or pedagogical sense, must be of the nature of work actually performed in the economy, therefore presenting a bridge to the real work-a-day world.

    b. Because such work requires either technical supervision or technical adjustment to meet the conditions of handicaps, or both, work supervisors with technical and industrial knowledge and experience must be used.

    c. Contracting work for regular industry imposes requirements of meeting limits of time, quantity and quality. Only by mixing the work force so that the low productive patients are in the minority can these standards be achieved. In the smaller sheltered workshop, this principle would seem to be more greatly responsible for keeping the proportion of mentally handicapped low than would an adverse attitude of the physically handicapped to the mentally disabled.

5. Of great significance is the continuous emphasis upon rehabilitation. Use of the rating scale procedures referred to in the description of Centrale Werkplaats has the effect of regularly re-assessing the worker's potential. Even though a relatively small proportion of this severely disabled work force actually moves permanently into normal industry, the concern and effort towards this end is constantly there.

REHABILITATION OF THE MENTALLY ILL IN OTHER WESTERN EUROPEAN COUNTRIES

Industrial therapy for the mentally ill is at an earlier stage of development in the rest of Western Europe than either in England or The Netherlands. From this writer's personal observation in France, supplemented by correspondence and review of the literature, and for other countries based upon official records, descriptive articles and reports of colleagues who have visited, herewith is presented a summary of present developments.

FRANCE

The pioneering effort in industrial therapy in France is the work of Dr. Paul Sivadon at the hospital of the Ville Evrard, located outside of Paris. Here Dr. Sivadon has introduced work for pay, essentially through the use of handicrafts and work for the hospital community itself. More recently, in his development of a very modern and unusual mental institution for the Teachers Mutual at the Chateau de la Verriere near Versailles, Dr. Sivadon has established workshops for occupational and work therapy.

The concept of rehabilitation of the mentally ill is by no means a new one to France where reference to "ergo therapy" as a treatment approach appeared as early as in England, but in France the practical establishment of programs for this purpose has been very slow. French psychiatry has tended to resist the introduction of group and milieu therapies, but has laid much stress on individual approaches including shock treatments, psychochemical and "Pavlovian" types of retraining. Even for occupational therapy which often serves as the introduction to industrial therapy, Dr. Pierre Pichot, Professeur Agrégé of Psychiatry at the University of Paris, has this to say,

> Interest in occupational therapy has grown considerably in the last few years. A variety of such procedures has been initiated, and certain psychiatric services have been reorganized to give this method primary importance. . . . It should be noted, however, that occupational therapy is not without opposition; some workers have criticized its extremely superficial character and have pointed out the danger it represents, i.e., that it may lead to the neglect of more efficacious therapeutic methods.[135]

Even where pay for work is provided, it is more often for sale of handicrafts or for work performed for the mental institution than for tasks on contract with outside industry. At the Chateau de la Verriere this visitor saw fairly well-equipped woodworking and other shops, but the design and facilities were more those of an industrial arts classroom than of an industrial workshop. In line with a most interesting plan to afford areas of sharing and cooperating with the "normal" life of the adjoining village (already achieved in a playing field and in a theater, both built on the border of the hospital grounds and the village), Dr. Sivadon will construct new workshops in which contract work can be undertaken with villagers and patients working side by side.

Another interesting program in ergo therapy, also closer to occupational therapy, is carried on as part of the day hospital of L'Elan (Association L'Elan Retrouvé), a comprehensive mental health center located in the IX Arrondissement of Paris (Montmartre section). Somewhat similar ergo therapeutic services are described for the newer mental health center, established with public support in the XIIIe Arrondissement of Paris[144] and for la clinique "Clerambault" in Sceaux on the outskirts of Paris.[139] Two typically French approaches in mental hospitals are described by Drs. Rajotte and Denber in *Mental Hygiene*.[50] In Saint-Alban Hospital which serves the population of La Lozere, a department in central France, a cooperative of patients produces handiwork of a variety of sorts, from embroidery to wrought iron work, and sells it both within the hospital and in the village market. At Lannemezan Hospital, in the foothills of the Pyrenees Mountains, a club of patients has built and manages an amusement park, well patronized by the neighboring population. At Lannemezan, too, the patient group has opened a public golf club. The hospital church has been constructed so as to serve as the local parish church as well as the hospital chapel.[152]

One of the most interesting newer developments is a rural rehabilitation center near Nantes, in Brittany. Called the Centre de Postcure et de Readaption Sociale Agricole de l'Ouest, it offers a halfway station back to farm work for rural patients discharged from mental hospitals.[42] At the Centre are training courses in modern farm technology, but it is not clear from the literature or correspondence whether the element of work-for-pay is present.

Interestingly enough there is ample provision in French law and regulations for industrial therapy, sheltered work or ergo therapy.[119] By a decree of 1954, district guidance commissions for the disabled and handicapped were given official status. Under the leadership of the prefect of the departmnt (district) or of the district director of labor and manpower, these commissions include representatives of the various governmental and educative departments concerned. Among the professionals serving on these commissions are doctors, educators, psychotechnicians and social workers. The guidance commission carries official responsibility for evaluation of the needs of the disabled or blind referred to it, and it can recommend a range of services including disability pension, re-education in a specialized center, retraining in business or industry and placement in sheltered work or in home work. France has developed thus far, however, very few sheltered workshops, and though there is no legal barrier to their use for the mentally ill, in only two of the approximately 50 in operation as of 1964 had there been any real attempt to serve this group. One of these is the shop of the Association "Vivre," near Paris, and the other is a very small service for women at one of the Southern governmental re-education centers.

In 1960 the Ministry of Health issued a circular setting out the principles that are to govern the growth of mental health services in France.[120] These called for geographic coverage by sectors, a variety of services to be available in each sector, and provision of continuity of care for the patients. Among the services itemized, the circular specifies workshops for readaption (sheltered workshops). There is increasing interest in France in the idea of industrial therapy, and the picture will no doubt be much improved in a few years' time.

BELGIUM

As in France, Belgium has ample legislation to provide for industrial therapy programs for the mentally ill but has moved slowly in implementation. The law of 1958 set up a Council to undertake and support training, rehabilitation and resettlement of the handicapped. The fund set up by this law, paid for by employer and insurance company contributions, provides for a full array of medical, social and vocational rehabilitation services including to "organize placement in 'sheltered workshops' subsidized or set up by the fund, if necessary."[184] Additions to the act in 1963 make clear its applicability to the mentally, as well as the physically, handicapped. In 1964, Belgium reported that there were 40 sheltered workshops in the country serving approximately 600 people and that 17 per cent of those served were in the mentally handicapped categories, most of these obviously being mentally retarded.[68] For the most part, the Belgian sheltered workshops have been privately organized and supported, though the new legislation gives promise of much greater governmental financial support.

SWITZERLAND

In Switzerland, the mental hospitals are for the most part cantonal institutions. Their smaller size and close relationship to their geographical areas have led to greater emphasis on psychosocial efforts than is ordinarily true in mental institutions. Currently there is a great interest in what we would call "total push" programs, particularly at the Burghölzli University Mental Hospital in Zurich and the Friedmatt University Hospital in Basel. In these institutions there is intensive use of the "therapeutic environment" and greater use of occupational therapy.[16] To date there has been little development of hospital-centered industrial therapy in Switzerland.

The Federal Disability Insurance Act of 1960 set up a Federal Office which, in addition to the Disability Insurance Scheme, has supervision over programs of rehabilitation of the handicapped. The act clearly includes mental illness and disability among the categories covered. In addition to the direct benefits to the handicapped, the Scheme "pays subsidies to institutions of the assistance to the disabled, i.e., subsidies to the construction, establishment and renovation of institutions and workshops . . . and subsidies to the running of these institutions and workshops."[60]

The State Disability Insurance Scheme, however, does not itself operate institutions or sheltered workshops. In 1964 there were 55 sheltered workshops in Switzerland serving 1940 handicapped persons, 19 per cent of whom were listed as mentally ill or mentally retarded.

THE SCANDINAVIAN COUNTRIES

The Scandinavian countries, since World War II, have demonstrated wide interest in rehabilitation of the physically disabled; there is at present the beginning of increased attention to rehabilitation problems of the mentally ill. Social psychiatry occupies an important place in Scandinavian psychiatry, and concern for the living and working arrangements for patients is regularly part of treatment planning. Boarding out arrangements (family care) have become an important service for a large proportion of patients in Norway. The Danish institutions, particularly those serving the mental defectives, make extended use of "family care."[106] The mental hospitals in Denmark, Norway and Sweden, however, have but recently begun to introduce aspects of industrial therapy. Most notable in this regard is the State Mental Hospital at Glostrup, Denmark, which has within the past few years developed an occupational therapy scheme which includes a sheltered workshop for some 90 patients, half of whom are outpatients.

The Danish psychiatrists, and this seems to be true of the Norwegian and Swedish as well, look upon occupational therapy and occupational training as more commonly the responsibilities of the institution and make greater use of community-based sheltered workshops for industrial activities. Denmark and Sweden, especially, have networks of sheltered workshops, mostly under private auspices but with heavy governmental financial support. Both the Danish Rehabilitation Act of 1960 and the Swedish Royal Ordinance Regarding Governmental Grants for Workshops Within the Scope of Vocational Rehabilitation (1963) include mental illness among the eligible categories. This appears also to be true of the Norwegian Disabled Persons Act of 1958.

In replying to the International Survey of Sheltered Employment in 1964, the Scandinavian countries reported the following:[68]

	No. of Workshops	No. Employees	Per Cent Mentally Ill
Denmark	40	1200	35*
Norway	25	490	30
Sweden	119	6990	35†
Finland	20	1200	8

* Per cent estimated from table for 1963 supplied by Danish Ministry of Health. May include mentally retarded in the total.

† Possibly includes both mentally retarded and mentally ill.

INDUSTRIAL THERAPY IN EASTERN EUROPE

U. S. S. R.

Except for Russia, there is little information available to the West about industrial therapy for the mentally ill on the other side of the "Iron Curtain." The most authoritative explanation of the underlying philosophy governing what is a wide network of work therapy programs in the mental hospitals and psychiatric clinics in the Soviet Union was presented three years ago by the Deputy Administrative Chief of Psychiatry, Ministry of Health, U. S. S. R., writing in the *International Journal of Psychiatry*. He writes,

> The experience of pre-revolutionary Zemstvo psychiatrists and of Soviet psychiatrists alike shows the great curative importance for the mentally ill, particularly those suffering from protracted forms of psychosis, of work and occupation adapted to the individual and in the right amount. In view of this, the neuropsychiatric clinics in the U. S. S. R. possess occupational therapy workshops, sometimes as one of their departments and sometimes as a separate organization. Their close similarity to ordinary production workshops creates in them an atmosphere similar to that in ordinary places of work. This circumstance in itself gives the patient an opportunity of adapting himself better to his future productive work and makes easier his subsequent transfer to normal working life.[8]

According to reports from an increasing number of American professional visitors to the U. S. S. R., these "occupational therapy workshops" are similar in description to what is referred to in this text as sheltered workshops, both of the transitional and extended service varieties, and they are to be found associated with all of the mental hospitals as well as the day hospitals and outpatient clinics. The explanations given for the central position of work therapy in Soviet psychiatric services are both Pavlovian psychology and ideological. In terms of Pavlovian psychology, Field and Aronson report the explanation that "confusion of higher nervous activity can be helped by labor corresponding to the strength of the individual patient."[61] Wortis and Freundlich describe the therapeutic mechanisms involved in work therapy as involving the following Pavlovian concepts:

1. Relief of inhibitory tendencies by the stimulus of work.
2. Relief of excitatory tendencies by diverting energies into useful channels.
3. Elevation of the functional tone of the cortex through the arousal of pleasant excitation.
4. Distraction of the patient's attention from distressing preoccupations (Pavlovian "sore points").[185]

Field and Aronson were told that in schizophrenia "the length of remission increases with the use of work therapy," and that "Soviet clinical experience is that a sharp dislike of work often indicates a diagnosis of schizophrenia."[62]

Ideologically, the role of work carries a greater meaning to the entire design of cultural behavior in Soviet life than in Western society. Karl Marx wrote that "The mode of production of the material means of existence conditions the whole process of social, political and intellectual life. It is not the consciousness of men that determines their existence, but, on the contrary, it is their social existence that determines their consciousness. . . ."[113] Soviet theory holds, then, that productive work is essential for the maintenance of and the restoration of mental health. Wortis points out that Russian psychiatric tradition long predating the Revolution emphasized the use of work in mental institutions and immediately after the October Revolution work therapy became mandatory for all psychiatric hospitals.[186]

It was not until the 1930's, however, that its use flourished, as much for the badly needed manpower made available as for clinical considerations. Dr. D. E. Melehov of the Institute of Psychiatry, Soviet Ministry of Health, quotes from the reports of a 1941 all-Russian conference on work therapy that

> the Conference considers that the results of the experiments carried out by local authority hospitals in organizing day time departments have proved to be valuable and should be further developed. They allow an earlier discharge of the patient and follow-up treatment and supervision. In chronic cases they promote restoration to work and compensate for defect states by preparing for future work resettlement. The Conference specially recommends the organization of forms of outpatient assistance that will ensure a gradual passage from therapeutic to productive work and will combine, as far as possible, work reclassification and training of the disabled in the new vocation.[115]

World War II interrupted therapeutic work entirely, and for some years after the War the use of work therapy fell into a decline. In the middle 1950's, probably spurred by the same set of treatment developments (chemotherapy, open hospitals, etc.) as stimulated the organization of day hospitals and community psychiatric facilities in the West, interest turned again to industrial therapy. A comprehensive order (No. 166) was issued by the Ministry of Health in 1954 providing regulations for treatment and production workshops in psychiatric and neuropsychiatric facilities. There are both an Institute for Medical Work Assessments and an Institute for Vocational Resettlement of the Disabled in the Ministry of Social Security. According to Melehov, special psychiatric work assessment boards were set up after World War II and these have established methods of determining the degree of disability and of comparing progress and outcome in vocational rehabilitation. In various industries special workshops for the disabled have been set up and large numbers of rehabilitated patients work in open industry under the supervision of the factory doctors. In 1958 an All-Union Conference on Work Therapy was held; two all-Russian conferences on problems of work assessment and resettlement of the mentally ill were held in 1961 and 1964 and a conference on rehabilitation and social readaptation was conducted in 1965.[115] Except for the 1958 proceedings, reviewed by Wortis and Freundlich, the more recent reports have not been translated for Western rehabilitation professional review.

Wortis and Freundlich, as well as Field and Aronson, describe visits to the workshops at the Bekhterev Neuropsychiatric Institute in Leningrad. The latter professional team also visited the psychoneurological dispensary and workshops of the Kiev District in Moscow. In 1963 the Bekhterev shops, which were founded in 1932, employed some 220 patients in bench assembly of plastic and metal novelty items, in manufacture of a variety of items, such as belts, buckles, screwdrivers, in broom-making, sewing, shoe-making and weaving. The Moscow workshops employed 280 patients in industrial types of work with paper and cardboard, using cutters and punchers or in sewing or knitting.

The practices described in these two psychiatric settings show a number of similarities to the programs in England and Holland, outlined earlier in this chapter. The hours of work are reduced from the normal work day, usually to six hours a day. Though work therapy in Russia occupies a more focal position in the regimen for the patients, it is most always combined with other forms of therapeutic intervention, chemotherapy, psychotherapy (largely hypnosis and persuasion) and the use of sleep. Payment is always made to the patients for the work they do, usually related to a piece work rate, and is in addition to whatever disability pension may be paid. An attempt is made to select the type of work that will be most useful therapeutically or will be most closely related to former occupation. While the shops, allied with outpatient treatment centers, try to keep their patients for limited times only, seeking transition to normal employment, there are reports of a range of stay from six months to as long as three years.

Wortis and Freundlich, particularly, report that work therapy is widely used in other settings as well as in the sheltered workshop. They list the entire array as follows:

　　1. Ordinary work in the institution itself, such as cleaning, maintenance, kitchen help, library or professional, etc.;
　　2. Arts and crafts, similar to those we see in our hospitals, but the general trend is away from this;

3. Special work in production shops set up and run as regular factory units. These can be found in both hospitals and clinics and may be attended by both in- and out-patients;
4. Agricultural work on hospital grounds;
5. Assignment to agricultural collectives which serve as foster homes;
6. Participation in sheltered workshops, cooperative units for the disabled (Artels);
7. Reassignment to regular industry with appropriate placement and medical surveillance;
8. Foster home placement combined with regular industrial work.[187]

There are many intriguing questions about industrial therapy in the Soviet Union that cannot be answered from existing literature in the West. It would appear from what is presently known, however, that there are many similarities both East and West in the therapeutic uses of industrial therapy, even though the underlying explanations as to psychological and social values have marked differences. Whether any similarities exist in the business and economic facets, it is not possible to say. Obviously, the economic bases of the Soviet and Western societies are so dissimilar that one can only assume these differences to apply as between their industrial therapy programs as well.

POLAND

There have been almost no reports about the state-supported psychiatric services in Poland, or, for that matter, those of the other countries in the Communist bloc. Personal discussions with visitors from Poland, Yugoslavia and Hungary seem to indicate a rich variety of experiments and demonstrations, though nothing either as widespread as in Russia nor so scientifically disciplined as in England or Holland. There are in all of these countries, however, well-organized services for the physically disabled, and it is very likely that the mentally ill and handicapped to some extent are being included in receipt of these services.

In a special report in 1962 for the World Commission on Vocational Rehabilitation, the Vice Chairman of the Polish Union of Invalids' Cooperatives described his country's rehabilitation programs for the handicapped, particularly the physically handicapped. Rehabilitation activities began in Poland in 1948, predicated upon "The right to work, guaranteed each citizen by the constitution of the Polish People's Republic. . . . Besides pensions and social assistance, rehabilitation of the disabled constitutes an essential factor as regards social security of citizens."[182] Rehabilitation programs are the province of two public agencies, the Ministry of Health and Social Welfare and the Ministry of Education, and an interesting nongovernmental agency, the Union of Invalids' Cooperatives. In the counties and districts, medical rehabilitation is the responsibility of departments of health and welfare at the Presidia of the People's Councils. Medical Commissions for Disability and Employment operate from the Social Insurance Office branches to assess levels of disability. Institutions for the vocational training of invalids provide training in a number of the major cities. Some 18,000 severely disabled persons are employed in workshops, but it is not reported how many are mentally ill.

An example of rehabilitation development, including industrial therapy, is described by an American expert in rehabilitation services who visited Poland.[97] On the outskirts of Warsaw a modern factory building serves amputees, paraplegics, deaf, as well as mentally handicapped persons. The handicapped employees package tablecloths, perfume, and soap, paint puppets and dolls, and operate drill presses, stamping and rolling machines. This factory is one of 410 constituents of the Polish Union of Invalid Cooperatives. These cooperatives, owned and operated by disabled citizens, both military and civilian, are estimated to serve about a third of all persons vocationally rehabilitated in Poland. Figures for 1962 listed 1439 mental patients among the 72,205 handicapped employees in all of the units. Reference is made, however, to one sheltered workshop specifically for former mental patients. This shop had 80 workers, with a full-time psychiatrist as medical director.

The members of the Union of Invalid Cooperatives in Poland are subsidized by the state through financial assistance and funds for capital development as well as being exempt from various taxes. The wage scales are by law made comparable to those of positions in regular industry. Though production earnings of the handicapped may not equal those of regular industry, there are bonuses and other social benefits. A highly productive person may even better the going rate in the U. I. C. shop. The use of cooperatives to meet a social-economic condition is peculiarly unique to the collective philosophy of Polish life and may not be replicable elsewhere. Its reported success does, nevertheless, suggest an interesting possibility for greater attention to "self-help" principles in developing some forms of industrial therapy in the United States.

CHAPTER III

INDUSTRIAL THERAPY IN THE UNITED STATES

EARLY PROGRAMS

As has been seen in the European developments, the recent decades of growth of industrial therapy for the mentally ill in the United States has also followed two paths now converging. The first has been an increasing interest by rehabilitation programs for the physically handicapped in opening their services to the mentally disabled. The other has been the "psychiatric revolution" awakening interest in community care for mentally ill patients.

A good case can be made that, with the possible exception of the Soviet programs, rehabilitation for the mentally ill in the United States predated similar efforts in Europe. In the voluntary agency or "private" sector, two early demonstration services are worth noting. Altro Work Shops, set up in the Bronx, New York in 1917 for the rehabilitation of persons with tuberculosis, in the 1920's added psychiatric consultation to its services.[92] Over the years, many mentally ill tuberculous patients were successfully rehabilitated in Altro's garment manufacturing plant. When Altro added cardiac rehabilitation in the 1940's, its psychiatric program was augmented with group therapy. Thus, as will be seen, this agency was equipped by staffing as well as experience in the early 1950's to pioneer in industrial therapy for the mentally ill.

The other quite early voluntary effort was established in 1924 by the American Rehabilitation Committee, Inc., a nonprofit charitable corporation developed by a prominent orthopedic surgeon and the then district supervisor of the New York State Division of Vocational Rehabilitation.[56] The Rehabilitation Center, as its original "curative workshop" came to be called, employed a psychiatric consultant in 1946 and began to accept neuropsychiatric patients to job training in clerical work, printing, messenger service and machine shop practice. The industrial aspects of this program never developed, though for some years the work therapy philosophy of this Rehabilitation Center had a significant effect in shaping the attitudes toward industrial therapy of rehabilitation centers and sheltered workshops serving the physically handicapped. The American Rehabilitation Committee still exists, in New York City, and carries on a small work therapy program for persons of a wide array of handicaps, including mental. In contrast to the Altro program, however, it did not enter the mainstream of psychiatric industrial therapy.

60

Possibly the most important legal and regulatory contribution to rehabilitation programs for the mentally ill in the United States, including industrial therapy, was passage by Congress in 1943 of the Barden-La Follette Act.[137] This law expanded the provisions of the vocational rehabilitation sections of the Social Security Act to include mental as well as physical disability and increased federal financial participation in state programs.

All 50 states, the District of Columbia and Puerto Rico operate programs under plans developed by the state governmental bureau or division of vocational rehabilitation and approved by the Federal agency, now known as the Rehabilitation Services Administration of the Social and Rehabilitative Services. Earlier names of the Federal agency have been Office of Vocational Rehabilitation and Vocational Rehabilitation Administration.[34]

Each state agency is a statewide administrative unit with district and often local offices. The professional staffs are made up of vocational rehabilitation counselors, most of whom have had college preparation in the psychological or social sciences or education. Their preferred prior work experience is usually in vocational counseling, psychology, employment guidance or teaching. Increasingly, though not at a pace to close the increasing demand, the state agency staff members are coming from the masters degree rehabilitation counselor training programs established in 71 universities by the Federal Rehabilitation Services Administration.

Soon after the passage of the Barden-La Follette Act some of the state vocational rehabilitation programs began to give service to the mentally ill. Little of this early work found its way into the literature. There was evidently very little specific industrial therapy involved in these programs, but reference to two which have been documented illustrates how the ground was laid for later developments.

In Vermont in 1944, the Vocational Rehabilitation Division of the State Department of Education appointed a Neuropsychiatric Advisory Committee. Staff work and liaison with the Advisory Committee was assigned to a vocational rehabilitation counselor who was a trained psychologist. In 1945 the counselor was deployed full-time to investigation and evaluation of mentally handicapped individuals referred and to psychological testing.[55] Most of his work was with psychoneurotic cases, and this was true in most of the similar state programs so far as this writer has been able to ascertain.

In 1948 the Vermont counselor became the clinical psychologist at Vermont State Hospital and began to refer an increasing number of hospital patients to the Vocational Rehabilitation Division "for assistance in vocational planning to be put into effect after leaving the hospital and for

various services to implement that planning once they had left."[54] By the
time Vermont State Hospital was ready in 1957 to inaugurate a research
project in rehabilitation of chronic schizophrenic patients, including industrial therapy, both the hospital and the state vocational rehabilitation
agency had had a decade of valuable experience.

In Colorado[177] the program developed a somewhat different format than
in Vermont. The Colorado Division of Vocational Rehabilitation established in 1947 the position of supervisor of special services for the mentally
and emotionally handicapped. The office for this supervisor was based in
Pueblo and drew its clientele primarily from the Colorado State Hospital
nearby. During the first three years of the program, two thirds of the cases
were from Colorado State Hospital, the others being referred by the public
welfare departments, the state employment service, other psychiatric hospitals and institutions. Thus, it can be seen that in contrast to the Vermont
experience, the Colorado program began by dealing with a very high proportion of patients in the psychotic categories.

While the vocational rehabilitation supervisor was based in the nearby
community, he was given complete access to the hospital staff and its
patients. He spent some weeks in intensive indoctrination and orientation
to the hospital and its procedures and participated in staff conferences in
which cases entering or leaving the hospital were discussed. A somewhat
informal procedure of referral to the vocational rehabilitation supervisor
was developed so that any staff member of the hospital ostensibly had the
opportunity of calling potential clients to his attention. In keeping with the
patterns already established by the State Divisions of Vocational Rehabilitation in dealing with referrals from hospitals serving the physically handicapped, no attempt was made to give service to the patient until just before
or at the time he was scheduled for discharge from the hospital. Vocational
rehabilitation services consisted mainly of "counseling" and referral to jobs.
A very small amount of referral to training programs was provided, the
counselor noting that,

> We have just about concluded that the client stands a much better
> chance in making a permanent adjustment if he is capable of
> entering a vocation with the necessary knowledge upon his release
> rather than having to embark upon a training period of several
> months' duration and at the same time make an adjustment neces-
> sary to integrate himself into the community and learn a new
> occupation.

The vast majority of the patients served in this program returned to jobs
at about the same socio-economic level as those they had been employed
at before hospitalization, and over half of them returned to the same or a
very similar job. Information as to the Colorado program was made avail-

able to the writer in a memorandum prepared for administrative use within the National Institute of Mental Health and is not available for publication. This is unfortunate for the memorandum is by an extremely skillful observer, Dr. Richard H. Williams, who was chief of the Professional Services Branch of the National Institute of Mental Health, and it is a fine description of the process of working with a state mental hospital prior to the advent of chemotherapy.

The report by Dr. Maxwell Jones and Dr. Allen Stoller of their review for the World Health Organization of programs of rehabilitation in psychiatry across the world was released in 1952.[96] This report documented quite briefly some of the European programs described in the previous chapter and mentioned that attempts toward half-way houses and industrial therapy as part of rehabilitation services were also being developed in South Africa, Kenya, Uganda, Sudan, Australia and New Zealand. The greatest emphasis of the report was on the developments in Great Britain, and it aroused great interest among psychiatrists wrestling with the problem of giving services in hospitals which were increasingly adopting the "open door" policy. Visits to the British programs and some of those in Holland were made available to groups of psychiatrists representing educational institutions or State Departments of Mental Hygiene under the auspices of The Milbank Fund and of Federal and state governments. The visitors from the United States came back with glowing reports about developments in community psychiatry and particularly about the possibilities in sheltered work or industrial therapy.

One of the very fine voluntary psychiatric hospitals, Hillside Hospital, in Queens, New York, turned to Altro Work Shops for vocational rehabilitation services to its patients. Early in 1953 an experimental program was initiated in which patients discharged from Hillside Hospital were referred to Altro Work Shops as a transitional stage, and they returned to the work-a-day world in the community. By the end of that year Altro's parent organization, Altro Health and Rehabilitation Services, was so satisfied with the results that it proposed to extend these services to patients from the public mental hospitals. Two local foundation grants made the service program possible, and Russell Sage Foundation joined in an experimental-control evaluation of the efficacy of the service.[116] It was decided to accept patients from the Bronx Aftercare Clinic of the State Department of Mental Hygiene. This clinic was organized to service all patients discharged from state mental hospitals who lived in the borough of the Bronx. This arrangement appeared logical because Altro Work Shops is located in the Bronx, and good working relationships with the psychiatric staff of the Aftercare Clinic made possible the carrying out of the research design.

Altro Health and Rehabilitation Services was established in 1913 as the Committee for the Care of the Jewish Tuberculous in New York City and

was concerned with offering rehabilitation services to patients discharged
from the tuberculosis sanatoria at that time. Over the years the Committee
for the Care of Jewish Tuberculous had given way to the Altro Health and
Rehabilitation Services, and enlarged its patient population to include persons suffering from heart disease as well as those with tuberculosis. The
Altro program included not only the full array of rehabilitation center professional services, including social casework, psychological, vocational and
medical services, but also Altro Work Shops. Altro Work Shops provides
a factory environment doing direct manufacture of light, washable cotton
garments as well as subcontract work of a variety of sorts. At the time of
its first experiment in industrial therapy for the mentally ill, the major part
of Altro Work Shops' industry was manufacturing of apparel for hospitals,
hotels, restaurants and industrial plants throughout the country.

The description of Altro Work Shops which was given at that time is
valid today except that Altro is now larger, both in size and in number of
patients, has a wider variety of occupations and has extended its professional resources for psychiatric patients. Writing in the *American Journal
of Orthopsychiatry*,[14] the leaders of both Altro and Hillside Hospital say,

> To the casual observer, the Altro looks, acts, and has the "feel" of
> a factory. There are two floors of modern, well-kept machinery,
> and a constant hum of productivity. Skilled efficient foremen and
> management personnel keep the wheels turning, and appear to be
> attending only to the usual concerns of factory production. There
> are the expected time clocks for punching in and out, and bells
> clang at intervals, apparently for shift changes. The working floors
> are very well lighted, clean, and in cheerful colors—much better
> than one expects to find in most factories in the New York garment
> district. To the visitor in the know, however, the time clock repre-
> sents the record by which the nursing and medical staff control the
> number of prescribed hours of work per day. The clanging bells
> signify rest periods at midmorning and midafternoon at which
> times refreshments are served on a medically prescribed basis.
> The management person is just as likely to be one of the registered
> nurses, who is not in uniform but who nevertheless keeps in con-
> stant touch with the health of the patient. She has the power to
> decrease the working hours or to arrange for immediate medical
> attention for any patient, and this in spite of production require-
> ments. In addition to nursing and medical personnel, each patient
> is assigned a caseworker; and the team of doctor, nurse and social
> worker becomes responsible for planning and supporting the re-
> habilitation program for the Altro "employee." The basic aim of the
> Altro program is toward return of the client to as normal a set of
> living conditions and working productivity as is possible in terms
> of his capabilities and handicap. The stay at Altro can be looked
> upon as a form of industrial convalescence. The vast majority of the
> patients graduate from the Altro Work Shops. At the point that
> the client has reached seven or eight hours per day of work

capacity, and is ready for graduation, the rehabilitation team, especially the social worker, helps him in the transition back to former employment, to an occupation in the garment trades if that is warranted, or to further training in some other occupation, oftentimes arranged with the help of the State Division of Vocational Rehabilitation.

In more recent years, the team referred to has been augmented by a vocational consultant, a regularly assigned staff member from the State Division of Vocational Rehabilitation and "industrial duty" social workers who relate to each of the major work divisions of the program. There are now in addition to the garment factory a jobbing machine shop, a bench assembly shop, Multilith printing, direct mail, and general clerical procedures and The Rogosin Data Processing Center for Rehabilitation, which offers work and training in key punching, tabulating and computer operations.

The experiment with patients from Hillside Hospital and the Aftercare Clinic of the State Department of Mental Hygiene appeared to be clinically successful. Unfortunately, problems developed in augmenting the research design, and it was not possible to obtain as good a control group as would have been necessary for definitive statistical findings. The results of the Russell Sage study are reported in a book by the social scientists who undertook the work, Drs. Henry J. Meyers and Edgar F. Borgatta.[116] The results suggested, but did not prove, a positive result from the type of rehabilitation program provided at Altro Work Shops, which in terms of this book are within the definition of industrial therapy.

What did become clear and very significant for the future utilization of community-based rehabilitation programs for state hospital patients was that once discharged from the hospital, it was extremely difficult to get the patient into an industrial therapy endeavor. If an individual is well enough to be discharged from the hospital, it is hard to interpret to him or to his family and friends his need for working in a sheltered setting. So great was the rate of relapse, however, that by the time it became clear to the ex-patient that he was not going to make the grade in the community, the exacerbation of his symptoms as well as the complex and very rapid provisions for readmission to the hospital made community-based rehabilitation pretty well out of the question.

In 1954 Congress passed Public Law 565 amending the Federal Vocational Rehabilitation Act. The amendments charged the Vocational Rehabilitation Administration with establishing standards, approving state plans, administering and certifying grants-in-aid and allotments to the states, and administering grants for research, demonstration, and training and in coordinating public and private programs in behalf of the handicapped. These amendments made it possible for Altro Health and Rehabilitation Services to receive Federal and state assistance in diversifying the kinds of occupations offered at Altro Work Shops. They also made possible a series of demonstration projects in a number of agencies offering industrial therapy to the mentally ill, which will be described later. In 1956 Congress passed the Health Amendments Act, Title V, which made grants available through the National Institute of Mental Health to state or local agencies, hospitals and voluntary programs for demonstration and research projects in treatment and rehabilitation of the mentally ill. On the basis of the experience with the Aftercare Clinic of the State Department of Mental Hygiene, Altro applied cojointly with the New York State Department of Mental Hygiene and the New York State Division of Vocational Rehabilitation for a mental health project grant under this act to move the base of services to patients back into the state mental hospital from which the major group of patients to the Bronx Aftercare Clinic were coming. This was Rockland State Hospital.

Two years prior to the establishment of this project, in 1958, Altro had placed a vocational counselor on a part-time basis at Rockland State Hospital. This initiated the first regular vocational services available at the hospital. Within that year a change in the state law permitted the New York State Division of Vocational Rehabilitation also to provide the hospital with the part-time service of a counselor. Attempts were made to have these two part-time counselors coordinate their efforts, but since both traveled from New York City, some 20 miles to the hospital, and Rockland State Hospital had a patient population of approximately 8000, little coordination ensued. The mental health project grant made it possible to place a team full time at the hospital and to provide that both Altro staff and DVR personnel would work together. The results of that cooperative effort have been reported in a book entitled *Guides to Psychiatric Rehabilitation.*[21]

The key project staff consisted of a consulting psychiatrist, a social caseworker and a vocational counselor. They worked closely with the psychiatric staff of the hospital, the occupational therapy department and the department of social service.

The project staff reports,[22]

> Characteristically, the staff referred patients they saw as needing "special help." Inherent in this need for "special help" were vocational problems frequent among psychotic patients which are not serviced by existing job training or placement agencies. Repeatedly the needs of the patients referred to us were identified as: in-hospital work experience to develop self-confidence, work tolerance, work habits; counseling to encourage motivation and to establish realistic goals; help in implementing post-hospital plans for transitional workshop experience, job-finding activities, living arrangments and support. Training and educational programs were not found to be

necessary for most of the patients; only five of the sixty-three patients accepted for comprehensive service required such programs as a beginning step. Undoubtedly, many other psychotic patients require primarily post-hospital job training or job placement services and their return to community living is accomplished through these efforts.

Interestingly enough, the low priority for training and educational programs found in the Rockland project corroborates the opinion of the supervisor of special services in the 1947–1948 Colorado experience. The Rockland project identified a group of hospitalized psychotics who could benefit most from a comprehensive in-hospital vocational service that developed broad ties with community services. The project staff reported,[23]

> When rehabilitation is viewed as a process of resocialization through activities and relationships that provide the opportunity for developing better adaptive behavior, actual work activities and work relationships assume a role of central importance and become an essential adjunct to vocational counseling. We attempted to provide work experiences at the hospital that would give the patient an opportunity to experience job satisfaction and to develop work tolerance, better work habits, self-esteem, and better interpersonal relationships.

Soon after the project began, the position of coordinator of employment was established by the occupational therapy department. This person was responsible for assisting the project team, particularly the vocational counselor on it, with locating jobs within the hospital that could be utilized toward therapeutic ends. It took a while for the project team to learn enough about hospital jobs and the supervisors who control them in order to set up a program to make effective use of work experiences. The project report pointed out that overprotection by supervisors was a more common problem than overwork or exploitation. Working hours in many jobs were limited by the hospital schedule; very few of the hospital jobs offered any payment. In time, job work experiences were developed in over 30 different hospital situations. Description of two of these illustrates their use[24]:

> Housekeeping jobs (cleaning offices and staff residences) were often used, especially for female patients, as a first step. Although many had worked in skilled or white collar jobs, they often preferred housekeeping jobs. These were generally supervised by "maternal" women who treated the patients with respect, sympathy, and interest. They were given recesses with coffee and cigarettes provided by the housekeeper. Socialization among patients and housekeepers proceeded at a pace set by each patient. The jobs permitted the patients to leave their wards—the desire of many patients. The housekeeping jobs therefore provided a suitable level of work

experience for patients who needed a period of trial with minimal demands, but with acceptance, interest, and encouragement in order to develop enough motivation and self-esteem to consider more challenging and demanding work experiences.

A typing program supervised by an occupational therapist was an excellent facility for assessing skills and work habits, for refresher training for some patients, for developing new skills for others, and as a work conditioning program very similar to a sheltered workshop. Performing clerical services for various hospital departments, this facility provided typing, stenographic, and clerical work on both an educational and industrial basis. The occupational therapist gave patients the type of supervision and instruction that encouraged them to develop self-confidence, tolerance for constructive criticism, work satisfaction, and improved relationships. In this way they were instilled with a sense of progress and accomplishment.

The Rockland Hospital project preceded most of the formal experimental and demonstration efforts in the United States to provide industrial therapy for the mentally ill, and its report has been widely used for reference and for training of personnel now in the field. The significant findings of this cooperative program between governmental and voluntary services are as follows[25]:

1. Our experience in adapting our services to the needs of patients and staff at Rockland State Hospital and in continuing post-hospital contact with discharged psychotics, clearly identified a group of patients without adequate help to bridge the gap to the community. Some patients recover so completely that they require no help; for others, the family, Aftercare Clinic, D.V.R., private psychiatrist, employment agency, casework agency, or financial assistance may alone provide the decisive method of help. In contrast, the very introduction of our comprehensive rehabilitation service stimulated the identification of patients with multiple needs and liabilities who require a variety of services coordinated into a unified program of help.

2. The needs of the psychotic patient clearly go beyond his protection and maintenance during the acute phase of his illness. His requirements in every one of the multiple facets of living must be examined and assessed, and provisions must be made for meeting those in which he may be lacking. These encompass the problems of dwelling, supervision, employment, job placement, social relations, family relations, and medical and psychiatric care.

3. Undertaking rehabilitation with a specific patient requires a comprehensive and thorough assessment of him. It is necessary to identify the patient's assets and strengths that can be further strengthened and that provide a basis for his life in the community. The assessment must also identify the weaknesses of the patient that will require bulwarking, watching, and care.

4. Identification and assessment of needs are meaningless activities unless resources are available to fulfill resulting plans.

5. The validity of assessment of a patient in the hospital or in the community depends upon the breadth of informational sources. In the hospital this means that everyone who knows the patient— the physician, psychiatrist, ward attendant, work supervisor, occupational therapist, social worker, D.V.R. counselor—must share or contribute information. In the community these sources will include the family, the employment agency, sometimes the employer, other social agencies, occasionally the police, and the psychotherapist.

6. In a psychotic's rehabilitation the process of assessment and implementation is ongoing. The complex variables in the patient, the hospital, and the community make predictions incomplete at best. Moreover, the unfolding experiences in the life of the patient after his discharge from the hospital involve him in unforeseen situations and with unpredictable stimuli that require the rehabilitation agency to be ready at all times for reassessment and reimplementation.

7. When the multiple needs of many post-psychiatric patients must be met to assure their return to the community, rehabilitation services unquestionably assume an important role. There is no mystery about the methods or concepts of the rehabilitation process. We are strongly impressed with the fact that the services and the personnel for modern rehabilitation programs already exist within the state hospital. What is required is a kind of administration catalyst to activate hospital staff toward an interdisciplinary approach to the patient's needs, provide the apparatus for communication, and stimulate communication between disciplines in order to integrate the hospital with the community.

8. Successful rehabilitation is crucially dependent upon a close cooperative relationship between hospital and community. No single service can be considered rehabilitation. Hospitalization, psychiatry, casework or vocational counseling, recreational services, employment agencies, sheltered workshops, residential arrangements, and financial support are not in themselves rehabilitation. Rehabilitation is all of these—not necessarily all working together with the same individual but all integrated into a program in which any, some, or all of them are available for an individual.

Independently of the vocational rehabilitation and industrial therapy developments resulting from the amendments to the Social Security Act and the vocational rehabilitation laws, the Veterans Administration had been developing a program unique to its own setting known as the Member Employee Program.[100] Soon after World War II, fear of exploitation of patients led the Veterans Administration to direct its hospitals not to assign patients to a variety of tasks in which they had been formerly used. These included work in the kitchen, the laundry, coal pile, etc. Objections were raised by patients who had enjoyed these assignments. Partly in response to the patients' requests as well as in recognition that occupations properly used could have therapeutic value, Dr. Peter A. Peffer, manager of the Veterans Administration Hospital at Perry Point, Maryland, initiated what came to be called the Member Employee Program. This program required the analyzing of all possible work assignments and their utilization for the patient in terms of his medical needs. Close coordination was called for with the vocational counseling service with a view towards relating his hospital work experience to his occupation after discharge. In 1953 Dr. Peffer was transferred as manager to the Brockton, Massachusetts, Veterans Administration Hospital, and there he developed a much larger Member Employee Program which has come to be coined with the acronym COPE, meaning Continued Opportunity for Productive Endeavors.[180] The idea was picked up by a number of Veterans Administration hospitals and in time has become one of the recommended rehabilitation programs in the Veterans Administration hospitals. These types of industrial therapy programs are available not only to the psychiatric hospitals but also to general hospitals of the Veterans Administration, wherever physical medicine and rehabilitation programs are provided. Dr. Goldberg[72] has described just such a program for the Chest Center at the Veterans Administration Hospital at Castle Point, New York, and Dr. Knudson[102] describes a program at North Little Rock, Arkansas, Veterans Administration Hospital, referred to by the initials VIP, representing Vocational Industrial Placement program or Very Important Person, as one may desire.

In 1955 a joint conference called by the Professional Services Division of the National Institute of Mental Health and the then Office of Vocational Rehabilitation was convened at the Massachusetts Mental Health Center in Boston, bringing together many of the leading developers of rehabilitation programs for the mentally ill in this country and Canada and including some representation of the British experience. This was the first formal exchange of knowledge and experience in this country. It led to the publication of the book *The Patient and the Mental Hospital*[74] which includes many of the principal papers presented at the conference. The experience of Altro Health and Rehabilitation Services was included and served to stimulate the interest of psychiatrists, psychologists and other social scientists present. Subsequently, the Massachusetts Mental Health Center itself inaugurated a rehabilitation program in which some simple bench assembly as well as designated work in the hospital was utilized as part of a therapeutic program. The supervisor of this program has reported to the writer that one of its greatest complications was arousing the interest of the young psychiatrists-in-training to make referrals to the rehabilitation program. In time this complication was for the most part overcome, and since the Massachusetts Mental Health Center is one of the foremost training settings used by the Harvard Medical School, it has over the years served to expose quite a number of today's "command" psychiatrists to a rehabilitation point of view. When Dr. Milton Greenblatt, who directed research including the rehabilitation program at Massachusetts Mental Health Center, moved to Boston State Hospital as director, he took the supervisor of the program with him, and an extremely interesting sheltered workshop was developed there as will be described later on.

Passing reference should be made to the effect of two therapeutic programs inaugurated in the state mental hospitals, for each of these has in its own way contributed to make fertile the ground upon which industrial therapy could develop. The first of these, growing in part out of the therapeutic milieu programs referred to in Chapter I and also through attempts at developing the therapeutic community, is generally referred to as resocialization. One of the later steps in resocialization is getting the patient interested in participating in work endeavors. Wherever a resocialization project is pointed out in a public mental hospital today, one can rest assured that industrial therapy will not be far behind. The other type of program that has had some influence upon the development of industrial therapy is known as the social remotivation effort. This is essentially a set of techniques used by the nursing staff or psychiatric aides in awakening very withdrawn patients to participate in their surroundings and in arousing their interest in their fellow patients and the staff. While this is not ordinarily thought of as a venture in rehabilitation it is a first stage toward leaving the hospital, and in many instances leads to the necessity for planning social and work activities for the newly-remotivated patients.

HOSPITAL-BASED INDUSTRIAL THERAPY

Reference was made earlier to changes in the Federal health legislation and Vocational Rehabilitation Act to make possible grants and allotments for research, demonstration and training. Both the National Institute of Mental Health and the Vocational Rehabilitation Administration have supported demonstrations in industrial therapy for the mentally ill. While the tendency for the NIMH demonstrations has been toward hospital-based programs, the Vocational Rehabilitation Administration has supported experiments both centered in the hospital and located in the communities. No attempt could possibly be made to describe all of what are now dozens of industrial therapy ventures of many sizes and of much variety. Selected here are a few that are illustrative of Federal-sponsored demonstrations under the National Institute of Mental Health, the Vocational Rehabilitation Administration and Veterans Administration sponsorship. In some instances no direct Federal monies were utilized for a state hospital project, though some of the cost may have been met out of Federal formula grants to the particular state.

MANHATTAN STATE HOSPITAL

Under a grant from the National Institute of Mental Health, the research department of Manhattan State Hospital opened a sheltered workshop in 1958.[49] It is interesting that the unit in the hospital, a 3000-bed institution of the New York State Department of Mental Hygiene located on Ward's Island in New York City, most interested in industrial therapy turned out to be that involved in experimenting with the new ataractic drugs. Dr. Herman Denber and his associate, Dr. Rajotte, "were struck by the lack of appreciation of the schizophrenic psychopathology in structuring the daily life on the ward; the absence of individual attention to specific details of each patient's symptoms and a non-recognition of the rehabilitative potential during the hospital stay." They pointed out that the traditional occupational therapy program was not consistent with the aims of a therapeutic community. They conceived of the sheltered workshop as a research undertaking.

A special act of the New York State Legislature allowed the hospital to obtain contract work directly from the community. Very simple bench assembly, mostly packaging novelties and colored construction paper, was obtained. The program was made available to the female patients assigned to the research division. The working quarters were away from the residents' wards in an old building of the hospital where it was possible to set up long benches in a light, airy room.

In the original conception, occupational therapists were assigned to direct the patients' work, supervise and make clinical observations. This did not turn out to be satisfactory for reasons explained in Chapter I, and Drs. Denber and Rajotte turned to the use of the nursing aide staff. This turned out very well. The attendants saw their role in the shop as ego-satisfying. The writer had the opportunity of reading a number of the personal descriptions by these attendants of their experiences in the industrial therapy program. There were few complaints, and most of the attendants felt they were being much more helpful to patients than in their traditional role. Also their attitudes towards patients seemed to have changed. They accorded patients more respect in the work atmosphere. They have become interested in the utilization of group experience and look upon the workshop as a tool uniquely available to them for therapeutic purposes.

Manhattan State Hospital is one of a number in which the initial interest for rehabilitation and industrial therapy has come from staff primarily concerned with research in chemotherapy. The Manhattan State Hospital project, like a number of others developed within hospitals, has suffered from lack of a consistent flow of contract work. It has also suffered from lack of a program of continuity in rehabilitation for the patients who move out of the workshop program.

MEDFIELD STATE HOSPITAL, MASSACHUSETTS

In 1962 a research demonstration project in rehabilitation for chronic schizophrenic patients was inaugurated at this hospital.[37] Out of the total hospital population of about 1200 patients at the time, about 300 were schizophrenic patients, 60 years of age and under and who had been hospitalized for at least one year. This population was randomly divided into an experimental and control group. For the experimental group, an extensive program in industrial therapy was inaugurated. In a report to the National Institute of Mental Health,[107] which financed this demonstration, the program director described the main components of the rehabilitation program as including the following:

1. An in-hospital and extra-hospital work program for patients under the supervision of a vocational counselor;
2. An evening activity program under the direction of an occupational therapist;
3. A discussion group program under the direction of a psychologist;
4. Intensive search for relatives and other sources of family and community support for the patients by the social worker;
5. Special training classes in groups;
6. A sheltered workshop providing training in factory-type work and with payment for it;
7. Involving ward and work area personnel in the assessment of and planning for patients;
8. Recruitment of volunteers for specialized jobs with activity groups and as assistants to the regular staff members;
9. The use of a ward building in a manner similar to that of a half-way house in which emphasis was given to the patient's own responsibilities in managing;
10. A standardized rating system under which each patient was evaluated at work and on the ward and was given previously-announced privileges on the basis of his ratings (known as the step system).

The project directors make note that,

> This program has been designed to utilize existing but as yet untapped resources for rehabilitation within the limited budgetary allowances of state institutions. In this it involves working with available personnel rather than with a numerically enlarged staff or with personnel specifically chosen for demonstrated talents in rehabilitation work.

They explain that the program tries to make the patients' life in the hospital as much as possible like life will be for them outside of the institution if they are released. It requires each patient to work during the day, to take part in avocational or recreational groups in the evenings, to attend discussion group meetings regularly and to gain their privileges and rewards by achieving specified levels of behavior. There is emphasis upon communication within the staff and between staff and patients, and the aim was to take the patients toward their release from the hospital through stages of increasing responsibility. Follow-up is provided within the community. There were 140 chronic schizophrenic patients in the experimental group. The rehabilitation counselor attempted to work out placements for each of these patients in jobs appropriate to their interests and abilities. In step gradation the privileges accorded patients on the basis of evaluation moved from work within the hospital, for which no pay was provided, to work in the sheltered workshop, where payment on the basis of productivity was afforded, to arrangements to work in the community and move out of the hospital entirely. The list of in-hospital work areas utilized by the project for training purposes is more varied than is found in most state mental hospitals utilizing hospital work for industrial therapy. It included the bakery; beauty parlor; kitchen; an electrician's shop; elevator operation; a garage; housekeeping tasks; some repair and furniture refinishing; a variety of laundry tasks; lawns and outside maintenance; the library; the building trades of mason, plumber, electrician and painter; the power house; the printing office; the record room and reception desk; the store room and a variety of tasks on the farm.

The sheltered workshop operated two shifts—one in the morning and one in the afternoon. It was used both for the evaluation of working capacity as well as for training in light bench assembly. Contract work came from outside firms such as the making of strings of Christmas tree light sockets; stringing key chains; engraving bake-a-lite dials; cutting flowers, ribbons and other millinery articles and assembling and packaging jewelry and novelties. Wages for individual patients varied with their productivity and was on a piece-work basis. It is of interest to note that since the hospital provided no working capital reserve, it was not possible to pay the patients until a shipment of completed work had been made to the contracting factory and a check issued in payment. This meant that the length of time between completion of the work task and payment for it varied from 1½ to 3 weeks. This is not an unusual situation in the early period of operation of a sheltered work program in a state institution.

The highest level of industrial therapy in the Medfield demonstration provided that the patients living in the hospital go out to work in the community. A variety of types of day work were obtained including assembly and production work in a local hat factory; chambermaid, kitchen work and caretaker maintenance in a hotel; housekeeping and upkeep and repair work on lawns and houses; work in the housekeeping kitchen and maintenance services of nursing homes; jobs in a bakery and pressing and marking at a local cleaners. To an increasing extent, assistance in obtaining work in the community was provided by staff from the state's official vocational rehabilitation agency, the Massachusetts Rehabilitation Commission.

The Medfield State Hospital program maintained a close teaching liaison with Northeastern University. Sheltered workshop supervisors were students from the Northeastern University cooperative program. Students also assisted in the liaison with the in-hospital work areas, with individual and group counseling and with assisting in the locating of community resources for the patients. The students worked two or three days a week throughout the semester. It is significant that this rehabilitation project considered industrial therapy alone to be insufficient and linked it with the array of other services as listed. It was the firm belief of those who originated the project that for the chronic schizophrenic patients to be served, the program must be concerned with their living arrangements, recreational and diversional activities, their family life and socialization as well as the work they would be doing. For patients moving out into the community who still needed a structured living setting, the project developed a half-way house.[134]

Three aspects of the Medfield State Hospital program should be of particular interest to those considering industrial therapy or services for chronic patients. The first is the frank recognition that motivation for rehabilitation would be extremely low. Many of the patients had spent years in the hospital under a system that trained them in dependence on others. Their bedtimes and mealtimes were fixed. They remained in bed for a good part of the day because there was very little else for them to do, and so long as they were quiet, they gave staff members no trouble. The more recent introduction in many of the state hospitals over the past decade of more active programs, open wards, etc., will do little to remotivate this group of patients unless special efforts are taken. The Medfield project required that the nursing employees spend a great deal of their time in urging and helping patients to take increased interest in their behavior and in their personal grooming. The remarkable changes possible are illustrated from the second progress report:[108]

> At the start of the project, forty-five of the male patients had not shaved themselves in years. With the emphasis on getting the patients to accept responsibility, ward personnel had gotten all but three of the men to do this for themselves without supervision. There were twenty-seven patients who were incontinent day and night at the start of the project. By April, 1963, only four were occasionally incontinent. Of the original 140 patients there were only six women who could or would make their beds. Now there are only seven patients who need help in making an acceptable bed.

It is obvious these are very first steps in moving the patients on into the work-a-day world.

The second aspect of the Medfield experience that is worth more than a second look is their so-called "step system." This, as has been said, was a program providing a series of incentives and rewards for patients according to accomplishments in both the ward and the work areas. Two rating scales were used, and these, along with the measure of the number of hours of work per day, were tied to a schedule of rewards for accomplishment. The two evaluation scales were made up of 4-point ratings based on the patient's behavior on each of the 11 items. The work supervisor was asked to rate each patient at 2-week intervals on the following: (a) willingness to work; (b) amount of work accomplished; (c) ability to learn and remember work; (d) ability to work when the work piles up; (e) amount of supervision needed; (f) quality of work; (g) relationships with other workers; (h) personal behavior on the job; (i) ability to make use of suggestions, directions, and orders; (j) ability to work alone; (k) punctuality. Behavior on the ward was also rated every two weeks and covered the following items: (a) ability to do things for oneself; (b) ability to converse with others; (c) relationships with other patients on the ward; (d) consistency of acceptable behavior on the ward; (e) personal appearance and dress; (f) willingness to do off-ward work; (g) interest in leaving the hospital; (h) personal behavior on the ward; (i) response to authority of ward personnel; (j) willingness to perform ward work routines; (k) posturing or gesturing.

The totals of the scores received on the two rating sheets, correlated with the number of hours of work per day, determined the step of progress; for example, a total of 44 points or less on the two scales with work performance at two or less hours of work a day added up to 0 step. A total of 65 points with not less than 27 on each scale but with five hours of work performance per day yielded step 5; a total of 80 points with at least 37 on each scale and with seven hours of work per day placed the patient at step 12. A patient with more than 81 points and with eight hours of work capacity was ready to move out into the community. As the points and hours increased, the privileges increased. A patient at step 1 was allowed two hours a day of ground privileges and one hospital social event per month. At step 2, the ground privileges increased to three hours a day, the social events to two a month, and the patient was allowed a half a day off the ward on the grounds for a visit from the family. At step 5, in addition to the three hours a day of ground privileges, the patient had one hospital social event a week, an overnight visit with his family, his ground privileges were unescorted, he was allowed one trip a month with staff, and three hours a week of work, earning money on the grounds. At step 10, the visits to the family had been increased to weekends, the patient had all-day ground privileges unescorted, two trips a month with staff, unlimited opportunity to earn money on the grounds, was eligible to live on the rehabilitation ward and allowed a nonhospital event with a volunteer each week, was allowed to earn money off grounds, could have a vacation on grounds one week every six months or a vacation off grounds for the same length of time. The privileges continued to increase, to add trips to the town of Medfield and eventually trips to other areas, by which time plans were being made for the patient's discharge from the hospital.

A third facet to the experience of the Medfield program relates to the question of motivation on the job. An experiment was conducted in operant conditioning to see whether the speed of production could be increased, particularly for very slow patients, by reducing the length of time between which the work was completed and there was actual payment. The conditioning process was tried over a period of a few months with a number of women patients working on stringing the Christmas tree lights. A 3-week period was used as a base. The average length of time each patient took to make each string of lights constituted the baseline. In the first phase of the conditioning, each patient was paid 4¢ immediately upon the completion of each string. In the second phase, the patients were paid immediately for all light strings produced faster than the second slowest one produced by him the day before. By the end of the experiment, the patients were not given cash but were informed immediately of how much money they were accumulating by means of numbered cards which the supervisor placed in front of them upon the completion of each string.

The operant conditioning turned out to be quite successful in increasing the interest of the patients in the work they were doing. Clock-watching stopped, smoking decreased, the workers kept their seats and tended to their work. Whether the operant conditioning as a training process was responsible for the successful outcome or simply the greater attention paid to the patients at work cannot be determined, but certainly the need for close, personal attention is emphasized.

MIDDLETOWN STATE HOSPITAL

Like Medfield State Hospital, Middletown State Hospital is a "middle-sized" state institution, close to a small semi-urban city. The director of the hospital, who had long been interested in community affairs and in the development of tie-lines between his hospital and the home areas from which his patients came, became interested in industrial therapy when he served as part of a New York State team sent by The Milbank Fund to visit programs in England and Holland.

The director of the hospital, Dr. Hyman Pleasure, assigned responsibility for the development of the sheltered workshop to the occupational therapy department of his hospital. Utilizing space in hospital buildings with some of the activities being carried on close to the wards, a combination of in-hospital work and subcontract work for local industry was developed.[128] Occupational therapists supervise and instruct patients on such contracts as folding in the edges of large shopping bags, hand weaving, cutting and bailing remnants, salvaging cloth and hemming the edges, lacing leather pieces to be assembled into shoes and a variety of other simple hand bench work. The hospital woodworking shop is used for training, and the hospital furniture refinishing shop not only does work for the hospital but takes in orders from private individuals as well.

A cadre of long-term patients is retained to maintain the flow of work. One of the hospital staff members is assigned the responsibility of soliciting additional contract work from sources in the Middletown area. The prospective orders obtained are analyzed into piece-work rates, and of the rate determined, 80 per cent is paid to the patients on the basis of their production and 20 per cent is retained by the workshop to provide for items not included in the hospital budget, such as radios for providing music in the working area and other small luxuries not otherwise available to the patients.

The hospital provides a trucking service for transporting the work from one part of the hospital to the other. Customers are expected to pick up their work and deliver the raw material to the hospital. The method of pricing the work is rather unique. The customer specifies the price and must certify by letter that the price paid by him to the hospital is based upon the minimum wage paid by the customer in his own plant for the same job. While this process denotes a rather high rate of trust of the sources of work, it may be one way of satisfying the Federal Wage and Hour requirements with regard to sheltered workshops that the prices charged for contract work truly reflect the normal business conditions of the community.

Working areas are spacious and well lighted. Over the years there has been increasing interest on the part of patients in participating in the program, and a closer liaison has been established with the local unit of the State Division of Vocational Rehabilitation and with a community sheltered workshop in the town.

The staff consists of one overall supervisor who is the responsible head for the business management; a senior occupational therapist who is concerned with the therapeutic aspects of the program; a supervising occupational therapist for each of the shops operated in the hospital, assisted by ward attendants. There is a vocational counselor and placement director who is psychologically trained and who is directly responsible to the director of the hospital.

The community workshop referred to was a small program set up to serve retarded adults under the auspices of the Association for Help of Retarded Children. In recent years it has been reorganized, and with assistance from the State Division of Vocational Rehabilitation, now functions as a community sheltered workshop available to a wide range of handicapped people. Some of the patients from the sheltered work program at Middletown State Hospital move to the community workshop. At one point, as many as 300 patients in the hospital participated in the industrial therapy operations.

A couple of years ago the director of Middletown State Hospital became the Deputy Commissioner of the New York State Department of Mental Hygiene for local services, and he is influential in the stimulation of rehabilitation programs elsewhere in the State. Plans are now in prospect for the opening of a new rehabilitation center building at Middletown State Hospital in which the sheltered workshop along with other modalities of rehabilitation service will be housed. This will also be a cooperative venture with the New York State Division of Vocational Rehabilitation and use will be made of provisions of the 1966 Amendments to the Federal Vocational Rehabilitation Act which make possible additional Federal sharing for staff and services to public services under the aegis of the state vocational rehabilitation agencies. In other words, it is planned that the vocational rehabilitation part of the total rehabilitation program at Middletown State Hospital will operate by agreement officially as a unit of the New York State Division of Vocational Rehabilitation. The partnership does envision proper coordination between the two state agencies so that a schizoid rehabilitation service does not ensue.

Both the Medfield State Hospital and the Middletown State Hospital sheltered work programs suffered from the problem pointed out in some of the earlier British industrial therapy endeavors when hospital personnel became deeply involved in the management and operation of the contract work program. Beyond a rather minimal beginning level, the hospitals find that they cannot properly develop their programs without turning for help outside the institution. The following three examples are of mental hospitals that have developed rather unique patterns of organization, admitting of a development beyond what is possible in those previously discussed.

Boston State Hospital and Its PROP Shop

Boston State Hospital is located within the city limits of the city of Boston. It has had a number of years of developments in the forefront of community psychiatry. It was one of the first institutions in the United States to draw upon the experiences of Dr. Querido of Amsterdam in introducing crisis intervention programs for psychiatric emergencies and in experimenting with open wards and day-and-night hospital service. Before 1963, when the decision had been reached to establish a sheltered work program, the hospital had been carrying on a patient-employee program in which likely patients were identified and placed on a 6-month trial visit to work in various capacities in the hospital for which they received pay at the rate of $16.00 a week. The newly designated rehabilitation department desired to complement the patient-employee program with a sheltered workshop rather than to replace it.

The first step was taken in the form of a direct mail campaign to manufacturers within a fifteen mile radius of the hospital, and this netted one tentative contract job.

The work offered was the stitching of linings for a handbag manufacturer. The head of the rehabilitation department, who had come to Boston State Hospital with previous experience in supervising the rehabilitation program at Massachusetts Mental Health Center previously referred to, and the head occupational therapist worked with the manufacturer in setting up a program.

It was not successful, however. As the director of the program reported,[75]

> The machines were too light; the stitches were too loose; the supervision was too permissive; and the screening of workers was too haphazard. There was no money to pay the stitchers for their work, and the manufacturer was dissatisfied. The project was shelved for a time.

An interim job of stuffing envelopes and mailing them for the local tuberculosis association provided a temporary crutch but was not sufficient to get the program under way. A joint all-out effort, cooperatively between the industrial therapy, the housekeeping and the occupational therapy departments of the hospital, managed to acquire a couple of sewing machines from the hospital sewing rooms, reconditioned them and a new attempt was made to take work from the handbag manufacturer. The program then limped along awhile and, it appears, would have died again excepting that the director of the hospital and the rehabilitation director obtained the interest of a prominent retailer in the Boston community.

The businessman proposed the setting up of a nonprofit corporation, with the interest of industry and individuals in the community to stimulate the development of a flow of work to the hospital.

The corporation was called Patients' Rehabilitation Occupational Program, Inc., which is reduced to the acronym PROP, and a charter under the laws of the State of Massachusetts provided for the following purposes:

1. To enlist support of industry and individuals in sponsoring PROP.
2. To furnish machinery and supplies where necessary.
3. To solicit business for the shop.
4. To subsidize the workers until the operation was solvent.
5. To assume responsibility for payroll and clerical considerations.

The organization of the separate corporation had a number of advantages over the hospital-owned and operated program. The negotiation with the manufacturers who were to supply the work was made officially between PROP and them. PROP had a corporate entity. It obtained a Certificate as a Sheltered Workshop from the United States Department of Labor, Wage and Hour Division, and this allowed it to pay the sheltered workshop minimum wage which, though based upon actual production in relationship to normal Federal minimum wage, provides for lower payments to handicapped personnel. As a nonprofit corporation, its operations were freed of many of the business taxes, and the business office of the hospital was freed of the complicated financial record-keeping necessary to an operation manufacturing on the open market. PROP pointed out to prospective customers a number of advantages which would pertain to manufacturers who might be interested in using the PROP shop. Without assessing their validity, for these will be discussed in Chapter V, they are as follows:

1. *Cost of Production*

PROP points out that the wage cost would be lower than in outside industry because of the sheltered workshop minimum wage allowed under the Federal wage and hour laws.

2. *No Fringe Benefits*

There should be a further saving of 10 to 20 percent in labor costs because the workers in the PROP shop are not regular work force employees of any manufacturer.

3. *Federal Employer Taxes—Under Regulation 31.3121(d)(-1) of the Internal Revenue Code*

In view of the fact that the workers are all in-patients of a mental hospital, the shop was exempt from Federal Employer Taxes.

4. *State Unemployment Compensation Taxes*

The Commonwealth of Massachusetts ruled that the sheltered workshop project at the hospital is not subject to Unemployment Compensation Taxes.

5. *Workmen's Compensation*

The Commonwealth Department ruled that Workmen's Compensation was not applicable since the patients in industrial therapy are not employees of the company for which the work is being done and they are not carried on the company payroll.

6. Rental Equivalent

Since the state hospital furnishes space, light, heat and power, this reduces the cost of production and at the same time may help the manufacturer by freeing his valuable space for other work activities.

7. Supervisory Personnel

Supervision is provided by the hospital and is not treated as a cost to the manufacturer since the supervisory personnel are primarily for training patients in good work attitudes and habits as a preparation for return to the community.

8. Personnel Problems

The sheltered workshop project reduces the problems of recruiting, training, record-keeping and labor turnover for the company which contracts to it.

9. Medical Examination

Pre-employment medical examinations are not needed inasmuch as the workers are all patients under medical care.

10. Employer Liability

All necessary care and treatment are borne by the state hospital, and no public liability need therefore be carried by the cooperating manufacturer.

11. Military Re-employment Rights

The PROP report says, "With the possibility of increased draft calls and enlistments, the problem of re-employing persons following military service can be avoided."

12. Convenient Location

PROP points out that the hospital is easily accessible, and therefore the expense of delivering raw materials and picking up finished products is at a minimum.

13. Capital Investment

PROP points out that, "Capital investment in defective products can be greatly reduced by repair and salvage operations which can be handled in the sheltered workshop project."

While all of these can be construed to be advantages to the manufacturer contracting with the PROP shop, there are disadvantages as well that will be made clear in Chapter V, and there are reasons why some of these advantages can be and are being looked upon by the Federal Wage and Hour Division, by Congress and by the labor union field as exploitative of labor and possible unfair competition.

Nevertheless, the establishment of the PROP corporation made it possible to set up a business-like operation calling for the cooperation of the rehabilitation department, the occupational therapy department, and the social service department. A set of rules was established and agreed to by the departments concerned. Some of these are particularly interesting in that they tend to force a closer approximation of the industrial therapy unit to that of a normal industrial shop.[76] Thus, for example, the requirement that "each worker shall report for work at 8:30 A.M. on every work day, and shall work steadily and with a minimum of conversation except with the supervisor, and also excepting the periods of rest specified." Provision was made for time clocks. Workers were not allowed to leave their tasks except for regularly-scheduled group meetings or individual therapy with therapist or counselor. Admission to the program involved a formal referral and an application procedure. Before assignment to work, the patient was evaluated by a screening team composed of psychiatrist, nurse, social worker, occupational therapist, shop supervisor and rehabilitation counselor.

A close working relationship had been established between the occupational therapy department and the Massachusetts Rehabilitation Commission, and it was arranged that this should continue and be augmented for patients accepted by the PROP shop. The social service department, as well as the occupational therapy department, shared in agreements to insure that the services of the Massachusetts Rehabilitation Commission would become available for any patient the Commission judged eligible. When additional supervisors became necessary in the PROP shop, they were supplied by the occupational therapy department. Nonproductive worker positions such as payroll clerk and secretary were recruited from the patient ranks. Supervisors in charge of each of the shops were selected on the basis of qualifications which included familiarity with the process being attempted. The rehabilitation department took responsibility for coordinating the preliminary screening, for correlating the weekly reports on evaluation of work, for whatever psychometric testing and vocational counseling was required and for the necessary lines of liaison with the PROP corporation. It was expected that PROP, Inc., would be able to employ staff, independent of the hospital, to assist in job placement, perhaps even for the establishment of an employment agency.

In reporting on the experience to date, reference is made to the cooperation by the nursing service since it is through the ward personnel that the initial recommendation of patients for assignment to the PROP shop originates.

CENTRAL ISLIP STATE HOSPITAL

The sheltered workshop at Central Islip State Hospital on Long Island, New York is one of the largest in the country's state hospitals. Central Islip is itself one of the very large state hospitals and was located out in Suffolk County, Long Island, some 40 miles from New York City, in an era in which assignment to Central Islip was to all practical purposes removal from society. This tremendous hospital which, with its great cutback, still has over 4000 patients, serves only persons from New York City and then only those from the upper half of Manhattan.

About 10 per cent of the hospital's population is employed in its sheltered workshops. The hospital superintendent, Dr. Francis J. O'Neil, was one of those who had visited the British and Dutch programs on The Milbank Fund trip. With the assistance of his supervisor of occupational therapy, he initiated industrial therapy in the woodworking shop in 1957.[162] Later, shops were added for the sewing of women's underwear, auto repairs and a variety of small bench assembly including that of ballpoint pens, novelty items, women's jewelry and the like. In contrast to the struggles which some of the hospitals already discussed have had in obtaining work to be done, Central Islip State Hospital has been highly successful. Over 50 different customers have supplied work of one kind or another for the hospital to do and evidence their satisfaction with the work done by fairly large scale repeat orders.

Many of the processes followed in the Central Islip sheltered workshop are similar to those already described at Boston State Hospital, Middletown and Medfield. The work areas are hospital buildings converted from ward use. Central Islip State Hospital has gradually eliminated the traditional occupational therapy almost entirely in favor of the industrial therapy programs. In fact, as of this writing, all occupational therapists on the hospital's staff are utilized in the industrial therapy program. A new rehabilitation program incorporating the other modalities of rehabilitation therapy is being planned, and there is some concern as to how it will be possible to reintroduce occupational therapy and still preserve the industrial therapy lines in the hospital's budget.

Two of the forms of work developed at Central Islip involve rather sophisticated semi-skill levels. One of these is the woodworking program where contracts had been for the manufacture of small condiment shelves, mostly in Early American furniture design. The other was the garment manufacturing shop sewing ladies' panties and half slips. In both of these shops, commercial-types of equipment was being used and well maintained.

In the selection of patients, somewhat the same process is followed as described for Boston State Hospital. Referrals come from any of the wards of the hospital. A formal application is required from the patient. There is an interview with the sheltered workshop supervisor or with a senior occupational therapist assigned to the program. There is a formal process of evaluation of performance and reportedly referrals of patients to outside employment. Central Islip State Hospital, however, has a very large long-term chronically ill population. Some 3000 of its 4000 patients have been in the hospital for 2 years or longer. Their tielines with New York City are tenuous, if they exist at all, and there is little likelihood that very many of them can be relocated in the surrounding community. The supervisor of the program and Dr. O'Neil are addressing themselves to the problem of sheltered work on an extended basis for a fairly large number of patients. The questions at issue have to do with whether this hospital will remain the domicile for most of these people and whether their place of work should also be in the hospital or whether some form of hostels or hotels, with work stations in the community, might be developed along the lines of the industrial therapy organizations described in England. In the meantime, Central Islip State Hospital has gone ahead with the expansion of its program and the raising of the level of the kind of work to be done and with the hope that they can further increase mechanical and electronic assembly procedures. It should be pointed out that the automobile repair shop referred to is used mostly for the repair of the institution's own equipment.

What is most interesting about Central Islip's sheltered workshop is the way in which it has developed support and assistance from the business community quite differently than the nonprofit corporation idea of Boston State Hospital. What Dr. O'Neil has accomplished has been to contract with small business in the local area to bring its work into the hospital. Thereby, the woodworking job was provided by a lumber company, the president of which served as the primary business advisor to the Central Islip sheltered workshop. In fact, he also contracted with the hospital to serve as an individual entrepreneur in obtaining work from manufacturing establishments and giving it over to the sheltered workshop to be assembled. Manufacturing contractors made their arrangements with this businessman, understanding that he was backed by Central Islip State Hospital. As an independent businessman, he made payments to the sheltered workshop and its employees from his collections on the contracts he had made with manufacturers. As in the Boston situation, the patients of the hospital are not employees either of the business contractor or of the manufacturers who supplied the work, and therefore a great deal of red tape, as well as cost, has been avoided.

The work done for the garment manufacturing plant is similarly a form of contract between the plant owner and the hospital. Hospital industrial therapy personnel insist that the pricing agreements between the manufacturer and the sheltered workshop are fair and equitable and do not constitute subsidization of the manufacturer and, therefore, unfair competition. Various visitors to Central Islip State Hospital have expressed reservations on this point to the writer. It is true that the recent death of the independent business contractor has presented the sheltered workshop program at Central Islip State Hospital with some interesting complications. Questions have to be resolved as to who owns certain of the business in the house and what the relationship of a businessman to the sheltered workshop might be if he does not have the security of his own business establishment in the Long Island area. Furthermore, changes in the Wage and Hour regulations of the United States Department of Labor resulting from congressional action in 1967 and interpretation of a recent ruling of the United States Supreme Court as to the liability of employees of state hospitals under the minimum wage laws raise doubt as to whether the independent businessman-contractor arrangement with a state institution will long be tenable.

Central Islip State Hospital's sheltered workshop program received the Silver Award of the American Psychiatric Association in 1967 for its outstanding contribution in rehabilitation of the mentally ill. It, in the opinion of this writer, is an alive and viable program. The interest and support given it by Dr. O'Neil in the face of almost overwhelming problems of bureaucracy and the staunch support evidenced by the occupational therapy staff of the hospital and the tremendous interest of the patients in participating are very great assets, and great care should be exercised in the addition of much needed components of a well-rounded rehabilitation program to coordinate with and make use of this strong industrial therapy service.

BROCKTON VETERANS ADMINISTRATION HOSPITAL—CHIRP

Out of the Patients' Employee Program at the Veterans Administration Hospital in Brockton, Massachusetts, as mentioned earlier, has developed an industrial therapy workshop program that has been designated as CHIRP, an acronym for Community Hospital Industry Rehabilitation Program.

CHIRP was established in 1961 by the hospital director, Dr. William Winick, to see whether it would be possible to rehabilitate the long-term chronic patient.[81] Dr. Winick was influenced by the programs that had developed in England and Holland. He turned the problem over to his chief of physical medicine and rehabilitation services, Dr. Francis X. Walsh, who put his coordinator of services, Mr. Earl S. Frost, to work on the problem. With the assistance of staff from the department of physical medicine and rehabilitation and the chief of manual arts therapy, Mr. Frost has developed one of the most successful sheltered work programs in a mental hospital in this country.

The Veterans Administration Hospital at Brockton, Massachusetts has about 1000 beds and is entirely a psychiatric hospital. Quarters for the workshop are separate from the wards of the hospital, requiring that the men leave their living areas in order to go to work. Assignment to CHIRP may be made by any of the psychiatrists assigned to the five different units in the hospital. Decision as to acceptance of the patient into the CHIRP program is on examination of the chief of physical medicine and rehabilitation services, Dr. Walsh. Dr. Walsh also passes opinion upon the type of work accepted into the program in terms of its value in industrial therapy.

While some of the work done in the CHIRP program is of the very simple bench assembly and packaging described in the previous hospitals, more and more of it is of a higher level of industrial work requiring the use of tools and equipment supplied by the manufacturers. Such work as inspecting and testing electronic components, salvaging parts from computers, grinding and soldering jewelry, buffing and polishing copper bowls and small drilling assemblies are some of the work that CHIRP has been doing for a wide array of industrial contractors. Brockton is located in an area of concentrated industry, and though it has not been easy, gradually the cooperation of a number of companies has been obtained. At a special meeting on Industry in the Mental Hospital arranged in New York City in 1965 by the Brockton Veterans Administration Hospital with the cooperation of Smith Kline & French Laboratories and with the assistance of some of the major contractors to the CHIRP program, representatives of the following companies spoke glowingly of the cooperative working relationship that had been established with CHIRP:[63] the Foxboro Instrumentation Company, the Polaroid Corporation, the Industrial Metals and Controls Division of Texas Instrument Company and the Smith Kline & French Laboratories.

The business representatives spoke not only of the satisfaction they had in contributing to the rehabilitation of veterans in the hospital, but how impressed they were with the sound business-management relationship between the workshop and their companies. They did not feel that they had to resort to a charitable approach and thereby accept anything less than the highest quality of production and of business standards in the relationship.

Contacts between the business firms and CHIRP were carried on by a member of the hospital's physical medicine and rehabilitation staff who had himself had factory work experience prior to professional training for work in the Veterans Administration.[64] The working conditions simulate those of a real factory. There is the use of time clocks and insistence upon acceptable work deportment. The supervision of the workers is by staff members assigned from the physical medicine and rehabilitation department, manual arts therapists and from the occupational therapy department.

The Federal minimum wage is paid to each patient employee. In accord with the regulations of the Veterans Administration hospitals, however, the accumulated earnings of the patient are credited to his account. The amount of money actually made available to the patient for his use at any one time is a medical determination.

The literature on the CHIRP program does not make clear just how the pricing arrangements are worked out between the contractor and CHIRP. The stated opinion of representatives of the major business enterprises from which CHIRP obtains its contracts is that the prices paid are fair and competitive. It is clear that the price includes provision for payment to the patient at the minimum wage level since, for all the higher level of industrial operation than simple packaging represented by the work CHIRP is taking, it is still true that most of this represents the lowest level of operation for the companies supplying the work. There must be some margin beyond the costs of direct wages, and this would be used by the CHIRP program for the necessary capitalization and for the payment of a variety of overhead costs which would not be borne by the Veterans Administration.

A few observations from personal visit and discussion with staff are pertinent.

A film of the CHIRP program entitled *Man Must Work* has been produced under a grant from the Roche Laboratories of the Hoffman-LaRoche, Inc., of New Jersey. The film makes clear that for adequate functioning, the CHIRP program requires an administrative trio. Mr. Frost functions as the overall coordinator. One staff person, as already mentioned, makes contacts with the employers. He also serves as a placement person for patients who do well enough on a particular job which is replicated in the industry from which it came so that the patient may be taken on for trial by the company. A third key staff member must be the inside overall supervisor for the CHIRP workshop.

It is explained to the prospective contracting companies that the hospital, in truth, can make no written contract with them. Agreement for completing the project must remain a "gentlemen's agreement." The manufacturing company must furnish raw materials, transport the materials to and from the hospital, provide initial instruction and pay the prevailing minimum wage in the area. In addition, on certain jobs requiring specialized equipment, the manufacturing company is asked to loan the machinery to CHIRP, and this they have been willing to do. Cooperatively between the industry contact man and instructional staff from the company supplying the work, production methods are ironed out. The film indicates that CHIRP's selling point to the industries is that it can take on jobs unwanted by the people in the factory, jobs which pose bottlenecks in their production line or those which occur seasonally and which the local labor pool cannot handle.

The film does clarify that the manufacturing company is billed by the hospital "at the end of a week for the number of hours worked by the patients. The company then remits a check to the hospital for those hours worked at the prevailing rate. The hospital then credits each patient's account with the sum of money he has earned." It points out that the patients are not employees of the company and are not hired by the hospital. Unemployment insurance, social security benefits and other fringe benefits are not paid. In this respect, it is similar both to the Boston State Hospital and the Central Islip State Hospital programs previously described.

The question of the attitude of the labor unions has come up a number of times in discussions with the CHIRP personnel, for the Brockton Hospital is in an area where strong unions predominate. Both Dr. Winick and Mr. Frost have explained that they have the cooperation of the key labor union involved. The unions' only concern seems to be that the prevailing wage be paid for work done.

A visit to the CHIRP program, accompanied by leaders of two of the British and one of the Dutch programs described in Chapter II, brought to light some interesting differences between CHIRP and the European programs as well as between CHIRP and what is developing in the state hospital system in the United States. In the first place, visitors were struck by the younger average age of the men working in the CHIRP program than one finds in the public mental hospitals. Secondly, one is struck by a greater sense of productivity on the part of all of the patients, and this is understandable when one considers the greater processes of selectivity that takes place in CHIRP. This is not to say that there are not many sick patients at work in the CHIRP program. It is only that the characteristics of slow movements and regressed behavior of the long-term chronically ill patients one sees, for example, at the Central Islip State Hospital program, at Glenside Hospital in Bristol, England or in certain of the units of the Dr. Van Der Kolk Stichting in the Hague seem to be completely absent at CHIRP. It is not clear whether this is an artifact of the patient population, the results of selectivity in assignment of patients to CHIRP or the results of highly successful industrial therapy processes which are nowhere described. One can only comment that a state hospital superintendent visiting the CHIRP program is as likely to be discouraged at the vast difference of his patient population from the people he sees working at CHIRP as he is to be enthused by the possibilities demonstrated in the cooperative relationship with industry and the kinds of work the patients are doing.

A final comment on CHIRP is that the winds of change may be already blowing. The tendency toward the reabsorption into the community of the less ill or more quickly rehabilitated patient is beginning to leave a less productive residue. The experiences elsewhere in the United States and abroad that hospital industry has a greater effect in increasing the rate of discharge from the hospital than in keeping the patient out in the community, thereby leading to a "revolving door" situation, is already producing some thinking about what form of community-based industrial therapy endeavor might be required for the more chronic patients who may require extended sheltered work care. The Brockton Veterans Administration Hospital may be an ideal setting in which to demonstrate the hospital-community continuum. It already has an excellent program of foster home care in the surrounding community for patients who either have no homes to return to or who require a transitional sheltered living arrangement before returning home. The foster homes are now being used for the domiciliary rehabilitation services for ex-patients of the hospital who work in the industries of the community. They might also be used to move patients out of in-hospital care who might work in a community-based version of CHIRP. Such a program would immediately be faced with many of the business and industrial problems which CHIRP, along with Boston State Hospital and Central Islip State Hospital, have been managing to avoid by virtue of their patients not being classified as employees of any organization.

Palo Alto Veterans Administration Hospital, California

The Veterans Administration Hospital in Palo Alto, California, established a psychiatric industrial therapy workshop in 1957. This program operates as a nonprofit corporation which contracts work from the outside and uses the patients of the hospital. Electronic repair work, manufacture of ski tow ropes and a variety of small assembly tasks constitute the work that is done. The workshop is under the supervision of the chief of the continued treatment service of the hospital, and he receives assistance in the operation of the workshop and in contacts with industry from the chief of the counseling psychology service. In its physical characteristics and in the principles of its operation, it is essentially similar to that of the Brockton Veterans Administration Hospital. There are other Veterans Administration hospitals which are also turning to the use of contract work as an adjunct to their member employee programs.

The Palo Alto Veterans Administration Hospital has been the location for one of the most interesting and significant experiments in applying small group treatment technique in conjunction with an industrial therapy approach. Under the supervision of the research psychologist for the hospital, Dr. George Fairweather, some projects of great future significance to the application of industrial therapy have been carried on. These will be described in Chapter IV.

Community-Based Industrial Therapy

After World War II, the rehabilitation centers and the sheltered workshops serving the physically handicapped found themselves facing new problems in their clientele. Modern medical treatment, as well as an increased economy, returned to the community, after treatment and physical therapy, a large number of handicapped people who had formerly been the mainstay of sheltered work programs. The rehabilitation services were dealing with increasing numbers of multiply handicapped in which the greatest barriers to employability often appeared to be in the psychological sphere rather than because of disabled muscles or joints. When the 1954 amendments to the Vocational Rehabilitation Act made Federal grants available for research and demonstration, the Jewish Vocational Service of Chicago proposed organizing a vocational adjustment center to test out ways of dealing with emotionally disturbed handicapped clientele. The Federal Office of Vocational Rehabilitation awarded that agency a special grant to set up what was to be a prototype of services that might be carried on elsewhere in the country.

The results of that prototype experience are reported in a booklet released in 1955 by the Chicago Jewish Vocational Service and Employment Center.[67] Following that experience, a number of the Jewish Vocational Services elsewhere in the country obtained Federal grants for replicating the Chicago program. Other agencies operating community workshops for the physically handicapped followed suit. Since these programs served as a backdrop for a series of later demonstrations in cooperative community-based industrial therapy with certain of the mental hospitals, it is important to understand their structure and purpose and what resulted from their experience. Three of these vocational adjustment centers, in addition to the Chicago prototype, will be described briefly.

The Vocational Adjustment Center
of the Jewish Vocational Service
and Employment Center of Chicago

Under the direction of a psychologist and social worker, Dr. William Gellman, the Chicago Jewish Vocational Service had pioneered in bringing work therapy to a wide array of physically handicapped people.[66] The history of this Jewish Vocational Service has parallels across the country. Employment services as part of the Jewish federations had been established in the 1930's in a number of cities principally to meet problems of religious discrimination in the private employment services and to combat this discrimination in the hiring practices of business and industry. With the coming of the public employment services and a gradual change in attitude toward Jewish applicants for jobs, the primary purpose for these Jewish Vocational Services faded. A number of them turned their attention to the special employment placement problems of the handicapped and disadvantaged. The Jewish Vocational Service of Chicago, in addition to employment placement, turned its attention to the task of preparing persons who presented difficulties in being placed in the job market to overcome their problems. A small sheltered workshop was opened, obtaining simple bench assembly and packaging operations from local industry, and the Jewish Vocational Service staff, under Dr. Gellman's direction, developed techniques for dealing with the more severely disabled, younger handicapped entering the job market for the first time, job placement problems of the older worker, and problems of the emotionally disturbed and mentally handicapped.

It should be kept in mind that the professional staff of the Jewish Vocational Service was psychologically trained and represented experience in clinical psychology, vocational counseling, employment psychology and social work.

Theories based upon six assumptions, out of experience with the physically handicapped, underlay the proposal of the Vocational Adjustment Center to the Federal Office of Vocational Rehabilitation.

1. Job turnover is more often due to inadequate vocational adjustment than to lack of job skill, and the majority of unskilled and semi-skilled positions require a "work personality" rather than specific skill experience.

2. When the work done acquires a positive value for an individual, his job performance, his job satisfaction and even his job seeking efforts will increase.

3. A successful work experience which leads to job satisfaction will help the person to attain the "work personality" which is admired in our culture.

4. If a person has a satisfying work experience and therefore develops the desire to work, his confidence in his ability to work will be enhanced, and he will be enabled to accept more realistic vocational goals and a vocational attitude consonant with his abilities.

5. A satisfying and successful work experience will stimulate the development of an adequate work personality, this in spite of cultural resistances to working.

6. Even where the resistance to entering the world of work is primarily the result of personality maladjustment, a guided work experience will help the individual to reach vocational adjustment.

These principles led to the development of a structured demonstration program with the following ingredients:

1. The organization of the workshop as a school for learning how to work and with a "curriculum" emphasizing skills and adjusting to the interpersonal demands of work.

2. The development of a program as close as possible to the real life setting of the competitive industrial work world.

3. Insistence upon intensively supervised, highly individualized approaches to meet the needs of the individual client.

4. A process of evaluating and interpreting the meanings of work to the client in terms of a psychodynamic orientation.

To meet these principles, only the simplest kind of bench assembly work was undertaken in order that supervision of the work could be done by the trained psychologically oriented staff members without their needing to acquire special skills in industrial production. The period of time the client might remain in the workshop was severely limited to 8 or 12 weeks. Although extensions of this time were allowed in individual cases, it was the minority of clients for whom the workshop period was extended. Elaborate rating devices were utilized by the supervisors toward a number of objectives, for the most part diagnostic, remedial or restorative.

During a prevocational or diagnostic stage, the client was usually tried out on a number of work samples of various gradations.

The Chicago project received its referrals from a wide array of community, health and welfare agencies. About half of the clients served could be diagnosed in the major psychiatric classifications of patients in the state hospital. Many of these persons had had mental hospitalization at some point in their lives. It became clear by the end of the demonstration phase, however, that while it was successful in preparing about half of those who went through the workshop training for return to normal employment, this was not sufficient to meet the needs of the large number of patients about to be discharged from the mental hospitals.

WORK ADJUSTMENT CENTER
OF THE JEWISH EMPLOYMENT SERVICES
OF PHILADELPHIA

This program, under a grant from the Federal Office of Vocational Rehabilitation, ran from 1958 to 1962, after which the program has been continued under the agency's own auspices. The project director describes[86] the intent of the Work Adjustment Center to "promote the employability of disabled individuals with emotional and mental problems by strengthening work attitudes and behavior and by stimulating the formation of an adequate work personality." The existing workshop was modified "to provide a psychologically true work environment which permitted the assessment of work capacity and encouraged the development of a work personality through controlled manipulation of psycho-social factors and work conditions."

The Work Adjustment Center of the Philadelphia JEVS was housed in a loft building in an old industrial neighborhood. It was surrounded by light manufacturing firms and wholesale and retail trade and was easily accessible by public transportation from any part of Philadelphia.

There were approximately 8000 square feet of loft space, and this was divided into work area, offices, storage, shipping and receiving. On the work benches clients were undertaking a variety of hand operations—sorting, counting and packaging novelties, toys, auto parts and accessories. In addition, there was some soldering, testing of electric plugs and the collating, counting, sorting and stapling pages for books. A few clients used patch presses, heat sealers or riveting machines.

The average population in the work area ranged from 20 to 30 persons. About half of them were referred by the Pennsylvania State Bureau of Rehabilitation, the New Jersey Rehabilitation Division, or through social agencies. A very small part of the client load was directly referred from hospitals. About 50 per cent of the population was listed in the diagnostic categories of psychosis or severe neurosis. About a quarter of the population was under 21, about half in the 22- to 44-age range, and another quarter in the 45- to 64-age range.

As in the Chicago center, the supervisory staff were for the most part psychologists and vocational counselors. Following a prevocational evaluation period in which the client was tested on five levels of work samples, he was assigned to the work adjustment training program for an 8-week period.

The vocational evaluation consisted of a series of work tasks of increasing complexity. The project director describes the lowest level, grade 1, as reflecting "behavior of a simple routine nature. Intellectually, it instigated a repetitive response to a single introduction and required no comprehension beyond the literal application of elementary knowledge. The motor equivalent was behavior at a reflexive level where spatial and visual arrangement aspects were at a minimum." Grade 2 was slightly more complex. Grade 3 involved multiple choices. Grade 4 involved judgmental activities. Grade 5 was described as incorporating "symbolic and problem solving activity in which reasoning and judgment of a more abstract character prevails; intricate visual motor arrangement, sequential processes, delicate tactual and dexterity factors pertained."

Since it was discovered quite early in the program that some clients did fairly well on the samples but failed miserably at maintaining a production schedule on actual work, the evaluative process was followed through when the client was assigned to the work adjustment training part of the program. The division of time between work samples and production work varied from client to client. For some, the prevocational evaluation took but a few days, for others it has to be extended beyond the upper limit of four weeks.

The psychologists and industrial foremen carried on a process of introducing the kinds of pressures that might be expected in competitive work. A series of procedures that might almost be called a curriculum were developed. Individual and group counseling were used to assist the client over problems which appeared to be inhibiting his adjustment. Among the techniques used in the work adjustment process were the following:

1. Stressing the need for good quality, requiring the client to redo a job on his own time if he had done it incorrectly.
2. Teaching the client to pace himself properly, encouraging a gradual increase in speed.
3. Emphasizing persistence, particularly in dealing with tensions.
4. Helping the client to gain a sense of responsibility by keeping track of his productivity.
5. Stressing attendance, punctuality and the importance of time.
6. Teaching the client to systematize his work in order to gain efficiency.
7. Teaching personal responsibility, such as the necessity of letting the foreman know if the client has to be absent.
8. Developing a tolerance for work by gradually increasing the amount of time spent in the shop.
9. Rearranging the seating arrangments to introduce the client to different kinds of group and individual working patterns.

In addition to these, clients were introduced to procedures of team work by assigning groups of persons to a common task and encouraging them to spend rest and lunch hours together to increase socialization.

Later in the project experience, the psychologists who had been serving as industrial foremen were replaced by regular trades people in an attempt to introduce somewhat more realistic controls and pressures as they might be found in normal industry.

Each client had available a JEVS counselor who reviewed his adjustment and gradually introduced him to considering placement in outside industry. Group sessions of clients were used for counseling purposes where a number had problems that were similar.

Wage rates were gradually increased from an initial pay of 30¢ to 60¢ an hour by the time of a client's third week in the Work Adjustment Center. After this, his earnings could rise to the Federal minimum wage of $1.15 per hour by the end of the program. A six-point pay raise schedule was established to provide motivational incentives.

The project director concludes that the program was effective in helping a wide array of seriously disadvantaged people to relearn work habits and to develop "work personalities." One professional to each five to seven clients was estimated as required to carry on the type of program described. Great stress was laid upon the value of time-limited nature of the program. The project director believes that the individual and group counseling services must be an integral part of the total program. He ponts out the value of mingling clients with diversified problems and disabilities as being closer to reality in the job world. Interestingly enough, the greatest rate of successful placement of clientele in jobs after the Work Adjustment Center was reported with the group labeled psychotic, and this constituted 40 per cent of the total.

THE VOCATIONAL ADJUSTMENT CENTER OF THE JEWISH VOCATIONAL SERVICE OF CINCINNATI

This industrial therapy program also followed the pattern of the Chicago prototype.[87] The workshop housing the Vocational Adjustment Center is in a building used for light manufacturing on the edge of downtown Cincinnati. There are approximately 4500 square feet of space on the ground level. It is well lighted and ventilated.

The workshop accommodates a maximum of seventy workers, but during the period of the demonstration project, from 1958 through 1963, approximately 10 workers at a time were referrals under the demonstration program. The project consisted of three phases: diagnostic phase, quite similar to the prevocational evaluation program just described for the Philadelphia agency; an 8-week adjustment phase, and a one-year post-workshop period during which a concerted effort was made to find suitable employment for the client.

The work carried on in the workshops was similar to that already described for the Philadelphia center. It included industrial subcontracts for the assembly of toys; assembly of advertising displays; packaging of hardware, candy and souvenirs; mailing, folding, sorting, addressing, minor printing and labeling and simple mechanical bench work requiring the use of staplers, drills, wire binders and small jigs. While some of the tasks required independent functioning, most called for some degree of cooperation with fellow workers.

The staff consisted of the project director, a psychologist, a part-time psychiatric consultant and a medical consultant.

The procedures of evaluation and the measuring devices were those developed by the Chicago agency with some modifications to meet local conditions.

The population served, however, seems to have had a higher proportion of psychiatric disability than was true in the other settings. The final report of the project says,

> The VAC population could be described as "seriously" disabled. Approximately half (49 per cent) carried psychiatric diagnoses of some form of psychosis, while the 23 per cent who were diagnosed

"neurosis" included a majority of individuals with profound charac-
terological or personality trait disturbances. Seventy-seven per cent
of all clients had a history of psychiatric hospitalization, many for
prolonged periods or with numerous readmissions.

A large majority (87 per cent) were receiving some type of
psychiatric treatment while they were enrolled in the VAC program.
A significant proportion (24 per cent) were in actual or technical
in-patient status, and, for this group, discharge from the hospital
was frequently contingent upon the successful completion of the
VAC program, including placement in gainful employment.

A quite careful follow-up was undertaken of the 127 clients covered in
the project period. Project staff expressed satisfaction with the end results
which, while the numbers were too small to be statistically significant,
showed a somewhat better outcome than had been true in either the Chicago or Philadelphia experiences. The project report points out that these
clients come from the lower and frequently the lowest socioeconomic strata
in the population. The usual expectation is that there is little possibility of
these people entering the job world if left to their own devices. The offering of the usual vocational counseling techniques available through employment agencies, and as had been previously offered in the Jewish Vocational Services, was unlikely to be effective, since few of these types of
individuals are capable of entering into the kind of one-to-one psycho-
therapeutic relationship called for in vocational counseling.

The project reporters, with great honesty, point out,

> There is no profit, either, in painting an unrealistically rosy picture
> of the vocational problems of such seriously disabled persons. In
> many cases their problems did not yield to the influences that the
> VAC could bring to bear on them. Even in those cases where the
> VAC was successful in improving work performance, other factors
> over which we had no control might interfere with, or totally undo,
> vocational gains. Not infrequently our clients were living under
> extremely difficult social circumstances from which work provided
> only temporary escape. . . . There is little reason to believe that a
> twelve-week experience, no matter how carefully designed to
> promote vocational growth, will have any effect on basic personality
> structure.

WORK ADJUSTMENT PROGRAM
OF THE GOODWILL INDUSTRIES
OF INDIANAPOLIS

The Indianapolis Goodwill Industries originated in 1929 in an old
garage. Today it employs over 350 persons and is housed in a new modern
building constructed and equipped specifically to meet the needs of handicapped workers.[145] It has a long history of interest in rehabilitation services. Goodwill Industries has employed a psychologist on its staff for over

20 years. It carries on a three-phase rehabilitation program including a 4-week experience on job samples, a work adjustment porgram of work therapy and a vocational training program on specific jobs. Among the areas available for vocational training are such fields as sales clerk, dry cleaner operator, medical secretarial, finishing furniture, switchboard operator, offset printing, electrical appliance repair, shoe repair, spray painter.

The demonstration project, which ran from 1958 to 1962 under a grant of the Federal Office of Vocational Rehabilitation, was also patterned after the Chicago Jewish Vocational Service prototype. A wider array of diagnostic categories are represented among the clients referred to this program than was true of the others described. The Indianapolis Goodwill Industries takes advantage of an extended array of workshop supervisor training programs made available through the national organization of Goodwill Industries. In preparation for the demonstration project, work supervisors attended supervisory training sessions focused on such matters as functions and responsibilities of supervisors, methods of job instruction training, human relations, work simplification, job layout, work planning and analysis, leadership, safety training, cost control, techniques for evaluating worker performance and methods of delegation of responsibility.

The Indianapolis Goodwill Industries demonstration covered 200 persons, 67 per cent of whom were men; almost 75 per cent of the clients were single. All of the individuals referred were severely disabled and considered probably unemployable by their referring agencies. Many of the multiple handicapped were sent to the demonstration project as a "last resource."

The techniques and the methods of evaluation follow the prototype systems already described.

The greatest difference between this program and the others is that the Indianapolis Goodwill Industries set a 12-week adjustment training period rather than eight weeks and was much more flexible in extending the time period beyond this limit. In their conclusions on the demonstration, the reporters pointed out that clients who achieved the highest job rating were some of those for whom the training period had been extended and that this was particularly true for mental patients.

In the main, this series of demonstration projects, supported by the Federal Office of Vocational Rehabilitation, served the following purposes:

1. It demonstrated to the community-based rehabilitation programs that it is possible to absorb mentally ill patients into a workshop population and to be somewhat successful in re-establishing them in regular employment.

2. It gave clear indication as to the complexity of the array of services necessary.

3. It brought the official rehabilitation agencies, the D.V.R.'s, to a familiarity with industrial therapy processes in workshops that had already established a fairly high level of performance with the physically handicapped.

4. It clarified to some extent that there were differences in the rehabilitation processes for persons with mental and motional difficulties that would require modifications in the programs that had become standardized for the physically handicapped.

FROM WORK ADJUSTMENT TO INDUSTRIAL THERAPY

Some of these same vocational and employment agencies moved on in their demonstrations and others joined them in working directly with mental hospitals. Again, the examples that will illustrate most graphically the processes used and the problems presented include the Jewish Vocational Services network and Goodwill Industries.

THE JEWISH VOCATIONAL SERVICE OF MILWAUKEE— MILWAUKEE COUNTY HOSPITAL FOR MENTAL DISEASES

The Jewish Vocational Service of Milwaukee has a number of years of pioneering experience with vocational training, employment and rehabilitation ventures. It is noted for a high level of professional competence and a willingness to experiment with the provision of vocational-educational training and rehabilitation services to a variety of handicapped groups. Its executive director, Michael Galazan, has long been used as a consultant in educational and rehabilitation services by the state of Wisconsin and on the national scene.

Although the grant received from OVR was for the operation of an employment-adjustment center for the emotionally disturbed, the Milwaukee Jewish Vocational Service modified the design of its demonstration considerably from that of the Chicago prototype.[89] With much more similarity to the Altro-Rockland project, heretofore described, the Milwaukee agency set up a cooperative venture with the Rehabilitation Division of the State Board of Vocational and Adult Education and the Milwaukee County Hospital for Mental Diseases.

All of the patients to the Employment Adjustment Center came from the Milwaukee County Hospital. In contrast, however, to the Altro program, which was primarily concerned with stimulating the interest and programming of rehabilitation within the state hospital, the contact between the Milwaukee County Hospital for Mental Diseases and the Employment Adjustment Center of the Jewish Vocational Service was through the Division of Vocational Rehabilitation which assigned a case supervisor to spend most of his time at the hospital.

The Vocational Adjustment Center workshop was one of a series of workshops operated by the Jewish Vocational Service and was set up to accommodate about 50 patients at a time. About 150 other patients with a variety of handicaps (including the mentally retarded, cerebral palsy, orthopedic, etc.) are served in adjacent quarters or nearby. For purposes of the demonstration as well as because, philosophically, the Milwaukee Jewish Vocational Service felt that there were advantages to the separation of clients with emotional problems from others, the Vocational Adjustment Center was available only for patients from the county mental hospital. Resources of the other shops were available on occasion when it was felt that the work in another shop was more suitable to the needs of a patient than that which was being performed in the Vocational Adjustment Center.

The work done was obtained on a subcontract basis from local industries. A full-time subcontract coordinator or procurer was employed by the Jewish Vocational Service to make the rounds of industries and obtain work for all of the workshops including the Employment Adjustment Center. For the most part, the job procuror obtained from a number of different companies the type of simple bench assembly and packaging work to be found in most of the workshops of this type.

One of the shops of the Milwaukee Jewish Vocational Service is engaged in manufacturing place mats, their own product, the sales of which are handled by a sales group not connected with the agency. Another shop is designated as the "high production shop" and manufactures headboards for beds using a variety of power tools. Clients are placed in this shop only when they have sufficient skills or where the training is intended to lead to an occupation in the woodworking or mechanical fields.

One of the most interesting hallmarks of the Milwaukee demonstration is the network of cooperative relationships set up. As mentioned, the project was a cooperative demonstration between the mental health institution, the public rehabilitation agency, and the Jewish Vocational Service with sponsorship by the National Council of Jewish Women. In addition, a professional advisory committee was organized with representation from the County Medical Society, the County Mental Health Association, the Psychological Association, the County Unit of Institutions and Departments, the State Board of Vocational and Adult Education, the United Community Services and local industry. In addition, a consulting committee of the local chapter of the American Institute of Industrial Engineers was turned to for advice.

This cooperative network served not only to broaden the availability of community resources for patients served in the demonstration but also gave support to the action of the governor of Wisconsin following the end of the demonstration in 1960 in which he made possible the continuation of the service of the Milwaukee Jewish Vocational Service to the Milwaukee County Hospital for Mental Diseases as a regular part of the on-going program of the State Board of Vocational and Adult Education, Rehabilitation Division. This latter action parallels that of the New York City Community

Mental Health Board which through New York State mental health service funding had, a couple of years before, made it possible for Altro Health and Rehabilitation Services to continue its cooperative program with Rockland and other state mental hospitals in the New York area.

In some other important respects, the Milwaukee demonstration differs markedly from the Vocational Adjustment Center projects developed from the Chicago prototype. These include the following:

1. A recreation director was added to the program and took responsibility for bowling teams for the worker-patients and for after-hours and evening recreational group programs. These latter included the organization of a formal club, a charm course for the women patients and the production of a newspaper distributed to all patients and alumni of the program.

2. The fixed time limit of the work adjustment programs was eliminated. No maximum was established. After a period of some months if evaluation indicated but little progress, some patients were moved into the permanently sheltered work program of the local Goodwill Industries. A few others remained on an extended temporary sheltered work regime with other workshop units of the Jewish Vocational Service.

3. While an evaluation period was utilized during the first four weeks, the formalized work sampling procedure was not used. A rating scale by the shop's supervisors was utilized along with a performance record critical incidence technique used by industry. A battery of psychometric and projective tests was administered as well as an intake questionnaire covering the patient's social history.

4. Individual and group counseling or psychotherapy was made available to all of the patients within the program, both while they were in the adjustment center as well as during an initial period on a job afterwards. Psychotherapy was provided at the Hospital for Mental Diseases or by private psychiatrists.

5. While operant conditioning in the context of learning theory has been the guiding principle in organizing the activities of the Vocational Adjustment Center, it would appear that greater attention was paid in this program to the interlocking effects of the psychiatric illness itself and the surrounding circumstances that produce disability.

The project directors speak of their theoretical orientation as basically eclectic.[90] They credit the influence of Dr. Robert C. Hunt in formulating their theoretical base. Dr. Hunt was the director of the Hudson River State Hospital in New York at a time it was first experimenting in developing community psychiatric services. Dr. Hunt expressed the opinion "that much of the disability associated with psychotic illness is not a part of the illness as such."[82] He believed that the potential for rehabilitation efforts "is therefore enormous if we think of rehabilitation as encompassing all possible measures for reducing the amount and severity of disability, including measures for avoidance as well as measures for alleviation." From these opinions, Dr. Hunt derives the following assumptions:

1. The disability associated with psychotic mental illness is enormous.
2. The illness and the associated disability are not necessarily homogeneous or synonymous.
3. Disability is only in part intrinsic to the illness.
4. Disability is in large part an artifact of extrinsic origin.
5. Since the disability is an artifact, it is not inevitable and something can be done about it.
6. The factors which produce disability are multiple.
7. The multiple extrinsic factors have a common origin in traditional attitudes toward the mentally ill in our culture.

It is pertinent to point out here that the concept that disability is only in part intrinsic to the illness and that help can be provided to the handicapped individual even though his basic medical condition may not be able to be changed is a well-known principle in the rehabilitation of physical disease and illness. One has only to think of the many physically handicapped people who have managed to re-establish themselves as productive members of society in spite of the fact that they are confined to a wheel chair or must wear a prosthetic appliance, or of the sufferers of heart disease who still find it possible to carry on productive work lives within the limiting capacity of what is actually their physical condition.

Jewish Vocational Service of Essex County, New Jersey— Essex County Overbrook Hospital

The Jewish Vocational Services of Essex County in Newark, New Jersey[88] set up its demonstration as did the Milwaukee agency in cooperation with the State Rehabilitation Commission and the County hospital for mental disease. Its plan embraced a research design, however, with the intent of attempting to measure the extent to which the use of its Opportunity Workshop contributed to the vocational adjustment of posthospitalized schizophrenic patients and to determine the usefulness of certain psychological instruments in predicting a patient's ability to profit from vocational rehabilitation.

Two small groups of patients, approximately 20 each, were randomly selected from among schizophrenic patients who were on leave status from the hospital. One group was supplied with the vocational counseling and regular services of both the Jewish Vocational Service and the New Jersey Rehabilitation Commission. The experimental group had added to these services placement in the Opportunity Workshop. The Opportunity Workshop looks very much like those already described for the other Jewish Vocational Services. The procedures of placement, the type of work, the relationship of counseling services to the workshop supervision were all quite similar to those of the Milwaukee demonstration; in fact, the project director in the Milwaukee agency had transferred to the Newark agency about midway in the project. As in the Milwaukee program, the official rehabilitation agency—in this case the New Jersey Rehabilitation Commission—was responsible for providing the professional rehabilitation services at the hospital and assisted in the selection of patients for referral to the project.

So far as the goals of the project were concerned, the findings were somewhat inconclusive. Little statistical significance was determined in the outcome for patients in the experimental group from those in the control group. The psychological instruments failed to predict the success or failure of a client. There were no clear indications as to any demographic or behavioral characteristics that distinguished the patient who would be successful from the patient who would not be successful. In a negative way, these bore out the findings of Meyer and Borgatta whose analysis at Altro Work Shops was reported on earlier in this chapter.

The positive results were sufficiently indicative, however, to stimulate the interest of the New Jersey Rehabilitation Commission in expanding its services to the other mental hospitals in the state. This demonstration, added to those previously reported, served to keep the interest of the Federal rehabilitation agency in continuing to support demonstrations and research in vocational rehabilitation to the mentally ill.

In the final report of the Essex County project, the project leaders refer to a number of problems that crop up with each of these experiences. These include:

1. The need for rehabilitation services beginning in the hospital rather than waiting until the patient is discharged or ready for discharge before starting the processes for vocational adjustment.

2. That social and recreational services are required concomitantly with vocational rehabilitation. Difficulties with housing and domiciliary plans and with recreational services get in the way of the patient's participation in vocational rehabilitation.

3. Question as to whether a diagnostic work-up in the vocational sphere may be necessary and, if so, whether it should be separate from the vocational adjustment program.

4. The recognition that some patients are not going to make the grade back to normal industry no matter how much service is rendered them and this raises the question of a long-term rehabilitation facility and where it should be located, whether in juxtaposition to the hospital or in the community.

5. Recognition that the revolving-door hospital results in a revolving-door workshop if many patients are to receive full advantage of the program.

Just as the Meyer and Borgatta study had led Altro Work Shops back into Rockland State Hospital, these adjustment center demonstrations led the Federal vocational agency to support others that provided even more of a bridge between hospital and community.

THE JEWISH VOCATIONAL SERVICE OF CHICAGO—
CHICAGO STATE HOSPITAL:
A WORK THERAPY RESEARCH CENTER

In 1965 the Chicago Jewish Vocational Service conducted a study as to the influence of a community-based rehabilitation center on the potential for rehabilitation of chronically hospitalized mental patients.[156] This was carried out in conjunction with the Chicago State Hospital and the Chicago Mental Health Center, a state aftercare clinic for discharged mental patients.

A rehabilitation program was established three miles from the state hospital in a remodeled factory building in an area of Chicago that was partly commercial and partly residential. The workshop was on a public bus route from the hospital, and after the first few months during which the patients were bussed from the hospital to the workshop, most of the patients were traveling from the hospital by public transportation.

Work in the workshop followed the usual pattern of simple bench assembly, packaging, packing and stock handling, with some light clerical operations. Following the earlier experience of the Chicago Jewish Vocational Service with its Vocational Adjustment Center, supervision of the work was provided by vocational counselors filling the roles of foremen. Every attempt was made, however, to maintain the semblance of the work atmosphere.

Before they entered the project from selected wards of the state hospital, patients were matched in groups of three according to age, sex, the ward from which they came, their length of hospitalization and marital status, and were randomly assigned to one of three service programs before their participation was solicited. With a certain amount of urging from the project staff and hospital personnel, almost all patients eligible agreed to participate. This design, therefore, did not run into the complication of dropouts and refusal to participate, experienced by the Jewish Vocational Service of Essex County and by the earlier Russell Sage study at Altro Work Shops.

The project design afforded three groups: one was the experimental group at the rehabilitation workshop; the second was provided a daily recreational therapy plan, also outside of the hospital but at the Chicago Mental Health Center; and the third group was provided the services routinely offered to all inpatients. Evaluation of the program was in terms of

1. The proportion of patients who were "successful," which was defined as being discharged from the hospital, working in competitive employment, and taking part in an on-going prevocational or activity program in the community.
2. The proportion of patients discharged from the state hospital within one year of the completion of their programs.

3. The proportion of patients, so discharged, who remained in the community six or more months without rehospitalization.

4. The proportion who remained in the community for at least a year following discharge.

5. Measure of the average number of weeks in the community for those patients who were discharged.

6. The proportion of patients who obtained competitive employment.

7. The proportion of the patients who retained employment for at least six months.

In addition to these criteria, the Chicago project also analysed the relevance of backgrounds and demographic factors as measures of success, the use of a behavior rating scale, a study of the relationship between performance on a series of psychomotor tests and the possibility of discharge from the state hospital and finally a study of the role constructs used by the professional staff in describing the behavior of clients in the workshop.

Although the number of patients was small, this was a tightly constructed design and the greater success by the groups served in the workshop was statistically significant from the control samples. Interestingly enough, the sample provided with recreational services was significantly more successful than the group provided only the normal inpatient services. The project directors conclude,[157] "The workshop program results were most superior to the results of the 'regular' state hospital program on those criteria where the staff exerted the most direct influence on subjects." They go on to point out that once the patients were in the community or employed and their contacts with staff diminished or stopped, these differentials vanished. The background in demographic variables, as was true in the Essex County study, showed no significant relationship as to success in either the workshop or the recreational therapy programs. The behavior rating scale did not turn out to be useful. The most powerful predictor of successful outcome was a pinboard psychomotor performance test developed for the project.

One extremely important conclusion of staff was that

> While the results of the workshop program in securing competitive employment are clearly superior, the percentage of people getting jobs (25 per cent of the total workshop sample) is small. The percentage maintaining employment over six months is still smaller. The success of the program is much more striking in promoting discharge than in promoting employment.

They visualized a model of vocational rehabilitation for the psychiatrically ill patient as embracing work in the institutional setting, a transitional phase with community orientation and finally a phase of community integration. They pointed out that their project was not much involved in dealing with the goals of clients in the institutional phases of industrial therapy, that their primary responsibility was in the transitional phase with emphasis upon community orientation and that the community integration stage was one of the weaker aspects of their study. They say,

> Continued support appears necessary for many clients to imple-
> ment new roles and to learn still other roles. All aspects of the
> program are still necessary parts of the rehabilitation process, of
> the major goals of community living, social functioning and pro-
> ductive roles. The staff of the program will often need to remain
> a major resource to clients making the last stage of a long effort to
> achieve these goals.

These points should be kept in mind in terms of what will be said of more recent efforts in industrial therapy for the mentally ill.

GOODWILL INDUSTRIES OF FORT WORTH
U.S. PUBLIC HEALTH SERVICE HOSPITAL

Two other cooperative ventures between community rehabilitation centers and mental hospitals are worth mentioning. One of these is between the Goodwill Industries of Fort Worth, Indiana and the United States Public Health Service hospital nearby. The Federal Office of Vocational Rehabilitation supported a demonstration project in the Goodwill Industries setting beginning in 1960. The characteristics of this program are very similar to those already described for the work adjustment program at the Indianapolis Goodwill Industries with the exception that all of the patients involved came from the one hospital. This project placed a good deal more emphasis on job training. The evaluation period was only for one week. A report on the project says,[78]

> It should be noted here that the majority of patients either con-
> sidered this a waste of time or considered the tasks too much like
> occupational therapy or psychological testing, or too distracting
> and confusing. They would prefer to concentrate on one type of
> work.

INSTITUTE FOR THE CRIPPLED AND DISABLED

The other program of interest is a psychiatric pilot project at the Institute for the Crippled and Disabled in New York City. The I.C.D. is a world-famous comprehensive rehabilitation center with more than 50 years of experience in very sophisticated social, medical and vocational services to the physically disabled. It has been the center of the development of many techniques in physical medicine and vocational rehabilitation, including the quite ornate Tower System as a method of evaluating an individual's skills on scored work samples. This has become the basic format for such prevocational evaluation both in the United States and abroad. I.C.D. took a small number of psychiatric patients into its program as a demonstration.[103]

The significance in the demonstration project at the Institute for the Crippled and Disabled is twofold. The fact that so prestigious a rehabilitation center has been willing to devote its facilities to serving the mentally ill should open an important new array of rehabilitation resources to psychiatric patients across the country. There are some 300 member agencies of the Association of Rehabilitation Centers, and although as of now only a handful have been willing to offer special industrial therapy or vocational rehabilitation programs for the mentally ill, more of them can be expected to follow I.C.D.'s lead. The I.C.D. demonstration has led to approval for continued funding under the New York State Mental Health Services Law. Since I.C.D. is truly a "comprehensive" rehabilitation center offering a wide array of medical, vocational, psychological and social services to its clientele and with an extensive program of followup, the possibilities are present over the years to come for more definitive studies of the rehabilitation needs of psychotic patients living in the community than could be obtained from the shorter demonstrations in the various Jewish Vocational Services.

THE HOSPITAL—COMMUNITY CONTINUUM

The two developmental streams, mental hospitals developing industrial therapy and then becoming concerned with services for their patients in aftercare and community sheltered workshops demonstrating service to mental patients and then suggesting that predischarge services for patients were necessary, have in recent years begun to converge. Two examples of programs which present the amalgam of such converging will illustrate the advantages and issues raised. Both, again, have been made possible through the Federal research and demonstration programs, one from the Federal Vocational Rehabilitation Administration, the other from the National Institute of Mental Health.

CAMARILLO STATE HOSPITAL— J.V.S. OF LOS ANGELES

Camarillo State Hospital, some 60 miles from Los Angeles, inaugurated a 3-year demonstration in 1963 under a grant from the Federal Vocational Rehabilitation Administration. This project, entitled "Coordinating Hospital and Community Work Adjustment Services," had as its purposes "(1) to use work as an instrument to help patients leave the hospital sooner, (2) to insure their tenure in the community and (3) to raise their level of instrumental functioning." An industrial therapy unit within the hospital, the bakery, was linked with a community work adjustment center, the Handcraft Industries of the Jewish Vocational Services of Los Angeles. Patients referred for the project were offered a "package" which included nonpaid work in the hospital bakery followed by placement in Handcraft Industries, with aftercare and supportive services towards job placement in regular employment.

The bakery was selected to be the hospital industry part of the demonstration because it was characteristic of hospital work stations, because it provided a number of different work activities from the most menial (sweeping and cleaning) to the semi-skilled (mixing dough, tending the bread machine, wrapping bread, frosting cakes), and because it already had a tradition of using patients as help. It had been decided not to establish a contract workshop on the hospital grounds

> because a great deal of real work already existed in the hospital which could be easily used for rehabilitation. This would eliminate the effort necessary to . . . finding space, getting machinery, negotiating contracts for work, transporting the raw material to the hospital and then transporting the finished product out of the hospital. All of this activity does not in itself contribute to patient rehabilitation. It is staff work that needs to be done to provide a work opportunity for patients.[70]

The bakery could absorb some 15 to 20 patients at a time, assigned for supervision to four or five bakers under the direction of a chief baker. The bakery work was production oriented, and to aid in the manipulation of the setting for therapeutic purposes, the project director, a psychologist with industrial experience, spent a great deal of his time in the bakery, learning the processes and counseling on assignments of individual patients.

The initial plan had been to "structure" the work experience so that each patient would go through three levels. Level one was to focus on work discipline, e.g., helping the patient to get to work on time; level two was to increase work tolerance by assigning more hours of work each day and by assigning some activities which were to increase his functioning abilities; level three required a full day's work and an increase in production demands, such as "assembly line" procedures.

This structural stepping up of work pressures turned out not to fit the working day facts of life. Most patients referred to the project already had achieved a 6-hour work day in other activities within the hospital; the demands of therapy sessions and medication, etc., did not allow for an 8-hour work day. In the bakery the entire crew was needed in the morning hours for the actual baking; even the advanced bakery staff pitched in for cleaning activities in the afternoon. It was left to each baker to arrange the work assignments for his patient assignees. The project supervisor on the scene aided in insuring that the tasks assigned provided sufficient challenge, for the staff were more inclined to be overly permissive and to make few demands of patients. Notwithstanding the flexible way in which work assignments were carried out, the project staff felt that the setting afforded an excellent testing situation for evaluation of work adjustment. They considered it superior to any psychological tests in assessing the patient's potential for work in the community.

During the project period, 146 patients were served. They were all schizophrenic men, 18 to 45 years old, whose home community was within easy commutation to Handcraft Industries in Hollywood. Length of hospitalization before admission to the project varied from just after hospitalization to a number of years. After an average time of two or three months in the bakery (range was seven days to nearly a year), the patients moved on to Handcraft Industries. Upon discharge from the hospital, however, they did not, for the most part, return to their family homes, for psychiatric advice was against this. Instead, use was made of "family care homes," foster homes under the supervision of the State Bureau of Social Work, a small halfway house and a small commercial hotel that was a block away from Handcraft.

Handcraft Industries has offered a work adjustment program for various handicapped persons since 1954. Its services for the emotionally disturbed and mentally ill follow the pattern set by the Vocational Adjustment Center of the Chicago Jewish Vocational Service. The work experience is bench asembly and packaging. Much use is made of heat sealing machines for blister and shrink packaging; these do require some training and involve dexterity and judgment. Of the 146 patients served by the project, 85 "graduated" from the bakery phase, and of these, 72 entered Handcraft.

After the first year of the project, there was less selectivity of patients, and a generally sicker group was referred from the wards. The bakery staff expressed unhappiness with the quality of manpower supplied, and while they were cooperative for the life of the demonstration, once the project was over, they quickly returned to the traditional use of "trained" long-term patients as bakers' assistants. Interestingly enough, although the sicker patients resulted in a proportionately smaller number who "graduated" from the bakery to leave the hospital, the same proportion of those who did leave went on to achieve self-support as of the "better" patients.

The final results of this project were twofold. Firstly, it demonstrated a method whereby a continuum of services from within the hospital out into the community can be designed, making use of existing facilities in both. Secondly, as had a number of the other Federally supported ventures, it has stimulated the interest of the state vocational rehabilitation agency and the state mental health authority in cooperating in rehabilitation services to state hospital patients. A cooperative agreement was made between the California Department of Rehabilitation and the California Department of Mental Hygiene, and a comprehensive vocational rehabilitation program was established at Camarillo State Hospital under direction of the project's supervisor.

Among the conclusions of the project directors are the following, of significance to cooperative industrial therapy ventures:

1. "It was clearly demonstrated by this project that monetary payment is not the only form of motivation that can be used with mental hospital patients. The promise and anticipation of leaving the hospital with a place to stay and a place to work can serve as an effective motivating factor. Motivation also is developed through relationship. When the hospital employee shows an interest in the patient as a person, not merely as a helper, the patient's motivation to work is enhanced, if only because he wants to please the employee."[71]

2. Patients working in the same industrial therapy program should be living on the same unit rather than in widely separated sections of the hospital. The support for vocational rehabilitation program that can be given by unit staff can materially enhance the chances for successful experiences for their patients.

3. There is need for some system of rewarding hospital employees for participating in patient rehabilitation. Specifically, publicity might be given to the work of hospital employees in industrial therapy and other rehabilitation programs.

4. Vocational rehabilitation must not be isolated from the total rehabilitation program for patients. This conclusion might easily be broadened to include the total therapeutic program of the hospital.

5. To maintain themselves in the community, mental patients need a wide variety of services. Housing, medical care, recreational and social activities must be available and also the assistance necessary to help such persons learn how to use such services.

6. There is a great need for helping many of these patients with learning the general skills of social living. Some of these skills may be developed in the work setting, but they may be more effectively learned in the living units away from work.

Altro Work Shops—
Hillside Hospital Young Adult Project

The conclusions of the Camarillo State Hospital—Jewish Vocational Service project are well borne out in the experience of Altro Health and Rehabilitation Services in a demonstration program just phasing into a continued service. The National Institute of Mental Health has just completed the funding of this project in supplying rehabilitation services to older adolescent and young adult schizophrenics. The program began in 1962 to demonstrate a hospital-community rehabilitation effort with young men and women, 17 to 22 years of age. Cooperation was designed as between Altro Work Shops and four mental institutions: Hillside Hospital in Queens, New York, a voluntary mental hospital; Psychiatric Institute, Manhattan, a state mental hospital; Jacobi Hospital, the psychiatric unit of the Bronx Municipal Hospital Center and Hawthorne-Cedar Knolls School, a voluntary residential treatment center. The results and findings of the demonstration are presently being compiled, but the service program is now being continued by New York State Mental Health Services Act funds. This description and these remarks relate to the part of the project involving Hillside Hospital, from which came the majority of project patients.

Altro's earlier experience at Rockland State Hospital had revealed a special set of problems applying to young people referred to the project team. It was difficult to motivate them to enter a rehabilitation program, and if they entered the sheltered workshop, the problems of coordinating the variety of services they required made any continuity of approach almost impossible. Rockland State Hospital was too distant from Altro Work Shops to make daily travel by patients feasible. Altro had already reached the conclusion that exposure to the rehabilitation program, particularly its vocational aspects, should begin as early in the hospital regime as possible. The professional leaders at Altro were also convinced that the very process of hospital discharge and referral to community agencies contributed to the very high rate of breakdown among the younger adult patients. A very great number of child mental patients were reaching the working age range and were either being discharged to a community for which they were unprepared or shifted to adult services in the mental hospitals where their chronicity was being reinforced.

At the point of discharge from the hospital, the young person was faced with three major life decisions all at once: where to live; how to support himself; what to do with his time. Failure in resolving any one of these is sufficient to promote relapse. The Altro project was designed to stagger the timing of these crisis points. The patient began work at Altro Work Shops early in his patient stay in the hospital. While living in the hospital and working in the workshops, to which he commuted daily, both Altro and Hillside Hospital social service staffs coordinated assistance with plans for living outside the hospital. When the move out of the hospital was made some weeks or months later, to own home, foster home, residence club or "Y," the patient had continued support of hospital aftercare, including social group, and of his Altro work. Move from Altro to a regular job in the community was phased to take place after the housing situation was resolved. The hospital guaranteed continued medical supervision for one year after hospital discharge; Altro continued social services and psychiatric consultation for up to a 2-year "adjustment period" after the patient left Altro Work Shops.

Since Altro Work Shops has already been described, it is necessary only to list the modifications in program necessitated by this project and to make some observations growing from the experience. The young people from Hillside Hospital were from the middle-class community with better than average schooling. Their initial interests were with white collar work activities and with higher skill work settings. Therefore, Altro pressed the development of its Clerical Service Bureau and the machine tool jobbing shop of its Mechanical Division. Interestingly enough, when these young folk were joined, in newer projects, by school dropouts and other disturbed boys and girls from the socially disadvantaged populations, these too preferred the white collar and machining jobs to the industrial garment sewing or the bench assembly and packaging operations.

Many of the schizophrenic young people were quite ill at the time they entered Altro Work Shops. There had to be a great deal of communication between hospital and rehabilitation center staffs about dosage of medication, about evaluations of performance both at Altro and at the hospital. Great flexibility was used in assignment to tasks at the workshop. A number of patients had to be shifted to the simpler demands of assembly work or direct mail, often after they had demonstrated to themselves that they could not perform at more complex tasks.

The transitions, from hospital to outside living, from Altro to outside work, from the hospital doctor to clinic or private therapist, were fraught with complications, frustrations and excitement. Altro's professional staff was practically on 24-hour call in some cases. The long tradition of dealing with tuberculous and cardiac emergencies served well. The nursing staff at Altro Work Shops, the Altro psychiatric consultants and the dedicated rehabilitation social workers combined with hospital services to snatch success from failure any number of times. Neither rehospitalization nor re-entry to Altro Work Shops was counted failure or the end of the demonstration period. Over the past six years the Altro experience has shown that with an adequate combination of services, especially with the younger patient, rehospitalization may be seen as a phase in the course of illness or a reconstituting phase in therapy rather than as a failure.

In direct parallel to the conclusion of the California project report, there was a close relation between ease in introducing new patients to the program and the level of understanding and support on the part of hospital unit staff. The movement of patients was much facilitated during the period that referrals were made from a single unit, whose psychiatrist and other staff were familiar with Altro. Also, as the Camarillo report pointed out, the fact that the patients lived together allowed for a commonality of interest and a reinforcement that was helpful. With this group of patients, however, the motivation for coming to Altro Work Shops was not really the lure of leaving the hospital. It was more that Altro was built into the total treatment plan and became part of the psychiatrist's prescription.

The experience of Altro Work Shops does not support those who prefer the separation of mental patients into a special unit in the sheltered workshop. Experimentation with different "mixes" of patients shows quite clearly the advantages of a heterogeneous grouping, in age range, sex, diagnostic leveling. At the community stage of industrial therapy, such a mixture is in greater attune to the normal work situation. At Altro Work Shops, when the proportion of schizophrenic patients in a unit reached 50 per cent, there was a noticeable lowering of productivity and a slowing down, even of foremen and nonpatients on the unit. Below that proportion the unit seemed to reach more normal levels, with the mental patients matching others.

Of approximately 80 patients in the project who have passed the one-year-after-Altro point, more than 65 have made a successful adjustment as measured by self-support and at least minimal socialization. These are chronically ill people, however, who may always need supportive care in the community if they are to be kept from serious relapses. Each goes through periods when his illness is in lesser remission. Most of them require supervision for a continued regimen of drug maintenance. Many of them require psychotherapy or a regular series of counseling sessions. All of them require what Altro in its tuberculosis heyday used to call "a stitch in time," or what the eminent expert in rehabilitation medicine, Dr. Howard Rusk, has called maintaining "the umbilical thread."[29] Of all the medical and social services, only the comprehensive rehabilitation centers have ever developed fully such a continuity of care. Whether the newly planned comprehensive community mental health centers can supply this kind of supportive service to rehabilitated mental patients remains to be seen.

While the Altro-Hillside project developed the community-based resources far beyond those in any of the projects described in this chapter, there were problems in insuring their availability when needed. Foster home care was supplied by a cooperating family and children's agency, a halfway house was made available by an Altro-Albert Einstein College of Medicine program, recreation was supplied by a Hillside-Educational Alliance (settlement house) project, etc. Problems of coordination came and went. Stimulation of the development of resources took almost as much staff time as direct service to patients.

It is also important to note that in this project, very like the community-based demonstrations described earlier in this chapter, Altro had no influence on the in-hospital phase of the program. In a new demonstration effort, this one called "Partnerships in Industrial Therapy for the Mentally Ill," Altro proposes to collaborate with Bronx State Hospital and two of its satellite comprehensive community mental health centers (Soundview-Throgs Neck and Lincoln Hospital) in a network of industrial therapy units in the hospital, community mental health center and community. Continuity of mental health care for the patient is to come from the mental health center; continuity of industrial therapy from Altro Work Shops. Whether such a pattern of care is practicable and, if it is, whether it will insure continuity of service to mental patients remains to be tested.

RESOURCES FOR PARTNERSHIPS IN INDUSTRIAL THERAPY

The idea for a relationship between a community-based sheltered work program and a mental hospital suggests itself naturally from the programs just illustrated. The thesis is that where a shop serving the handicapped already exists, it might extend its services to mental patients and also become the source of contract work for the in-hospital industrial therapy unit. In 1965, Altro Health and Rehabilitation Services undertook a survey of sheltered workshops in the United States serving the emotionally disturbed.[65]

In all, 490 workshops reported that they do serve the emotionally disturbed. Forty-seven of these workshops, of which 24 were already in mental hospitals, served almost one quarter of all the emotionally disturbed clients reported. The median number of the emotionally disturbed in the 490 workshops each day was only 11, so that the apparent room for expansion is very great.

Seventy-two per cent of these workshops began operation since 1955, showing the influence of the 1954 Vocational Rehabilitation Amendments. It is fair to expect a continuation of this trend, aided by new provisions in 1965 Vocational Rehabilitation Amendments to the Social Security Law.[168] These make financial support available to sheltered workshops and classify the mentally ill among the categories for which a rehabilitation regimen of as long as eighteen months may be approved for a patient by the state Division of Vocational Rehabilitation.

INDUSTRIAL THERAPY IN PSYCHIATRIC UNITS
OF GENERAL HOSPITALS

Almost all of the inudstrial therapy programs for the mentally ill developing in this country have been located in or related to specialized psychiatric hospitals. There has been a slowly growing and increasingly important number of general hospitals that have added full-fledged psychiatric departments. A very few of these have thus far introduced some form of industrial therapy program. The notable exceptions have been the work therapy programs in the army psychiatric treatment centers. The inpatient treatment of psychiatrically ill military personnel has over the years taken place on the psychiatric services of general hospitals.

The work of Dr. Maxwell Jones, particularly with British military men during World War II and his subsequent publication of *The Therapeutic Community*,[95] provided impetus to U. S. Army psychiatrists to introduce work therapy. Following the Korean War, the occupational therapists in Army hospitals led the field in creating programs that took patients out of their ward settings into crafts and then into work therapy. The first complete work therapy program was inaugurated at Letterman General Hospital in 1958. Since then, several other Army general hospitals have followed suit.[1]

The general format of work therapy is similar for each of the Army psychiatric treatment centers. Patients are referred to work therapy by the medical officer. The occupational therapist "makes an assignment that meets the requirements prescribed as well as the interests of the patient. Work therapy assignments are frequently available not only within the somewhat protective environment of the hospital but also in the more competitive outside atmosphere of the military community."[161]

It should be kept in mind that Army posts are really self-contained communities. Not only are all or almost all of the normal work activities carried on as in a small city, but on each base there may be a variety of industrial activities ranging up to quite technical manufacturing and assembly. The assistant chief psychiatric consultant of the Army describes the range of work therapy assignments as including

> auto repair, electronics, welding, aircraft maintenance, stock-room work, carpentry, painting, gardening, physical reconditioning activities, photography, laboratory work, research and development projects, ward attendant positions, acting as a messenger, cooking and mess hall duties, work with the Military Police, and various administrative assignments. An occasional patient has been assigned to a sophisticated research unit, some are assigned to relatively menial positions; but always an attempt is made to insure productive possibilities for the patient involved. Broom-pushing details are not considered part of the work therapy program nor are solitary, repetitious and non-socially oriented positions.[2]

The psychiatrists and occupational therapists closest to these programs have noted three major long-term benefits. First of all, the patients seem to have benefited. They have reported on survey that they considered the work therapy program as most significant in their treatment. The staffs noted a decreased need for medication and a decline in length of hospital stay wherever work therapy was introduced. Secondly, work therapy has furnished diagnostic and evaluative material not otherwise available. "Where a work therapy program has flourished, a more positive expectancy relative to patient's assets has developed."[3] Thirdly, the work therapy program has increased the acceptance of psychiatric patients by other divisions of the hospital and on the post. Job supervisors have been known to plead for a patient's retention an a job even though the doctor thought him too ill to remain on active duty.

Col. Allerton cites four problems presented by the Army work therapy programs which may be seen as common to industrial therapy elsewhere.[4]

First, "continuous attention is required to prevent the program from being utilized by the institution as a whole as providing a labor force." Second, it is necessary to assure that the physician, the nurse and the occupational therapist remain uniformly concerned with the patient's interests so that work therapy "does not degenerate into an artsy-craftsy type of endeavor." Third, there is the danger that overly great enthusiasm for work therapy will lead to interference with other necessary treatment modalities. Absence from work must be provided for individual and group therapy schedules. Finally, although information from the work therapy experience is valuable in assessing the patient's condition, it is extremely difficult to assess what part work therapy has contributed to the recovery or lack of recovery of specific patients. There are just too many variables. It should be noted, furthermore, that while the Army work therapy programs have relevance to the therapeutic aspects of industrial therapy in general hospitals and in the community, they represent an entirely foreign socio-economic aspect. In its economic respects, Army work therapy may be somewhat closer to industrial therapy in the U. S. S. R. than to the programs in the Americas and Western Europe.

Two examples in attempting to establish industrial therapy in community general hospitals deserve brief mention. For some two years, in 1963–1964, Altro Health and Rehabilitation Services collaborated with Montefiore Hospital, Bronx, New York, in operating a sheltered workshop in the hospital.[5] This workshop was primarily for patients of the hospital's department of physical medicine, but its relatively new department of psychiatry also referred patients. Complications in management-sharing and philosophy of operation led to Altro's withdrawal, but there was never any question about its value for patients. Altro at that time was wedded to community-based sheltered work and could not see its long involvement in a hospital-based program.

The other was the inauguration of a work therapy program for the acute psychiatry department of the District of Columbia General Hospital.[33] In 1966 an existing work therapy program for the Physical Medicine and Rehabilitation Services of the hospital was asked to extend services to psychiatric patients. Assignments were used in the maintenance department, business office, laundry, supply department, x-ray department, etc. Patients worked from a few hours to full time. Their progress was reviewed periodically by an interdisciplinary professional team. Some 33 psychiatric patients were so employed at the time of a visit by this author. The development of this and other general hospital psychiatric industrial therapy programs is limited by (1) the short duration of stay and rapid turnover of inpatients in psychiatric wards of general hospitals, (2) a limited number of positions that can be used for patients in the highly technical and specialized operation of today's general hospital and (3) the moves toward linking general hospital psychiatry with comprehensive community mental health centers, thereby requiring different forms of industrial therapy for a larger number of patients, including day hospital and outpatients.

THE USE OF INDUSTRY FOR INDUSTRIAL THERAPY

From time to time, the suggestion has been made that the best place to find a real work setting for industrial therapy would be in industry itself. Individually selected jobs have long been used by employment counselors for the handicapped and by vocational rehabilitation counselors either as transitional or as final employment for individual discharged patients. While such job placement has been much more frequent for the physically handicapped, an increasing volume of special placements has resulted for the post mentally ill.

Placement of groups of patients in a regular industry, such as was described for Glenside Hospital in England, is rare in this country. Some years ago this author at a national meeting proposed introducing the concept of "foster work," using regular industry in the way regular families are used for the "foster home" housing of dependent children and even mental patients, but no large scale efforts in this direction are discernible.[28] Two experimental programs are, however, "straws in the wind." These are the Fountain House Foundation arrangements with a variety of businesses in New York City and the Mental Health-Rehabilitation Project of the Sidney Hillman Health Center, Amalgamated Clothing Workers of America (New York Joint Board) and the New York Clothing Manufacturers Association.

FOUNTAIN HOUSE

Fountain House is a social vocational rehabilitation facility serving patients who have been released from mental hospitals.[12] Almost half of the patients come shortly after leaving the hospital. Three out of four Fountain House "members" are schizophrenics. A third have had hospitalization of over three years; two thirds were hospitalized before the age of 30. It is apparent on review of records or even upon observation of the 100 or so patients who use Fountain House facilities during any day that this is a very handicapped group of people, presenting the greatest difficulty in making a successful transition from hospital to community.

Fountain House provides services in four major areas: a social and recreational program on weekends and in the evenings; a daytime vocational adjustment program in which members, assisted by staff and well volunteers, keep the house clean, prepare luncheons, man the switchboard, make repairs and perform a large variety of office and clerical routines; a program of aiding members find living quarters, including an extremely imaginative apartment living project in which Fountain House underwrites the availability of apartments rented at reasonable cost to its members; and the transitional employment program. The latter has been in existence since 1958 and now has some 25 to 30 companies cooperating.

Through the efforts of staff members, volunteers and members of its Board of Directors, Fountain House obtains the cooperation of a business enterprise in earmarking one or more of its simpler jobs for use as a rehabilitation setting for ex-mental patients. These positions are messenger work in a printing company, clerical work in a department store, packaging in a drug firm, stock-room work in a wallpaper factory, porter work and others of a similar unskilled nature. A staff member tries out the job for a short time to assess its demands. Then a Fountain House patient member is assigned. When the patient has demonstrated his capacity to carry on productive work, even though these tasks are often below his potential or past skills, and to get along with fellow employees, he is helped to move from the transitional job to regular employment somewhere else. The initial job placement is then used for another patient member who needs it.[140]

Fountain House believes that this project best serves patients who have made the grade in the day program but who are not yet ready or able to assume regular employment. Placement in the project, which the patient knows is a temporary job, removes the threatened pressure of having to succeed in order to remain. A weekly meeting of all members on transitional job placements aids in stimulating member interest and serves as a group therapy supportive session. Representatives of the participating employers meet three times a year and exchange experiences.

Both the employers and Fountain House are enthusiastic about the program and its potentials. The firms consider that they are making an important humanitarian contribution. The possibilities for interpretation of mental illness are great. Considering the quite fragile mental health of Fountain House's members, this form of transition to the regular work-a-day world might have some advantages over the sheltered workshop form of industrial therapy. There is less formal "treatment" structure, and the next step to regular employment may be less formidable than between the sheltered workshop and industry. On the other hand, there seem to be fewer opportunities for diagnostic and evaluative observations in the Fountain House form of industrial therapy, and the opportunities are not present for upgrading skills or learning new tasks. To date, only a few hundred patients have been served in the Fountain House transitional employment program. Further service development is warranted before evaluative attempts are made.

THE SIDNEY HILLMAN HEALTH CENTER PROJECT

A joint labor union and management project in rehabilitation services to garment factory workers was initiated under a grant from the Federal Vocational Rehabilitation Administration and more recently extended to provide mental health services by a grant from the National Institute of Mental Health. The program was housed in the Sidney Hillman Health Center in New York. The Health Center gives a wide range of medical services to members of the New York Joint Board of the Amalgamated Clothing Workers of America, some 30,000 people who work in the men's clothing manufacturing plants which belong to the New York Clothing Manufacturers' Association.[57]

The physical rehabilitation phase of the demonstration had been very effective in identifying handicapped union members, insuring that they received medical and social services and that their conditions of work were protected or altered so as to enable them to be productive wage earners. Social workers and physicians on the project staff were joined by union business agents and shop stewards, with the cooperation of management, in seeing that needed services were given. There was "job protection" and, in a number of instances, experimentation with modification of job assignment or job content within the plant where the person was regularly employed to effect rehabilitation. With the expansion to mental health services, psychiatrists were added to the Health Center's staff and services were extended to persons with mental or emotional difficulties.[174]

The story of this total rehabilitation program under labor union auspices is extremely interesting in its implications for bringing mental health services to a blue-collar population. What has significance to industrial therapy, however, is the use of the employee's own work setting as the locus for rehabilitation.[35] This might be looked upon as a form of preventative industrial therapy. Thus far, no other labor union has developed this form of vocational rehabilitation of the mentally ill to such an extent.

INDUSTRY'S OWN INDUSTRIAL THERAPY

Increasingly, the medical departments of our country's largest industries have become involved in rehabilitation and mental health. The early identification of troublesome health problems, arrangements for their treatment and such necessary rearrangements of work activity to make therapy and rehabilitation possible are being tackled together by the company physician, the personnel department, and management. Such programs are becoming recognized as good economy, especially where the preservation of semi-skilled, skilled and highly technical labor is involved.[114]

Industrial managers are not inclined to look upon such practices as constituting industrial therapy. They are not open to accepting nonemployees who exhibit the same kinds of mental handicaps into their factories. It does not take much imagination, however, to translate the present efforts of many businesses who, with governmental financial aid, are giving training and jobs to "school drop-outs" and socially and behaviorally handicapped young people into similarly subsidized efforts for schizophrenics and other post mentally ill. After all, experience is revealing that a high proportion of the jobless, socially handicapped have psychiatric diagnoses.

CHAPTER IV

THE THERAPY IN INDUSTRIAL THERAPY

The purposes to which industrial therapy is put were described in Chapter I. These included use as a setting to occupy the time of patients, use as a substitute for occupational therapy, as a place in which to carry on vocational rehabilitation, as a bridge to the work-a-day world, as a program for developing ego strengths, as an observation post for diagnosis and evaluation of the patient's illness, as a new treatment modality. Some or all of these purposes are intended in each of the industrial therapy programs dealing with the mentally ill, and a variety of techniques and methods have been adapted or devised to translate the purposes into services to patients. Before considering methods and techniques, however, there needs to be consideration as to the nature of the population for whom industrial therapy is devised.

CHARACTERISTICS OF THE PATIENTS

It should be obvious that the clientele served by the work adjustment centers, described in Chapter III, is quite different from that of the hospital-based industrial therapy units. Both groups fit under the rubric of "mentally ill," but this is not at all a homogeneous category. It is an oversimplification to say that the mentally handicapped living in the community include a high proportion of neurotics, psychopaths and sociopaths, while those in the mental hospitals are mainly psychotics. Each of these categories covers a wide range, and the psychosis designations have frequently been used as catch-alls for many seriously inadequate people for whom no other easy classification has seemed to fit.

In the rehabilitation of the physically handicapped, there is a longstanding "rule of thumb" that 10 per cent of those disabled will finally need the services of a transitional sheltered work setting in order to return to the world of work. A larger proportion, perhaps double in number, should receive the vocational counseling or casework services they will need to move directly to school, homemaking or work. These percentages applied to mental hospital populations or to clinically diagnosed psychiatric problems in communities will yield numbers of handicapped that are staggeringly greater than the amount of resources now available to serve them. Therefore, it is understandable that mental health authorities should first direct their attention to rehabilitation programs for their usefulness in dealing with the long-term or chronic patient.

Even this is a category hard to define precisely. It is clear that the largest single group among them is the schizophrenic and that a large proportion of them are elderly or have serious additional physical disabilities. Length of hospitalization characterizes them more than anything else—the chronics are the 10 per cent of state hospital patients who have been in the hospital for over a year; many entered in their teens or early adulthood and have spent half their lives as hospital patients. The poor facilities, lack of attention, destruction of self-respect, denial of social amenities, all typical of state hospitals even today, have taken their toll. In a recent study for the National Institute of Mental Health, Helen Padula[132] describes the chronic mental patients as taking

> . . . on the protective coloration of their environment. Conditioning and illness produced indistinguishable results. Ironically, the more effective the patient's adaptation to the hospital, the more compelling the evidence for his continued hospitalization—and the more difficult, in fact, would his adjustment be if he were released.

She concludes,[133]

> Although chronic patients bear some likeness to one another, they are not peas in a pod. They differ in diagnosis and in the degree of scarring from their illness or from their institutionalization. . . They are young and old, clever and stupid, pleasant and irritating; they vary in interests, resources, and talents. But they all *look* much alike.

An important outcome of the "psychiatric revolution" that has come with the ataractic drugs and the open door policy has been recognition that frequently the irrationality and inertia, the uncooperativeness and untidiness associated with the patients are not symptoms of their psychoses but of the treatment they received. Chronically ill patients are not so different from those who do not become chronically ill. The classification of chronicity results from social and economic determinants rather than from any differential in the nature of the illness. Follow-up studies of patients discharged from the state hospitals, such as those done in California,[118] have made this clear.

The significance of these findings is that vocational rehabilitation and industrial therapy programs can be designed for mental hospital patients generally and need not be developed separately for the acutely and the chronically ill. Two additional facts bear out this contention. First, none of the measuring devices for predicting success outside the hospital have been able to demonstrate any difference in outcome between chronic patients and others; second, there is no statistically significant difference between premorbid states or prior job experience.

A number of demographic studies have shown that the major proportion of mental hospital patients come from the socially and economically disadvantaged areas of the population.[80] The California studies revealed[117] that

> approximately three-fourths of the patients released from a mental hospital had either meager prior work experiences or none at all. Those who did report prior employment had worked at the most marginal and unstable jobs. Thus, few could be expected upon release from the mental hospital to return to a steady job or to pick up on a "career."

Dr. John Cumming[46] has reported from his work at Syracuse,

> We know from studies carried out at the Mental Health Research Unit and elsewhere that as many as half of all patients of working age who are admitted to mental hospitals have an inadequate job history.

Interestingly, the Russian reports suggest much the same situation there.[11]

The implication here is that the problem to which industrial therapy for the mentally ill addresses itself is not unique to mental hospital patients. It may apply to a larger group of socially inadequate human beings with occupational handicaps from which the entrants to mental hospitals are drawn. Cumming suggests as much when he says

> we must learn to distinguish among the occupationally inadequate those handicapped persons whose psychiatric disability is playing a major part . . . we need to start experimenting with actual rehabilitation programs as a basis for developing imaginative techniques for dealing with those who have psychiatric difficulties or profound "enculturation" problems.

We now know that with help many of these occupationally inadequate and mentally ill people can and do leave the hospitals and live perfectly well in the community, making a living and participating, at least to an acceptable level, in some social life. Whether such help should be looked upon as truly rehabilitation, which connotes a return to a prehandicap level of performance or compensation from it because of residual handicaps, or should be considered as "habilitation," connoting initial learning to perform in the work and social world, is a semantic exercise. The needs of the patients are great and obvious. A variety of approaches have been developed to meet a complex of problems.

THERAPEUTIC USES OF INDUSTRIAL THERAPY

As a therapeutic instrument or as a setting for treatment, the industrial therapy unit can be used in a number of ways. For the sake of discussion, these uses may be grouped under four headings: (1) for assessment and evaluation, (2) for education and training, (3) for devising psychiatric prostheses and (4) as a setting in which techniques of dynamic intervention in the handicaps can be effective.

ASSESSMENT AND EVALUATION

The industrial therapy unit can be used for three kinds of assessment and evaluation of the patient's work ability. Its use in supplying information as to the behavior, attitude, functioning limitations of a patient to add to the psychiatric diagnostic or treatment evaluation has already been mentioned. Reaction to surroundings, tasks, fellow workers and supervisors can be directly observed and reported to therapist or evaluative team. A second form of evaluation frequently desired is some prognosis as to the rehabilitation potential of the patient. A third use is assessment of progress with a view to modifying the effective elements of the industrial therapy itself.

Many case examples can be given of the additional dimensions to medical-social diagnosis and treatment plans that are supplied from observation in an industrial therapy program. Mood swings become more noticeable; the effect of hallucinatory experience upon performance can be observed; hypochondriacal complaints can be noted, etc. The fragile nature of the remission of symptoms of some patients who look good in the structured and highly protected ward life of the hospital can be quickly unveiled in the industrial therapy setting. On the other hand, unsuspected ego strengths show up for some chronic patients in industrial therapy that are just not obvious upon clinical examination.

Along with its use in supplying clinical information for diagnostic or treatment assessment, the industrial therapy program offers an important resource to the psychiatrist evaluating employability after psychiatric illness. The American Medical Association's Councils on Occupational Health and on Mental Health have issued a guide for this purpose.[77] Among the 12 factors they list as "bearing on employment" are "on-the-job stress," "rehabilitation," "after-effects," and "placement and transfer." Generally, neither the family physician nor the treating psychiatrist can be in possession of facts about the patient's job world. Information from the trial in industrial therapy can be quite significant. The positive experience of Altro Health and Rehabilitation Services[19,91] and other rehabilitation centers and sheltered workshops with "work classification" for cardiac patients makes a convincing argument for this type of use for mental patients as well.

Vocational rehabilitation professionals have for many years been intrigued with the idea of devising a method of measuring a handicapped person's potential for benefiting from a rehabilitation program and returning to work. Psychometric devices and job analyses have been borrowed from industrial psychology and modified. Systems of "work-sampling" have been designed by the rehabilitation field, and various "situational" assessment methods have been more recently proposed. Walter S. Neff[124] has prepared a lucid summary of the strengths and disadvantages of each of these approaches.

Psychometric tests as instruments to evaluate a person's potential to work have the advantage of being quick to administer, easy to use and of objectivity and reliability. Unfortunately, they have very low predictive validity. Neff[125] concludes that

> The psychometric tests become entirely inappropriate when our problem is to appraise the work potential of an ex-mental patient with long-term hospitalization, a borderline mental retardate with no work history, or a socially and culturally disadvantaged school dropout.

Neff does believe, though, that

> If what we need is a mass screening device that will enable us to select for certain kinds of employment those persons who possess a necessary minimum of certain abilities, then certain of the psychometric tests may serve reasonably well.

For readers who may be interested, two of the most frequently used tests for this purpose have been those of Kuder and Strong.[104] Two more recent attempts have been the psychomotor test battery designed at Vermont State Hospital,[36] with its modification by the Chicago Jewish Vocational Service[38] and the Hunter Process Index[154] developed in the social therapy program of Philadelphia State Hospital.

Recognizing the inadequacies of the aptitude and achievement tests, rehabilitation psychologists after World War II turned their attention to combining the psychometric idea with the job analysis techniques of the industrial engineers and efficiency experts. The result has been a "work-sample" approach, already referred to. Basically, a work-sample is a simulated industrial procedure, designed to require the worker to perform the same essentials of work as would be required on the regular job, but under standardized conditions. The best known example of work-sample procedure is the TOWER System,[163] originated by the Institute for the Crippled and Disabled, in New York City. TOWER stands for "testing, orientation and work evaluation in rehabilitation." In this system some 93 occupational samples have been developed in the vocational areas of clerical, drafting, drawing, electronics assembly, jewelry manufacturing, leather goods, lettering, machine shop, mail clerk, optical mechanics, pantograph engraving, sewing machine operating, welding and workshop assembly.

Since the Occupational Classifications Handbook, issued by the U. S. Department of Labor, lists thousands of titles, obviously the TOWER System provides for testing in only a relatively selective sample. This is one of the limitations of any work-sample system. The advantage of direct trial on simulated real work tasks are offset by the practical limitation in the range of kinds of work-samples available, particularly in a world of ever-changing industrial tasks. As Neff[126] sums it up,

> The virtues of the work-sample approach are its strong reality orientation, its close simulation of actual work demands, and the unparalleled opportunity it affords to observe actual work behavior in a reasonably controlled situation. It is, however, an expensive and time-consuming procedure, requiring commitment to a virtually continuous process of revision and reconstruction. Not only are there unresolved problems of reliability and validity, technical obsolescence is also a continual threat.

PREVOCATIONAL EVALUATION

Closely related to the work-sample approach, but developed out of recognition that rehabilitation centers are dealing with an increasingly severely disabled clientele, has come the "prevocational evaluation" process. The earliest proponent of prevocational evaluation was the Institute for the Crippled and Disabled,[164] quickly followed by most of the rehabilitation centers in the United States. The Federal Rehabilitation Services Administration has urged the establishment of such units in all rehabilitation workshops.

Essentially, prevocational activities are under medical direction and include the processes of medical assessment, psychological screening, developing the social and vocational history and the use of speech and hearing or other evaluations including psychiatric, as the patient's condition may require. At the Institute for the Crippled and Disabled, work-samples from the TOWER unit are used to provide a vocational component for the team review. These prevocational work-samples are under the guidance of the occupational therapist, however, who may institute changes in method or setting to try to minimize the physical handicap of the patient. At the end of the prevocational trial, a matter of two weeks to two months, the patient may move formally into testing in the TOWER unit.

The Institute for the Crippled and Disabled describes its prevocational program as serving especially (1) those with no prior work experience, (2) those who have not worked for several years, (3) those who have lack of confidence or severe anxiety or fearfulness about adjusting to a work environment and (4) those who have finger or hand disabilities and lack coordination and speed to function at work. The prevocational units serves to assist the patient to learn good work habits, punctuality, regular attendance, concentration, neatness, grooming, etc. In this it sounds very like the resocialization efforts in state hospitals in which industrial therapy may be used.

During the past decade, particularly in programs serving the emotionally disturbed and the mentally ill, a "situational approach" to evaluation has been developed. The work adjustment centers and sheltered workshops described in the last chapter have for the most part preferred the "situational approach." In this, the workshop itself rather than simulated work-samples is used as the setting for evaluation. Instead of an assessment of specific work skills, the "situational approach," says Neff,[126]

> . . . focuses on what can be called the general work personality: the meaning of work to the individual; the manner in which he relates to important other persons on the job; his attitudes to supervisors, peers, and subordinates; the roles he finds it congenial to play.

The reader will remember that the occupational adjustment centers preferred to keep to very simple bench assembly work. They were more interested in the interactions that took place in the work settings than the value of particular work skills or occupational interests. As Neff points out, it is obviously impossible to reproduce all kinds of work settings in the "situational approach." Also, the measuring devices and reporting observations require the use of vocational psychologically trained staff who are not prepared to supervise more technical industrial procedures.

> As a result, the situational assessor tends to make a virtue out of a necessity and takes the position that *any* kind of work will do, so long as it gives him an opportunity to appraise the components of the work personality.

Some of the sheltered work centers have introduced a prevocational unit into a "situational approach" workshop, resulting in much confusion of objectives, particularly for mentally ill patients. It has long seemed to this author that the basic concepts of the "situational approach" are themselves in reality "prevocational." They are designed for the marginal or inadequate worker. Beyond assessing his condition, this approach alone can do little to raise his level of job skills and his placeability in industry. For a great many years Altro Work Shops maintained that its sewing machine factory could meet all of the vocational needs of its tuberculous patients because "work hardening" (a medically oriented form of prevocational preparation) was paramount and it really did not matter what occupations the patients were interested in or likely to pursue. What was true was that so long as 70 per cent or more of New York City's industry was garment manufacturing, the sewing factory sufficed. As the labor and industry picture in New York changed, additional skill areas had to be provided.

A great deal more research is necessary before it will be possible to identify with any precision the factors that describe the "good bet" for industrial therapy. In the meantime, the greatest usefulness of the evaluative mechanisms is for continuous assessment throughout the patient's rehabilitation.

EDUCATION AND TRAINING

Industrial therapy and what has come to be known as "educational therapy" among the specialties that have erupted since World War II are quitedifferent therapeutic modalities. Still, they can work well together, particularly with industrial therapy supplying a setting in which educational services may be carried on. The work setting supplies many opportunities for remedial education. The reading of instructions, counting, paycheck recognition and the processes of quality and quantity control afford splendid opportunities to teach fundamentals of the ABC's should the patients need brush-up or initial teaching, and many patients do.

Higher educational skills can fit logically into many semi-skilled work processes. For example, while one does not have to know how to read to turn the buttons on and off on an automatic lathe, to set up the machine requires knowledge of fundamental decimals and fractions, and one who cannot read will have difficulty with a blueprint. Similarly, an IBM numeric keypunch operator needs no more than to recognize numbers; but infinite flexibility is afforded the operator who can read and work an alpha-numeric machine and punch from data that does not have to be recoded in numbers.

A progression of increasing skills in the industrial therapy shop offers unusual opportunities for in-service, on-the-job training. The techniques of combining education for the next higher job level with experience at it is an old industrial training method. Unfortunately the low level simplicity of work tasks in most industrial therapy programs has masked this possibility for all except, perhaps, the mentally retarded. Even for this group we, in this country, have not applied the training and educational efforts the Dutch have shown to be effective.

The value of combining educational with work training on the job has long been recognized in the rehabilitation of the physically disabled. It was this understanding that spun vocational rehabilitation off from vocational education in the first place, exemplified by the many state rehabilitation bureaus that are divisions of their state education departments. For the physically handicapped it has long been a principle that rehabilitation should provide them with skills above those necessary for the jobs for which they apply. The handicapped need this extra benefit if they are to win a spot in the competitive labor market on grounds other than sympathy. This principle is just as applicable to the mentally handicapped. The discharged mental patient who is familiar with heat sealing machines, pneumatic nut fastener, automatic box stapler and motor driven assembly belt, for example, does have the edge on his untrained "mentally well' counterpart applying for a bench packaging job. The machinist's helper who also can read a blueprint and who understands a milling machine set-up can apply for entry level work in a precision machine manufacturing shop rather than in a jobbing repair shop. The confidence aroused in the patient by his possession of this additional knowledge and experience represents another kind of therapeutic value.

The vocational rehabilitation field refers to the process of developing ability to function adequately on a sheltered job as "personal adjustment training." In this, the emphasis is on the variety of other skills in working than on the technical ability to produce the work itself. In addition to the interpersonal skills required, there are a variety of behaviors that make up a working man or woman, or what Gellman[67] and his associates have labeled a "work personality." These include such matters as acceptable dress and grooming, adhering to hours of work, deportment at coffee breaks and lunch hours, methods of addressing a superior, dealing with transportation to and from the work setting, etc. When one considers the disadvantaged backgrounds from which so many patients come, it can be seen that symptoms of the illness may aggravate a set of behaviors already difficult for the "middle class"-oriented job world to accept. Frequently, the actual disease symptoms appear little more than somewhat extreme "normal deviations from the norm" when the patient has learned the essentials of "personal adjustment."

The question is frequently asked as to how much training in job skills should be included in industrial therapy. As has been seen, so very few such programs call for anything other than the simplest of hand bench assemblies that there is little opportunity for teaching technical skills. It is this author's opinion, from his own experience, that to provide training in anything more complex than the entry-level positions in the semiskilled trades is not warranted. In the first place, very few patients will reach the level of ability and productivity during their sojourn in the industrial therapy program to make such training feasible. In the second place, it is unlikely that the mental health or rehabilitation center will have teachers equipped to impart such skills. Finally, it is highly beneficial for those patients who have such capabilities to take additional training in the normal technical or professional school as a further test of their ability to use the skills. Otherwise, it is as though one prepares drummers with unusual ability to beat intricate sounds but they are completely unable to desist when the music calls for other instruments.

Devising Psychiatric Prostheses

From a medical and public health viewpoint, almost all psychotics may be considered as suffering from chronic illness, no matter what the state of remission of their disease. Like the diabetic, for example, they will need periodic medical attention for the remainder of their lives. The use of the psychotropic drugs, counseling and psychotherapy may keep the disabling symptoms under control. The right combination of housing, recreation and work conditions may help to minimize the handicap.

For many patients the rehabilitation process has been able to develop supports which might actually be considered psychological analogies to the prosthetic devices created for the physically disabled. For example, there is the well-educated young man whose schizophrenia erupted while he was in graduate school. For the past 10 years, after rehabilitation, he has worked comfortably as a statistical clerk in a brokerage house. This is a job well below his educational potential but in keeping with his productive capabilities. In addition, it is in "Wall Street," and this supplies status and climate that is important to him and his family. This young man's capacities and the training in confidence he needed in order to enter the job world were learned in industrial therapy; the understanding that revealed the nature of the task for specialized job placement and the lesson he learned to avoid promotion to supervising others came from the counseling sessions provided him.

Just as with an artificial limb, the patient should be expected to try out the use of his "psychological prosthesis" under supervision, and provision must be made for followup to insure that the device or the conditions that make it operable have not changed. Obviously, the analogy between physical and psychological prostheses can quickly be stretched too far. These two points of comparison are, however, worth emphasizing. Just as the fitting and conditioning for an artificial limb is a skillful, time-consuming process based on careful observation of both medical status and experience in use, so should be the creation of the psychological support. Careful psychiatric and life history is required as well as all the observations from industrial therapy and experience from the hospital, residence or home and from counseling contacts. Secondly, a "bridge in confidence" must be supplied so that the patient will attempt to use the device. For the mentally ill the industrial therapy program can supply that "bridge in confidence."

Techniques of Dynamic Intervention

The industrial therapy setting is a good one in which to stage various treatment approaches. Among these are opportunities for reality testing, examining transference manifestations, matching choices of work to personality characteristics and manipulating closeness and distance. In addition, industrial therapy can supply the patient's needs for gratification and security. It can also supply a number of opportunities for utilizing the techniques of the group therapies.

Reality testing in the industrial therapy unit has two aspects. For many mental patients there exist unreal and often bizarre ideas as to their working abilities, either too great or too small. There may also be skewed ideas as to what the conditions of life really are in the work-a-day world. Industrial therapy, the sheltered workshop or the work-for-pay unit, represents the adult world—but with a difference. If things do not turn out as expected, the patient will not be fired. The professional counselor, psychiatrist, occupational therapist or social worker, will also be there to ease the shock. The man with grandiose ideas of his mathematical ability can be faced with his inability to add and be shifted, often at his own request, to a task in which his finger dexterity is useful. The patient who underrates his achievements can be started at lowly tasks and slowly be helped to have confidence for greater skills. Many young people who have spent years in institutions have romantically unclear ideas about working. They are inclined to run from their initial discovery that much of work is repetitive and boring. In industrial therapy, interpretation is possible as well as changes of pace or work tasks during the "personal adjustment" stage.

Every intervention of a therapist involves the relationship that has come to be known in psychodynamics as transference. Positive transference frequently gives way to negative ones; and unless these can be dealt with in the therapeutic relationship, therapy breaks off or becomes self-defeating. The patient in industrial therapy is in a setting where transference manifestations are present with fellow workers and supervisors in addition to those with his therapist. It is much less anxiety-provoking to be able to look at one's attitudes and behavior in relation to a fellow-worker than in relation to the therapist. One can afford to damage his relationship with his fellow-worker more easily than to risk anger at the much needed therapist.

We know that in this complex society of ours there are many job options for people. In many endeavors people shift from one type of work to another or from one job setting to another until a "fit" is obtained in which it is possible for them to work with acceptable degrees of comfort. Of course many factors, such as availability of work, requisite education and training, etc., determine the jobs people take. But there are persons who prefer outside to inside work, night work to daytime work, dealing with numbers to writing words, selling to clerking, handling tools to holding a pencil, etc. Some attention to these interest differences can be paid in industrial therapy. Within the limits of the variety of work to be done, attention should be given to vocational interests of the patient. Where the range in kinds of work available in the industrial therapy unit is limited, a combination with work tryouts in regular employment might be devised with the help of the state vocational rehabilitation agency. This can only be successful if the patient knows he can return to industrial therapy if his choice outside is for any reason unsatisfactory. In the extreme case, this job of personality matching comes close to the concept of "psychological prosthesis" previously described.

The value of industrial therapy as a place to manipulate closeness and distance to other human beings was mentioned in Chapter I. This "porcupine effect" in therapy can be used both diagnostically as well as therapeutically. In some of the work adjustment centers referred to in Chapter III patients are deliberately tested for their behavior in work groups and at solitary work, at tasks requiring teamwork or tasks on a production line. The resulting observations are fed into the assessment of the working personality and into recommendations for the work rehabilitation training and job placement plan.

There are great dangers in depending on the diagnostic value of "closeness behavior." There are too many variables in any particular situation to permit generalization. While it may be homosexual panic, for example, that immobilizes a young schizophrenic male assigned to work alongside a strongly masculine older man, the disabling factor might also be due to a cultural or language differential, the fear of failure, poor supervision or by real aggressiveness on the part of the working partner. The panic or immobile behavior should be dealt with in counseling or psychotherapy; shifting the patient to a work task in which the closeness is removed or diluted through participation in a group can be manipulated in collaboration with the therapist.

The normal worker usually has the capacity to engineer changes in his work arrangements or in his behavior to fellow workers so as to produce the distance or closeness he is most comfortable with. If this is not possible on the particular job, he finds the means to make a change. The mental patient does not have this capacity, and his tendency when uncomfortable is to leave the setting. Industrial therapy dropouts should be reconsidered in these terms. Some of these mentally handicapped people can be helped to acclimate to a larger range of personal closeness even if individual or group therapy is unavailing.

MILIEU AND GROUP THERAPIES

Every work setting is a group setting. The total unit is a milieu and the techniques of milieu therapy may be applied. There are groups performing the same set of tasks, groups with the same foremen, groups in the same work stations, groups at the same stage of therapeutic rehabilitation, groups with similar cultural backgrounds, similar recreational interests, etc.

Maxwell Jones[94] pointed out the therapeutic value of work groups in his experience with industrial therapy in the Belmont Hospital Social Rehabilitation Centre more than a decade ago. There the patients chose their work area in one of five groups: furniture repair, tailoring, painting and decorating, building maintenance and building construction and repair. These groups functioned with a staff member as leader, and included all of the patients assigned to the work area. Patients served as foreman, deputy foreman and timekeeper. Each group met daily in a session for open discussion. Problems about rivalries, authority, leadership, lateness and the myriad of other difficulties in social interaction were included in the discussions. Minutes of the meetings were shared with all patients and staff in the other work groups. Thus, the entire industrial therapy program became a series of therapy groups, using the now widely recognized techniques of milieu therapy. Jones made clear, however, that this conversion to group therapy has greatest relevance to short-term patients before they leave the hospital. Production-oriented work settings in the community are also a necessity for transition of patients to the world of work; these present difficulties in lending themselves to group and milieu therapy.

Many "work-for-pay" and sheltered work units in mental hospitals and mental health centers now use combinations of milieu and group therapies. This is particularly true when the industrial therapy is in proximity to a day hospital program. Altro Work Shops has for some years used therapy groups in conjunction with its work settings and for a variety of patient needs. For example, an orientation group composed of all arrivals to the Work Shops within the month meets with key therapeutic and management personnel until the major problems of introduction and "getting started" have been clarified. Groups of workers within a program (e.g., machine shop or multilith or key punching) meet regularly with a social worker, much as did Jones's groups at Belmont. In addition, the Altro program provides for formation of special groups to meet current problems. Examples of these have been groups of patients getting ready to leave the workshop who meet for a number of sessions with the vocational consultant about the problems of job hunting. There have been groups of parents of adolescent patients meeting with a social worker, a group of young unmarried women who have children, groups interested in developing recreational activities.

In addition to the specific problem solving value of such groups, there is an indirect effect in improving behavior on the job. As Oseas has pointed out in discussing work requirements and ego defects, the individual in a work group has to learn to abide by the rules of two regulatory systems: the formal one of spoken or written rules and regulations and the "unwritten standard the work group society itself establishes as a condition of group participation."[130] Participation in therapy groups aids the mentally ill patient to learn or relearn the methods of relating to peers and authority so as to manage the much more subtle second system.

Fairweather and his associates at the Veterans Administration Hospital, Palo Alto, California[59] experimented with task-oriented small groups as a means of rehabilitating chronic patients. In a rigorous experimental-control design study, a ward made up of small groups of patients having a high degree of self-government was compared to a regular hospital ward. The groups in the experimental ward were assigned work tasks in the hospital, and each group was held accountable for the performance of its members. Pay was given for the work. The study conclusively demonstrated that this small group system released patients to the community at a significantly faster rate than did the usual hospital procedures, and the patients remained in the community longer than did patients from the traditional hospital program.

One highly significant finding of the study was that in selecting patients for a group, the optimal patient-mix comprised two-thirds socially active and one-third socially inactive members. Such a group demonstrated more adequate behavior in problem solving than a more homogeneous socially active group. The implications are great of such a program for moving less adequate patients out into the community in a group with more adequate ones. Present systems have the effect of "creaming off" the more socially active and productively adequate patients, leaving a residue more and more difficult to deal with.

For all the success of experimental program over controls, some 52 per cent of the population had remained in or returned to the hospital by the 6-month follow-up. Fairweather therefore proposed moving the task group system out of the hospital.[143] A patient task group was organized in the hospital and, while there, was presented with the kind of problems it would have to face outside. The task organized was the operation of a janitorial service. After a few weeks the group moved into a community lodge and set up a small business. Leaders emerged for housekeeping, business management, etc. Gradually the group has sloughed off formal ties to the hospital's professional staff and is demonstrating a successful operation. In over a year, the lodge group reduced its rehospitalization rate to less than one third compared to over 50 per cent and two thirds, respectively, for the two control groups. With these encouraging results, there should be interest in further trial with this small group system.

In the author's experience at Altro, wise use of the group system provides for an important component of good worker-management relations in addition to any therapeutic value. The groups allow for communication of grievances, for patients to participate in many policy decisions that affect their working conditions. Especially where the staff leader is not "management" of industrial therapy, the group provides the opportunity for developing "indigenous" leadership, thereby giving the patients their own self-selected spokesmen.

MOTIVATION AND INCENTIVES

Few patients enter industrial therapy highly motivated to participate or succeed. The nature of the illness with its unrealistic expectations, the secondary gains developed while not working, the cultural unfamiliarity with the demands of the work world, all hinder the process of rehabilitation. Therefore, it is not surprising that without efforts directed toward overcoming these barriers, even the best structured sheltered work setting will be little used. Even when the patient expresses great interest in work therapy, it cannot be assumed there is motivation to build on.

> Let it be stated at the outset that verbal expression of motivation is hardly to be taken at face value. All Altro social workers have heard clients talk readily about their desire to work while finding it impossible to keep appointments, coming an hour late, somatizing, staying away from the workshop, and in many other ways obviously presenting problems in motivation. Conflicts, conscious and unconscious, take many forms and meet defenses of equally numerous types. It requires all of the special skills available to determine how and if motivation is present and can be induced.[18]

The root of lack of motivation, or of poor motivation, may lie in the patient—his illness, his past experiences with work. It may lie, however, just as much with family attitudes and values, or with cultural anomie.[112] Motivation or its lack is not a fixed condition. It is possible to arouse or increase motivation. The techniques and values already discussed offer clues to this process. The use of individual therapies (counseling, psychotherapy, the psychotropic drugs) can aid in overcoming resistances, freeing psychic energy tied up in defending against aggressive impulses, increasing family tolerance and understanding, building up norms and values. It is because dealing with motivation takes professional services in addition to the industrial therapy setting itself that effective industrial therapy must be a partnership between treatment teamwork and sheltered work. In the words of the old song about love and marriage, "you can't have the one without the other."

A few industrial therapy programs have experimented with incentive systems as a means of increasing productivity, the assumption being that productivity and motivation to work are highly correlated. Carstairs and his associates at the British Medical Research Council[44] demonstrated the effectiveness of money payments over a decade ago. "It was soon clear," they reported, that the opportunity to earn a few shillings a week was a potent incentive for long-stay patients. . . . It was noted that on pay-day even the most autistic patients would talk relevantly and sensibly about their money and would discuss among themselves the resources of the hospital shop. For a time, their delusional pre-occupations ceased to dominate their attention.

There have been attempts to modify methods of paying patients toward increasing production. Johnson, Haughton and Lafave used operant conditioning, reinforcing correct work behavior and using competition with average past performance.[93] They were able to show significant changes for the better, both in production and in work behavior. More recently a group at the Missouri Institute of Psychiatry[153] compared an operant conditioning system using tokens with direct money payments per hour. They found both systems equal in raising productivity, but, of course, direct money payments were much easier to manage.

In a study of normal workers, William R. Schriver[146] has demonstrated that many employees should be classified as "sensitive-to-approval" rather than "sensitive-to-wages." While Schriver found a direct correlation between high sensitivity to wages and productivity, this was not outstanding for workers sensitive to approval. He concludes that "output control," production norms developed by informal groups in the work force, has greater incentive effect upon those sensitive to approval. Such a finding is significant in explaining the effectiveness of the Medfield Hospital Step System referred to in Chapter III, in which awards of increasing privileges were given rather than money.[84] Goldin, Margolin and Stotsky[73] describe more recent successes in using nonmonetary incentives. They say,

> Living as we do in a society where money and prestige connote status, it is possible to regard them as the primary factors in motivating handicapped clients to perform and to reduce their dependency. However, observations carried on during the experiment strongly suggest that other factors are at times more important as incentives. For example, the interpersonal relationships between the professional staff and the rehabilitation client can in certain circumstances more strongly motivate the client than any material or nonmaterial award. Approval or disapproval of staff . . . can be of vital importance in influencing the performance of the client.

THE REHABILITATION SPECTRUM

For the most part, industrial therapy has been referred to as though it were a single entity. Actually there are as many varieties of industrial therapy as there are therapeutic settings for patients. In former years, mental patients were either hospitalized or ambulatory. It was conceivable to establish sheltered work units within the hospital or attached to an after-care clinic for those who were on "convalescent leave." Today, as has been described, there may be industrial therapy units on the wards, separately housed in the patients' treatment building, in separate quarters on the hospital grounds, in the day hospital, attached to a "halfway house," in a mental health center, in a community rehabilitation facility, in a unit of local industry. Each of these settings has usefulness for mental patients with different degrees of illness and at different times in their patient careers.

It is convenient to think of the course of treatment and rehabilitation as constituting a spectrum from hospital to community. Industrial therapy units may be introduced at any number of points along the spectrum. Each should then take on the coloration of the "treatment band" in which it is introduced. The therapeutic purposes and the therapeutic techniques utilized would vary. However, the essential principles of industrial therapy would remain constant, and as will be seen in the next chapter, its industrial and business aspects do not change. In planning rehabilitation programs in mental health services, it is useful to remember that the variety of uses for new facilities increases geometrically with their number. Thus, an industrial therapy unit in a hospital has use for patients in the hospital. Two units, one in the hospital and one in the mental health clinical center, can be used four ways, independently and in tandem. By adding a community sheltered workshop, nine permutations of use can be offered. Combining such transitional work situations with varieties of domiciliary rehabilitation, such as foster home care, hostels and halfway houses and with social and recreational services, as is done in some of the English programs, provides for very flexible treatment to meet a wide array of patients' needs.

A question that will occur to the reader by this time is whether one can reconcile the therapeutic manipulations listed in this chapter with the goals of work productivity referred to in almost every description of industrial therapy. Before answering this question, it is necessary to examine more closely the business and industrial aspects of industrial therapy.

CHAPTER V

THE INDUSTRIAL IN INDUSTRIAL THERAPY

As an organization for producing goods and services, the industrial therapy unit may be looked upon as a small business. In fact, from the point of view that rehabilitation for the world of work is best carried on in a setting that teaches real work habits and methods, the closer industrial therapy approximates many elements of a business enterprise, the more useful it becomes for therapy. It is the purpose of this chapter to examine industrial therapy as a small business or industry, for unless it is so recognized, it is unlikely to be successful in staying alive either clinically or economically.

TYPES OF WORK

Three general sources of work are available to industrial therapy units: direct manufacture of products; subcontract manufacture or assembly; service trades activities within the institution or mental health center or on contract outside. The European and American illustrations have described some of each of these. For example, direct manufacture is one characteristic of the Altro Work Shops garment plant and of the party favors factory of industrial therapy at Cheadle Royal Hospital in England. Most of the American work adjustment centers and mental hospital "work-for-pay" programs subcontract for simple bench packaging, while CHIRP, at Brockton Veterans Hospital and the Dutch shops emphasize contracting for light bench assembly. Many mental hospitals include service activities (laundry work, repair and maintenance crews, gardening, etc.) in their industrial therapy; the Palo Alto Veterans Hospital set up such a cleaning and maintenance crew to contract its services out into the community.

The moment an industrial therapy program contracts to perform work for a business organization or sets out to sell its products or services on the open competitive market, it has entered the business world. Business is a set of social organizations with entirely different goals and purposes than the therapeutic ones of the treatment center. Industrial therapy then becomes subject to conditions, regulations and laws which were set up or have evolved to meet the needs of commerce and industry. These business standards include the "rules of the market place," various wage and hour regulations, the procedures of fiscal controls, personnel practices and conditions of work, acceptable methods of quality and quantity control and the regulations for safety.

First of all, a word about direct manufacturing versus contracting. There is great appeal in manufacturing one's own product and selling it directly to the consumer. Many an industrial therapy manager who has struggled with the exigencies of assembly or packaging when the contractor sends the pieces at irregular intervals, or his source of work dries up at inopportune times, expresses desire for his own product—if he could only find the right one. As Dr. Wadsworth[170] puts it in describing Cheadle Royal,

> In the unit producing its own product, one is probably taking on more difficulties because of the problems of finding the right product both from the point of view of the range of the patients' working abilities, and the hospital's ability to find suitable markets. On the other hand, there are oportunities for designing tasks which are particularly suitable for patients. One is able to modify tasks to suit the varying abilities of the patients and so make their work easier and themselves more efficient and successfully adjusted. While more staff are required in a self-contained sheltered workshop than in a subcontract workshop, for such extra functions as tool-making, work preparation, inspection, dispatch, office work, etc., the resulting profit margin from the sale of one's own products nevertheless more than pays for such staff and may also pay or contribute to overhead costs as well as permit extra payments for patients. . . . When one is involved from beginning to end in the manufacture of the product, it does mean that one can create a variety of jobs, and, of course, the bigger one's factory becomes, the better chance there is of finding the right job for the right person. Inevitably, in subcontract work, there is a tendency for reduced choice of tasks for patients to perform, and one is much more exposed to a fluctuating market with consequently less control over supply and demand.

On the negative side, direct manufacturing has some very great dangers aside from the problem of finding the right product. First of all, there is the problem of marketing. "Marketing is the combination of business activities that direct the flow of goods from producer to consumer. Three important elements are involved in the distribution of manufactured goods. The product must be saleable, priced realistically, and merchandised intelligently."[148] Assuming that the elements of saleability and pricing are met, the industrial therapy unit still faces the problems of merchandising. As the Handbook for Sheltered Workshops[149] points out,

> Establishing a market and maintaining it requires skill, imagination, ingenuity, and the assumption of some risk. Industry pays large sums of money annually for product development, testing, promotion and many other aspects of the distribution of goods. The workshop cannot afford to approach the problems of marketing and merchandising in an amateur fashion.

In the experience of Altro Work Shops, the advances in technology of manufacture have led, on the one hand, to ever-increasing capital expenditures for newer equipment in order to stay in the price competitive race and, on the other, to the gradual elimination of low-level "fringe" tasks (thread snipping by hand, for example) that may still have therapeutic value. In a shop as large as Altro, fortunately the latter problem can be met through shifts to bench assembly contract activities. The technological cost problem, however, poses a serious threat, not so much of financing as of growth. Dr. Wadsworth hinted at the extra value in size in affording better choices of therapeutic tasks. This is true, up to a point. After a while, the very size of the industry freezes requirements for maintaining the establishment and the demands for production may counteract flexibility of assignment for therapy. It is almost an economic truism in business today that unless an industry grows larger each year, it is losing ground, particularly in sales. Growing larger can place strains on an industrial therapy program having a limit to its patient intake and particularly one in which the average productive capabilities of patients is declining with successive patient residual loads.

For these reasons, as well as the fact that "good" products to manufacture are not easily come by, most industrial therapy programs begin with and stick to contract work from industry.

WORK PROCUREMENT

Obtaining an initial subcontract to get industrial therapy started is not usually very difficult. With a focus on simple hand packaging or assembly, what is called for is contact with a number of potential customers, corporations, companies and small businesses that are likely to have work of this sort. The major selling points are that industrial therapy can supply a work force, thereby saving a company from having to hire and train temporary personnel, eliminates the use of skilled labor when unskilled labor will do, helps the company avoid unnecessary plant expansion and overhead and saves the company the cost of record-keeping for tax and other governmental purposes. Many producers of novelty items, small plastic parts and toys, on which there are large runs for short periods, are willing to use sheltered workshops and industrial therapy units for the assembly and packaging. The company supplies all of the parts and packing cartons and frequently arranges for pick-up and delivery. If the industrial therapy unit produces effectively, additional work or repeat orders will most likely come. In time, selection can be made of work most beneficial—in longer runs, better pricing, greater flexibility or range for therapy.

To be effective in procuring work, the contacts with industry must be made at a top level. Except with a few large corporations which have over the years developed a know-how in dealing with sheltered workshops (e.g., I.B.M., Western Electric), scattershot mail approaches to company purchasing agents and production managers yield poor results. The Managing Director of I.T.O. (Bristol), Ltd.,[165] succinctly advises in a leaflet "for the benefit and guidance of those interested in such matters,"

> He must make a personal approach to local industrialists and seek their aid. The support of the Senior Trade Union Officer at this stage would make his task very much easier. He will almost certainly fail if he attempts in the first instance to obtain work by writing letters or by sending out a deputy to make the first approach. Top level negotiation is most likely to succeed in the first instance. Delegation can come later. He must aim at finding at least one influential Industrialist and one highly placed Trade Union Officer willing and able to take an active and personal interest in the project. Having found such men, lean heavily on them for support and a useful industrial unit will soon be on its way.

The gentleman who gave this advice is just such an industrialist.

Even after the initial contact, the successful industrial therapy organization should keep channels of communication open with the top management level of its corporate business customers. It is the man at the top who should be conversant with the aims and goals of industrial therapy. The man on the firing line, who daily parcels out the work and receives it back in finished state, no matter how sympathetic he may be to the clinical or philanthropic aims of industrial therapy, has to place business considerations above all else—such matters as quality and delivery, for example.

At the same time, a corporation executive has suggested[111] that top level communication can be beneficial to the businessman. In speaking before the National Association of Sheltered Workshops, the president of a large plastics company told how such conversation has led to work for a number of sheltered workshops near his plant locations. This company manufactures thermal cups used by the airlines. A percentage of cups are below the quality acceptable to the airlines but are prized by nurseries for plantings. It does not pay the corporation to use its skilled labor in sorting cups for sale to the nurseries, but this turned out to be a most profitable undertaking for sheltered workshops.

An excellent reference that gives in detail guides to work procurement procedures was prepared in 1963 as a research project of the National Society for Crippled Children and Adults under grants from the Federal Vocational Rehabilitation Administration and the Easter Seal Research Foundation.[51] This manual covers such matters as industrial purchasing practices, promotional aspects of contract procurement, methods of pricing on bids and factors to be considered in accepting or rejecting contracts. The recommendations were developed after studying the actual practices in

35 sheltered workshops across the country. This author served as a member of the advisory committee to the project. In addition to this manual, the reader should turn for advice on contract procurement methods to the graduate schools of business or commerce of the universities in his area and to the local businessmen serving on the boards or advisory committees to his own or nearby industrial therapy units.

Two further notes on the issue of work procurement. This author is firmly of the belief that the increasing technology of industry and the cybernetics of automation are producing more tasks useful to industrial therapy rather than eliminating them. Many smaller runs of industrial processes remain for replacement purposes even when the newer models have been converted to automated long runs, huge quantity productions. It takes industrial know-how and ingenuity to keep abreast of the changes in business needs. With the changes in mental health services that are taking place—with shorter hospital stay and greater reliance on community-based services—this author strongly recommends a closer liaison between existing community sheltered workshops serving other disabilities and the clinical industrial therapy services for the mentally ill. In many places across the country, the work procurement process could be held as the responsibility of the sheltered workshop under a "partnerships in industrial therapy"[30] arrangement which will be discussed later.

WAGES AND PAYMENTS

WAGE AND HOUR LAWS

The examples given in previous chapters of industrial therapy programs have referred to a variety of wage payment methods. Some units pay piece-work, that is, a rate per piece of work completed. Others pay on an hourly basis, and still others pay amounts related to arbitrary standards of patient's financial needs or amounts judged to provide incentives to work or simply a splitting or sharing of whatever income is yielded by the contract being worked on. Actually, in the United States, with a few exceptions the wage rates paid to employees in an industrial therapy or sheltered workshop are governed by Federal wage and hour laws. In addition, there may be state or local laws that set higher standards. The Federal laws involved are the Fair Labor Standards Amendments of 1966 (Public Law 89-601, 80 Stat. 830)[167] and the Walsh-Healy Public Contracts Act as amended. The Walsh-Healy Act was established to apply to all workers, sheltered or not, who help manufacture, handle, assemble or ship items called for by a Federal Government supply contract which may be in excess of $10,000. Since such contracts are unlikely in industrial therapy units for the mentally ill, consideration here will be given only to the Fair

Labor Standards Act. Both Acts are administered by the Wage and Hour and Public Contracts Divisions of the United States Department of Labor.

The Fair Labor Standards Act, first enacted in 1938 and most recently amended in 1966, applies generally to employees engaged in interstate commerce or in the production of goods for interstate commerce. It puts a floor under wages that must be paid, requires weekly overtime pay and restricts child labor. At the time of this writing, the minimum wage rate is set at $1.50 per hour, with time and a half of work over a 40-hour week. The 1966 amendments make special provision for wages to handicapped workers in sheltered workshops under special certificates issued to cover

> individuals whose earning or productive capacity is impaired by age or physical or mental deficiency or injury, at wages which are lower than the minimum wage applicable . . . but not less than 50 per centum of such wage and which are commensurate with those paid non-handicapped workers in industry in the vicinity for essentially the same type, quality, and quantity of work.[138]

The administrator of an industrial therapy program which is manufacturing or subcontracting should keep in mind that, with few exceptions, most business activities today fall wholly or partly within the definition of interstate commerce. The only exceptions listed by the Wage and Hour and Public Contracts Division are "manufacture of handcraft and hand- or machine-sewn articles sold locally through fairs, bazaars, etc., and renovation of used clothing and other materials when the finished articles are to be sold at retail within the state"; also, the "selling of goods in retail establishments when there is reason to believe all the items will be sold for consumption within the state. . . ." The law also covers practically all employees in an enterprise engaged in interstate commerce, even though these employees, such as clerical, watchmen, porters, etc., may be divorced from the actual manufacturing or shipping processes.

The Fair Labor Standards Act sets additional conditions for the issuance of the special certificate for handicapped workers. The state vocational rehabilitation agency in each instance must certify to the adequacy of the rehabilitation program of the sheltered workshop applying. The employees can be carried under the special certificate at the "50 per centum" level of the standard minimum wage only so long as they are in a "training program" (maximum of 12 months) or an "evaluation program" (maximum of 6 months) or both. The training and evaluation programs also require approval of the state rehabilitation agency. In cases where an individual may require a longer rehabilitation regimen than the evaluation and training periods and is still capable of earning at 50 per cent of the minimum wage, it is possible, again with state rehabilitation agency approval, to obtain an individual special certificate stipulating a specific minimum wage below the 50 per cent standard. All special certificates are subject to annual review by the U. S. Department of Labor and, at its request, by the state rehabilitation agency.

A number of industrial therapy programs are carried on in state mental hospitals and in state schools for the mentally retarded. The provisions of the Fair Labor Standards Act do not now apply to workshops operated by a state or a political subdivision of a state. For a governmental official to assume that it is therefore not necessary to abide by the Federal minimum wage standards is to borrow future trouble. These are truly *minimum* standards, both in business practice and in rehabilitation. Undercutting them is likely to produce an inadequate program for industrial therapy and set a chain of dissatisfaction in motion with the local business community and the labor unions. It is significant that most of the programs in state mental hospitals described in this book are covered under special Federal Wage and Hour certificates.[39] The industrial therapy programs in Europe described herein are also subject to governmental standards and regulations.

WAGE RATES AND FRINGE BENEFITS

It should be kept in mind that the Federal minimum wage is but a standard. It supplies a floor below which wage rates must not fall or the spectre of exploitation of labor arises. The actual wages an individual receives while in industrial therapy should be related to the prevailing rates paid in industry for such work and to the actual productivity of the patient. This means that if the normal rate for producing "x" items per hour is $2.00 and the patient is producing "x" items in 2 hours (one-half normal productivity), he should be paid at the rate of $1.00 per hour and not at the 75 cents which is half the Federal minimum. If his productivity is actually less than 75 cents an hour, he will have to be paid "make-up" pay to bring him to 75 cents, unless the patient is eligible for one of the individual special certificates mentioned above.

Where it is possible to convert prevailing rates of pay to piece-work, or pay rate per piece, this is the easiest and preferable method of wage computation. If the going industrial rate is 5 cents per unit assembled and the patient is assembling 17 per hour, he is paid 85 cents for the hour's work. In many instances, however, the piece-work measurement is not possible. Then an hourly rate must be determined. Often called the "time rate," this amount is determined either from the prevailing rates paid normal workers in industry for the same or similar work or by time studies of the job undertaken using nonhandicapped persons. Sheltered workshops and industrial therapy programs frequently use staff members for this purpose. The productivity level produced in the time study is matched against prevailing wages for this level of work to yield either a piece-work rate or an hourly rate. Where patient-employees are shifted from one operation to another during the day and piece-work rates are not available, an average hourly rate is often used. Specific instructions for time studies and piece-work rate computations are available in several of the references quoted herein.[166]

It is generally recognized that the wages paid directly to employees do not constitute the employer's total wage bill. Social Security taxes, fringe benefits for disability insurance, health and hospitalization, Workmen's Compensation and sometimes retirement benefits are additional wage costs. The extent to which these must be included depends upon such factors as state laws, whether patients are in-patients of a hospital while in industrial therapy and whether long-term or transitional service is intended. It seems clear from the advice given state mental hospital industrial therapy programs by the Social Security Administration that patients in a hospital need not be considered as "employees," thereby relieving the unit from Social Security wage deductions. Similarly, some hospitals have been told that they need not deduct for Workmen's Compensation and disability insurance. All of this seems eminently fair for in-patients, but the issue is in doubt for out-patients and day-hospital patients, and certainly where such persons use industrial therapy programs that are community-based.

In this writer's opinion, every effort should be made to cover as many mental patients as is possible under all of the fringe benefits normal to local industry. Such treatment, in addition to its soundness business-wise, is meaningful in conditioning patients to successful occupational adjustment in the community.

SUBSIDIES TO WAGES

When a patient-employee in industrial therapy fails to be sufficiently productive to earn the minimum wage, he must be paid the difference in "make-up" pay. A number of patients, particularly those on out-patient or day-hospital status, may be unable to earn sufficiently in the industrial therapy program to meet their basic economic needs. For these workers, additions to earnings must be provided or they will have to drop out of the program and the aims of rehabilitation may well be defeated. These additional costs or "subsidies to wages" must be looked upon as beyond the normal business costs of industrial therapy.

The subsidies to bring actual earnings up to the Federal minimum wage are not really "make-up" as the business world interprets them. "Make-up" pay costs are normal during training periods for new personnel and in regular industry are expected to be made up by later increased productivity of trained personnel. In industrial therapy the productive employee is more than likely to be ready for discharge to the work-a-day world, and the industrial therapy program can never recoup the subsidy costs. The subsidies to bring family income to a minimum economic level are in reality relief costs and should be charges against public or voluntary welfare rolls or against veterans or other disability pensions.

In some states, provision has been made in welfare regulations to allow persons in industrial therapy who are eligible for public assistance to keep all or part of their earnings in addition to welfare payments. This provides a meaningful added incentive to remain in industrial therapy. The 1968 amendments to the Social Security Act[155] now provide for such "incentive pay" for welfare recipients in job training programs, possibly including industrial therapy. Patients eligible for service from the state rehabilitation agencies may also have certain living costs, over and above the costs of training and above earnings, met by direct grants-in-aid.

It is well for an industrial therapy program to have financial resources to meet wage subsidy costs for certain patients in economic crises who may not be eligible for welfare, pension or vocational rehabilitation coverage. If such resources cannot be generated by income from business production, and this is generally unlikely, assistance may have to be sought from the social services of the community.

FINANCING AND FISCAL CONTROLS

Too often, while there is much professional concern with management of the patients in industrial therapy, there is too little attention paid to financial management. The industrial therapy program that focuses its fiscal eye only on the wage rates paid the patients is headed for failure in the long run. There must be adequate concern for such matters as costing and pricing of work, valid accounting practices, provision for capitalization and the proper handling of funding of deficits.

COSTING AND PRICING

In computing the cost of manufacturing or assembling a product, a business firm includes a number of items besides the cost of labor. In a careful cost analysis the firm would add, in general, to the labor costs of producing a set quantity of the product the following items: cost of direct supervision of the labor crew; a proportion of the cost of administrative salaries; applicable costs of light, heat, rent (or building depreciation if the firm owns the premises), insurance; costs of raw materials, if the firm supplies them; costs of transporting materials and supplies and of delivering finished goods; depreciation of tools and equipment; costs of storage of raw materials and finished goods; costs of borrowing money to pay for wages, supplies and equipment in advance of receipt of payment for work done. In addition to these, a profit-making firm would include a proportion for profit, out of which stock or share owners would be paid and a reserve established for future expansion.

It may easily be seen that an industrial therapy program which accepts the customer's labor costs as a valid price to charge, on the grounds that the customer's labor is more expensive than the cost of patient-employees, may actually be pricing too low and thereby running at a loss. Where some of the costs enumerated are supplied through other sources, they are often eliminated from the pricing calculations. This is entirely valid, as for example, if the customer supplies the raw materials or loans the machines or picks up and delivers. This practice is questionable, however, where the costs are borne by the therapeutic institution as in the case of work supervision costs included in the salaries of nurses, occupational therapists or ward aides, or if the hospital supply truck makes pickups of work materials and delivers finished products.

The industrial therapy program that does not figure overhead costs in its pricing calculations or allows the shifting of valid production and support costs to the hospital or mental health center may actually be guilty of unfair business competition. If the shop is subject to the supervision of the Fair Labor Standards or Walsh-Healy Public Contracts Act, such underpricing may be looked upon by the Wage and Hour Division examiner as a violation. On the other hand, however, it is considered valid to provide a reduction in pricing where a customer is willing to accept lower standards in quality or in delivery time from the industrial therapy unit than he would from another business subcontractor. Sometimes "built-in" inefficiencies occur because of the therapeutic requirements of the work operation. The added costs resulting in time and increased supervision or special overhead are not valid charges to the customer.

As a rule of thumb, particularly for new units, or where fiscal records are not readily available for detailed costs calculations, overhead for simple bench assembly is often estimated at 100 per cent of direct labor costs. This rule has proven acceptable to the Wage and Hour Division. It is also closer to the average being used by the larger, more experienced sheltered workshops, as the report by Dolnick[52] revealed. In that study of 35 sheltered workshops, divided almost equally between small, medium and large (under $50,000 a year business; $50,000 to $100,000; over $100,000), the small shops were adding 47 per cent for overhead to their labor cost base; the medium shops, 88 per cent and the large shops, 127 per cent. It should be kept in mind that the higher overhead costing for the large workshops included costs for semi-skilled work much more expensive than the simpler work performed in the smaller shops. However, as the study points out,[53] "Any contract price based on direct labor plus approximately 50 per cent, as is the case in many small workshops, could very well be set below actual production costs."

ACCOUNTING PRACTICE

It should hardly seem necessary to point out that industrial therapy programs must have bookkeeping and accounting systems. The fact is, however, that many industrial therapy and sheltered work programs have very inadequate or nonexistent bookkeeping. Frequently the director has had no experience with financial management and the need for an accounting system does not appear pressing until the embarrassing questions occur of cost or explanation of deficit. A set of books for financial record-keeping need not be difficult to set up, nor must it be complex.

The controller for the Kenny Rehabilitation Center in Minneapolis[99] has listed five major elements in designing an accounting system for a sheltered workshop, as follows:

1. The accounting system should reflect your organization.
2. Income and cost to produce that income are related.
3. The manufacturing function should not subsidize industry.
4. Accounting and estimating procedures for manufacturing are related.
5. The cost of a unit of rehabilitation services is a major factor, but not the only factor in setting prices for these services.

Substitute "therapeutic" for "rehabilitation" in the last element and it fits industrial therapy.

With these five elements in mind, accounting help should be sought in setting up the records. An accountant familiar with systems for small businesses would be helpful. One also familiar with nonprofit enterprise bookkeeping would be even more helpful. A worthwhile guide, prepared a few years ago, may be obtained from the National Association of Sheltered Workshops and Homebound Programs. Entitled *A Manual of Standardized Accounting for Sheltered Workshops,* it suggests a chart of accounts, the basic journals to be used, and the formats for balance sheet, income and expense statements and departmental cost and income reports. A simple and straightforward set of double entry bookkeeping records will be sufficient for a beginning industrial therapy program. As an increasing variety of work is obtained, however, cost accounting methods should be introduced.[98] In no other way will it be possible to have the information on which business policy questions must be answered. Pay rates, overhead and pricing require cost accounting records showing the expenditures required by job and the income applicable.

CAPITALIZATION AND FUNDING

One of the business problems in industrial therapy given least consideration is that of capitalization. By this is meant the capital available for investment in equipment, methods, overhead, purchasing power, and credit. The industrial therapy program has to have free cash available to meet a variety of contingencies. For example, the gap of time between completing a job and receiving payment from the customer may unduly delay ability to pay wages to staff and patients. It is also not infrequent in assembly work that jobs can be only partially completed if one assembly element is delayed; then, although labor has been expended, income for paying labor is delayed until total completion. The only other alternative is for the unit to defer even beginning on a job until all parts are at hand. This will often prove uneconomical, for work demand gets "bunched up" and the shop loses flexibility.

Other common examples of the need for capital are the following:

1. Jobs in which the shop must secure the raw material itself and include the cost in its price. This type of work must be turned down unless the industrial therapy program can borrow the money needed.

2. Opportunities for buying supplies more economically in larger quantities. A letter shop should be able to stock quantities of regularly used paper instead of buying only enough to satisfy the job on hand.

3. Jobs where there is greater complexity in initial learning or the need for redesigning jigs and fixtures during the early phases must be rejected if the program cannot afford to invest money on which the potential return will come only later with increased productivity.

4. Special problems of supervision or teaching, requiring additional temporary staff, call for funding as a capital risk.

5. Investment in new equipment to increase work potentials is possible only if free money is available.

In this country the limited availability of capital funds to sheltered workshops and industrial therapy programs presents a hardship that should be overcome. In the Netherlands, as was seen in Chapter II, government assists. Here, the only avenues open are (1) including a "profit" or "surplus" amount in each job contract to accumulate a capital reserve, (2) obtaining a foundation or philanthropic grant for this purpose or (3) borrowing the money from a bank. Actually, the first and last approaches are closely related. Borrowing must be resorted to if the capital is currently required; the repayment cost plus interest charges is then included in the pricing structure. If the capital funds are for future use only, the bank interest rates may be saved. One of the advantages of having the industrial therapy organization a nonprofit corporation of its own, with a board of directors including local businessmen, is the backing and accessibility to commercial bank funding. This is usually not available to a hospital-based industrial therapy program.

Most industrial therapy programs have at least part of their "business" costs subsumed under "patient management" costs met through health and welfare funding. Thus, hospitals or mental health centers pay for direct work supervision under the nursing or occupational therapy items in their budgets. Others receive direct grants or payments for service from the community funds (Red Feather agencies), mental health service funds of the state or from state and federal vocational rehabilitation fees and subsidies. For the most part, it should be remembered, the public and private health and welfare funding makes no provision for capitalization. This kind of funding is line item and deficit funding in contrast to the business approach. Thus, an amount for depreciation of equipment is rarely included in a health agency budget—when the machine wears out, application is made for a grant to replace it. The careful consideration of the effect of decreasing equipment efficiency upon the pricing structure and ability to meet competition, so characteristic of the business world, rarely enters the health or welfare agency financial planning.

Of course it may be assumed that if nonbusiness funding can meet some of the overhead costs, then it is easier to provide for capitalization in the job pricing. This should not be overlooked.

PERSONNEL AND MANPOWER

Two groups of people are employed in industrial therapy programs: One, the patients served by the program; the other, the group of supervisors, instructors, and in some instances, nonpatients on the assembly line, who insure that the necessary supervision and training and management are attended to.

From a business standpoint, such as in discussing the Fair Labor Standards Act, the patients who work in industrial therapy must be considered in the same light as employees in industry. They are eligible for protection under the law, and their needs as workers deserve the same attention from their supervisors and from management as do those of employees any place else. It has now become a recognized standard for good sheltered workshop management that working conditions and employment practices be spelled out for patients and clients as clearly as would be expected for nonhandicapped employees. Generally speaking, such delineation of personnel practices becomes more clear as one moves from industrial therapy units within a hospital, serving patients on a ward, to industrial therapy units operated in a community for patients on ambulatory status. While the group of in-patients will not have the protection of Workmen's Compensation, liability insurances and perhaps even Social Security, all of these should be built into the operations of the community-based industrial therapy operation. Policies must be clear and consistent as to hours of work, holidays, vacation time with pay, whether overtime will be allowed and, if so, how compensated, and attention must be given to such matters as health and hospital insurance, and, for patients working in long-term or extended service workshops, the possibilites of a retirement plan.

As has been illustrated in the examples of industrial therapy programs in the earlier chapters, a variety of backgrounds and disciplines have been utilized to provide supervision for the patients. Generally speaking, it can be understood that the closer the patient is to in-hospital status, the greater is the necessity that his immediate supervision in industrial therapy come from trained personnel in nursing or occupational therapy. The farther away from the hospital base, the closer to the community, and when the type of work performed is at a somewhat higher skill level, the instructors and supervisors should be persons with business and industrial training and experience. An interesting approach has been described by Dr. Wadsworth and his colleagues at Cheadle Royal Hospital in England. They say,

> We have dealt with this by arranging a gradation from supervision by ward nurses to industrially-experienced floor supervisors. We have done this by seeing that those most handicapped patients working in the "worst" department of the sheltered workshop are handled entirely by ward nurses. The ward nurse may be given, say, a family of six to eight patients, her first duty being to get them up in the morning, dress them, see to their breakfasts, take them to the workshop and then work with them while they are there, helping and assisting them whenever necessary, to provide the most primitive form of group activity. . . . As improvement occurs, patients can be split off from the "family" to work in smaller groups and ultimately by themselves, at this stage coming directly under the charge of the factory supervisors, who ideally should themselves have had nursing as well as industrial experience.[171]

In this country there is still a difference of opinion between those industrial therapy units of the "work adjustment center" persuasion and the rest of the field as to whether supervision should be by industrially trained personnel or by vocational psychologically trained individuals. In this author's experience, the answer lies more in the intended skill levels to which patients are to be raised than in the therapeutic demands of the setting. It appears to be easier and more productive in the long run to train foremen and supervisors who have had experience in industry in the variations and approaches which will be necessary for dealing with a specialized employee force than to train professional therapeutic staff in the industrial processes and the methods of training and supervision in them.

Until very recent years almost no attention was paid to special preparation of the staff detailed to work with patients in industrial therapy. Outside of internal in-service training programs of Goodwill Industries for the physically handicapped and the National Industries for the Blind, there was no formal training available. Under the amendments to the Vocational

Rehabilitation Act of 1966, the way was opened for establishing a few college-based programs in sheltered workshop administration and supervision. These are very few at present, but it is hoped that they will increase as time goes on.

In a study financed by the Vocational Rehabilitation Administration, Dr. Everett H. Barton, Jr., analyzed the personal attributes, background qualifications, and the special training of persons working directly with handicapped clients on the sheltered workshop floor in 28 sheltered workshops serving a variety of handicapping conditions on the West Coast.[10] Three hundred and twenty-two workshop staff personnel participated, and the following are the ranking personal characteristics the study revealed as most important for effective workshop supervision:

1. Can plan, organize and schedule work well.
2. Remains patient with slow learners and slow thinkers.
3. Can speak in terms understandable to the persons with whom dealing, no matter what their education level.
4. Has good skill, and knowledge in his line of work.
5. Can keep confidential information to himself.
6. Is skillful in motivating and stimulating others.
7. Believes that handicapped persons are not basically "different" from non-handicapped people.
8. Does not lose track of organization's major objectives in day-to-day operations.
9. Can observe and report behavior impartially and accurately.
10. Strives for high quality work, believing that "a job worth doing is worth doing right."
11. Can maintain a friendly, warm interest in workers but avoids becoming emotionally involved in their problems.

Sheltered workshops and industrial therapy units which take in a variety of work to do, particularly anything higher than the simplest bench assembly, also find it necessary to have employees who are not handicapped work alongside the patients. Such "cadre" employees may be looked upon as on-the-job instructors or pace setters or, in terms of modern psychological theory, as role setters. For some kinds of work, as many as one cadre staff member to every five or six patients may be necessary in order to prevent the setting from taking on the attributes of a day hospital rather than that of a real work environment.

INDUSTRIAL OPERATIONS

New managers of industrial therapy programs, particularly if they have not had industrial or business experience, are inclined to forget that quality and quantity control are necessary elements in any industrial operation.

When work is subcontracted from industry, it is always wise to learn from the contractor the acceptable measures of quality control and to introduce these into the industrial therapy program. The cost of quality control is almost always higher in a shop dealing with the mentally ill than in one dealing with the physically handicapped. This is in part because consistency in behavior is not one of the attributes of the patient-employee. Too often inexperienced supervisors watch a patient at a task for some time and then assume that because all is going well, it will continue to do so and then discover sometime later, to their consternation, that without his necessarily being consciously aware of a problem, the patient's quality of performance has declined and work is ruined or not done. Either provision must be made for an on-going spot check by supervisory personnel or provision must be made for a testing procedure on the product before it goes into its final preparation for return to the contractor. If the latter process is used, then it is possible to have other patients do the final testing. Provision, which would be somewhat different than in normal industry, for change-over of personnel and regular spot checking would insure that batches of work do not leave the industrial therapy unit at below the quality acceptable.

Quality control is related to cost setting and to the computation of pay rates. Lack of attention to the count of amount of work done connotes a sloppy enterprise and immediately raises questions as to the economic stability of the program.

Some of the more modern programs in industrial therapy for the mentally ill have turned to the field of production engineering for help, as had a number of the programs for the physically disabled in earlier years. The aim here is the development of work processes engineered to provide the simplest and the quickest way of performing each task. Cheadle Royal Hospital[172] has perhaps considered the industrial engineering aspects of work for schizophrenic patients more fully than have other industrial therapy programs here and abroad. They point out that the pattern of schizophrenic motor behavior in a work situation should be kept in mind in planning a job. "(1) Movements should be simultaneous . . . (2) Movement should be natural . . . (3) Movements should be rhythmic. . . ." The *Handbook of Sheltered Workshops*[150] recommends that

> Almost any community able to support a workshop can call on engineering consultants to advise the workshop management and supervisors on time-motion studies and the best and most efficient operating methods. The local chapter of the American Society of Training Directors can often help to obtain such volunteer assist-ance, and other industries in the community are frequently willing to give services from time to time.

Two adages from industrial engineering are almost self-truths. One of these is that "The best way to handle materials is not to." Many people operating industrial therapy programs do not seem to be aware how the extent to which moving materials about increases their costs. The use of ward space in a hospital so far removed from the delivery point of materials that extra loading and unloading processes must take place, and in which inadequate elevator service may require lugging materials up stairs, may turn out to be so economically inefficient as to offset whatever therapeutic values the program might suggest. The second adage is that fixtures and jigs should be used wherever possible; in other words, wherever equipment is available to do the job more efficiently, it should be substituted for hand labor. Almost every industrial therapy unit will in time run into situations in which the introduction of mechanical equipment may eliminate work which has therapeutic value for certain patients. It may therefore seem more valuable in the long run to continue with older methods, even though somewhat more costly. While this may be true for a short time, in the long run it is more efficacious to find some other type of work requiring similar hand productivity to the original process and not to keep the patient-employees performing on obsolescent tasks. The lack of such basic equipment as trucks, dollies, conveyor belts, fork lifts and power-driven screw drivers, etc., is frequently related to the aforementioned inability of industrial therapy programs to provide funds for capitalization. Those beginning new industrial therapy programs should keep in mind the need for such equipment as the program grows.

PHYSICAL LAYOUT

It hardly seems necessary to refer to the need for safety precautions in an industrial therapy workshop. The Sheltered Workshop handbook recommends the following safety measures as minimum:

1. Well-marked, strictly maintained free aisle space.
2. Clean floors, uncluttered by objects which may cause stumbling or falls.
3. Orderly arrangement of all materials and objects within the shop.
4. Proper stacking of materials to eliminate the possibility of objects falling on persons.
5. Regular safety training and proper methods of lifting, carrying, bending, etc.
6. Safety devices on all machines and insistence on their proper and consistent use.
7. Adequate first aid service, with a designated and qualified staff member immediately available.
8. Thorough training of staff members and key personnel in what to do in emergency situations.[151]

In planning for the physical space layout, inexperienced managers often take into account only the working space required for the patient-employees and supervisors and do not include space for the storage of raw material and completed goods. A general rule of thumb has been developed in the sheltered workshop field to the effct that at least 100 square feet of working space per employee is a good minimal standard. This will insure that for assembly operations there will be at least space to hold the packaging and the units to be worked on.

It is also readily recognized that one of the necessary attributes of an industrial therapy program must be its accessibility to those who will use it. Industrial therapy in a state mental hospital may be ideal for patients on the hospital grounds but quite inaccessible for patients on aftercare. This may be true even though provision is made for periodic transportation of patients from the community back to the hospital for re-examination or the filling of drug prescriptions. Arrangement for clinic visits is not comparable to arrangement for daily travel to a place of employment.

INDUSTRIAL THERAPY VERSUS THE BUSINESS WORLD

It is interesting that the literature on sheltered workshops and industrial therapy programs is devoid of reference to those aspects of the business world relating to competition and customer relations, to public relations, and to the general problems of relationship with organized labor. The comments included herein are from the author's personal experience and out of his discussions over many years with those responsible for operating industrial therapy programs, both in this country and abroad.

COMPETITION AND CUSTOMER RELATIONS

Competition is a common and well-understood component of business, and industrial therapy organizations are as subject to the results of competition as is any small business. On the one hand, it is unfair practice to expect that the philanthropic or welfare nature of industrial therapy should give it preference in contracting from some industry over some profit-making small organization doing the same kind of work. To depend upon charitable influences to establish relations with a customer is also very dangerous. Expectations arise on both sides that have little to do with price, quality of product, delivery, etc., which are the hallmarks of a successful business enterprise. The quality of the work done deteriorates, the usefulness of the industrial therapy setting as a rehabilitation program declines, and "for sake of charity" becomes substituted for "intent of rehabilitation." The industrial therapy program must see itself as in the open competitive market, having to maintain the same kind of customer relations as does a business enterprise. Regular contacts must be made with the customer, proper service must be given him, the industrial therapy program must be prepared to meet his needs and there must be the pride existing that goes with quality of product and a job well done.

PUBLIC RELATIONS

Because an industrial therapy program depends upon the support of the general community, it should institute a regular program of public relations. One or another of the following factors depends for its attainment upon adequate understanding on the part of the general public or the specialized business and professional groups representative of the more general community:

1. Referral of handicapped people to the industrial therapy program.
2. Opportunities for the placement of rehabilitative patients back into the work world.
3. Understanding on the part of industrial leaders with whom initial contact will have to be made to obtain work.
4. Appreciation of the value of the program on the part of governmental authorities who control funding.
5. General support by health and welfare leaders who control financial support through the foundations or Red Feather agencies, etc.
6. Knowledge of the program on the part of business and professional leaders to whom the industrial therapy program may want to turn for advice and guidance.
7. The support of organized labor.

LABOR UNIONS

In recent years organized labor has begun to pay some concern to the growth of sheltered workshops across the country. Some of the larger sheltered workshops represent capital investments in buildings and equipment of well over a million dollars each. Some of them have hundreds of clients working on any given day. As of March, 1967, there were 973 sheltered workshops holding Wage and Hour Certificates from the U. S. Department of Labor and employing 52,494 handicapped people.

While the total impact in terms of productivity in relation to the business and industry in the United States is infinitesimal, there had been a number of instances in which local union affiliates of the AFL-CIO charged violation of Fair Labor practices. Attention was called by the labor unions to instances in which the workshops had avoided the Fair Labor minimum, to instances in which the bidding practices on the part of sheltered workshops constituted unfair advantage, particularly when bidding against unionized firms doing the same kinds of work, and to some situations in which the right to collective bargaining had been denied handicapped people working in the sheltered workshops. In a few instances, more particularly at a sheltered workshop for the blind in Canada and at sheltered workshops doing machinery-type work on the West Coast, there had actually been strikes of the sheltered employees and supported by the local labor unions.

During 1965 and 1966, a series of meetings between representatives of sheltered workshops in the rehabilitation field and organized labor were held in Michigan, New York, New Jersey and a national meeting was called at the University of Chicago. Out of these sessions some understandings developed, and the Fifth AFL-CIO Constitutional Convention adopted a resolution on sheltered workshops for the handicapped[129] which resolved "that organized labor continue to support the sheltered workshop program wherever workshops meet the following standards":

1. Sheltered workshops should adhere to Federal and state Wage and Hour regulations, where applicable, and maintain wage standards comparable to prevailing piece-rate standards for similar work in private employment.
2. The workshop should conform to national, state and local codes and standards covering safety, health, sanitation, lighting, heating and ventilating.
3. The right of workers in sheltered workshops to organize any unions of their own choosing for purpose of collective bargaining should be recognized by the boards and administrators of sheltered workshops.
4. Sheltered workshops should not seek to deprive workers in competitive industry of their jobs by bidding for work, usually performed through normal industrial channels, on the basis of substandard wages paid to sheltered workers.
5. The policy-making boards of sheltered workshops should be representative of all community interests related to the workshops, including representatives of organized labor.

It should be kept in mind that while industrial therapy for the mentally ill presents some differences from the sheltered workshops for the physically handicapped, increasingly the support of organized labor becomes important. It may be true also that if industrial therapy units supply more extended services to mentally handicapped persons who might remain in a sheltered environment for the rest of their lives, the working conditions insisted upon by the labor movement become directly important.

BUSINESS ADVICE

A local Board or advisory committee to the industrial therapy program, including influential business people as well as labor leaders, is highly recommended. There have been a number of examples throughout this book of ways in which availability of top flight industrial and business advice can help in the successful operation of the industrial therapy program. Such a committee can be looked upon either as a component part of the business operation of industrial therapy or as a primary public relations responsibility of the program. Either way, it can make the difference between a faltering service or one soundly conceived as a small business venture.

STANDARDS AND ACCREDITATION

For a number of years, the National Association of Sheltered Workshops and Homebound Programs and the Federal Vocational Rehabilitation Administration have been working on the development of standards for sheltered workshops. This has recently culminated in the establishment of a standards and accreditation program under the auspices of a Commission on Accreditation of Rehabilitation Facilities, housed in juxtaposition to the Commission on Accreditation of Hospitals at the offices of the American Hospital Association in Chicago. Assistance for the Commission on Accreditation of Rehabilitation Facilities is provided from the Rehabilitation Services Administration of the Federal government, the Association of Rehabilitation Centers, the National Association of Sheltered Workshops and Homebound Programs, and from the National Rehabilitation Association. The commission has developed a survey and evaluation procedure by which rehabilitation programs are accredited for one or more of their service programs in the areas of physical restoration, social adjustment, vocational adjustment or sheltered employment. Interestingly enough, sheltered employment in this classification now carries the European interpretation and refers only to "permanently" sheltered workshops, or in today's parlance, "extended care facilities." Most of the industrial therapy programs described in this book would fall within the areas of social adjustment or vocational adjustment or both. Detail with regard to the accreditation procedures and their self-survey and evaluation forms may be obtained from the Commission. It is pertinent here, however, to list the eight basic standards for rehabilitation facilities which the commission looks for:[160]

A. The purposes of a rehabilitation facility shall be established and stated so as to govern the direction and character of its programs. Its operations shall be directed to the primary objective of fulfillment of these purposes.

B. The rehabilitation facility shall be organized and administered so as to effectively implement its programs.

C. The rehabilitation facility shall provide services essential to implement its programs. These services must be of high quality and effectively applied through its programs.

D. The rehabilitation facility staff shall be competent, ethical, and qualified to provide the services essential to the conduct of its programs. It shall establish and maintain personnel policies which contribute to the effective functioning of its staff.

E. The rehabilitation facility shall maintain accurate and complete records necessary to the conduct of its programs. It shall prepare and distribute reports that demonstrate and interpret the level of fulfillment of its purpose.

F. The rehabilitation facility shall manage its fiscal affairs consistent with the purposes of the organization and in accordance with sound practices and legal requirements.

G. The rehabilitation facility shall be designed, located, constructed, and equipped so as to promote effective conduct of its programs and to protect the health and safety of its clientele, staff, and equipment.

H. The rehabilitation facility shall actively participate in community planning, organizations, and programs, as they relate to rehabilitation.

It would appear that as time goes on, the condition of accreditation, whether by this national standard-setting Commission or by the individual state divisions of Vocational Rehabilitation or even by local bodies concerned with rehabilitation and sheltered work, will become a requirement for participation in governmental funding programs and for eligibility for fees for service from both public and voluntary agencies. Industrial therapy has become accepted as a component of the sheltered workshop program in the United States and will increasingly be expected to share both in the benefits and the responsibilities adhering to the field.

CHAPTER VI

BALANCING INDUSTRY AND THERAPY

Industrial therapy for the mentally ill has been described in this book both as a therapeutic endeavor and as a business type of enterprise. Actually, a good description can be made of industrial therapy from at least three points of view: (1) that it is essentially a community mental health modality, (2) that it is after all a form of social welfare and (3) that industrial therapy is a means of preserving and training manpower otherwise lost to the labor market. In the United States today it would be difficult to support still a fourth description, that it is a means of producing commodities for the assembly of which there is no other manpower available, even though this argument can sometimes be used to obtain specific work tasks for the industrial therapy shop.

As a medium in the rehabilitation of mental patients, the mentally retarded, the emotionally disturbed and the socially disadvantaged, industrial therapy and the related sheltered workshops are becoming increasingly important. The oft referred to concept of "continuity of care," now included in all the planning for comprehensive community mental health centers, falls short in practice unless there are transitional work and vocational training resources. Industrial therapy is therefore increasingly being experimented with as part of the mental health–public health network in many communities. As a rehabilitation resource, dealing with people handicapped by social and economic problems in addition to their medical and psychological ones, industrial therapy is of the highest order of social welfare. Moses Maimonides, the renowned religious scholar of the twelfth century, defined as most meritorious the charity that prevented poverty by teaching a trade or setting up in business "so that he may earn an honest livelihood; and not be forced to the dreadful alternative of holding out his hand for charity."[147] This is in essence the philosophy of industrial therapy. It is heartening in this regard to note that recent reorganization of the United States Department of Health, Education, and Welfare has brought the major welfare services as well as rehabilitative functions under a new division of Social and Rehabilitation Services.

Although each of these "faces" reveals different aspects of the program, industrial therapy is but one social institution, not three. There has to be a single physiognomy. What has been said about sheltered workshops in general applies particularly well to industrial therapy for the mentally ill.[31]

> The sheltered workshop is a socioeconomic institution that, in business parlance, deals with two products—the items it makes,

160

packages, or distributes, and the ill or handicapped people it serves. For each of these products, there are problems of demand and supply, of productivity, of quality control, of management, of personnel, of marketing and sales, of public relations. There is an eternal balance required, but in this sheltered workshop "business," the service to client comes first. However, we have learned from long and sometimes sad experience, that the adequacy of service to customer and to community often determines the preservation of service to client.

It is with the "eternal balance" that this chapter deals.

Work As Therapy; Work As Work

To a greater extent in the description of the European industrial therapy programs than is true of those in America there is reference to choosing the type of work in terms of its therapeutic value to the patients. Statements to the effect that the psychiatrist-in-charge decides upon the acceptance of work in terms of its therapeutic value must be accepted somewhat sceptically. In a very limited sense is it possible to match work tasks with therapeutic prescriptions. The instances are few where work in a photographic darkroom, for example, can be made available to the withdrawn but artistic patient, or work loading heavy trucks can be assigned to the overactive young man or the assembly of beads in pretty colors can be obtained for the overly meticulous woman. This is a concept from occupational therapy that rarely fits the industrial therapy picture.

Somewhat more likely is the opportunity of refusing work contracts of a certain type because these do not appear to have therapeutic value. This is clearly possible, however, only in its gross respects. Packaging the components for embroidery crewel work may appear unseemly for men patients, while cutting firewood may seem unfitted for the women. In one instance a large order to assemble and package hypodermic needles was refused by the director of an industrial therapy program serving narcotic addicts. While the decisions to turn away work under such circumstances may be interpreted in terms of the work's antitherapeutic value, it must be obvious that other more culturally determined issues play a larger part. The acceptance or rejection of power sewing machine work for men may be clear on therapeutic grounds if the choice be between sewing work trousers or ladies undergarments. More likely the work will be refused for men in an area where there is little likelihood of such training carrying over into employment and there are other kinds of work available; it will be acceptable in a locale where garment manufacturing is a large part of the industry and the pattern of men sewing machine operators is already established.

The true state of affairs is that most industrial therapy programs have but little choice as to the kinds of work they perform. The economics of the area in which they are located and the productive capacities of the patients for whom industrial therapy is provided determine the work done and not the therapeutic desires of the professional staff. Since work in industry is not planned for its therapeutic value for the workers, but in terms of the profits it can generate while satisfying consumer demand, work performed by industrial therapy must be viewed from the same perspective. The difference between regular business and industrial therapy lies in the balance of choice available to industrial therapy after the true state of the business issues is clear. Industrial therapy can continue inefficient processes for therapeutic reasons, providing the added costs are met from social and medical funds (or out of a "profit surplus") and are not charged to the normal operating costs of the business; a commercial venture that followed such practices would in time go bankrupt.

The problem of balancing work production against work as therapy is illustrated by some experience at Altro Workshops with a sewing finishing operation, that of snipping excess threads from finished garments. From time immemorial this had been a job for women who sat in a group and wielded scissors. Some years ago the industry developed machines so that one woman could do the former work of five. The Altro force was by this time an "extended service" group of women, getting on in years, and with no possibility of absorption into the normal garment trade. Altro therefore paced the installation of the newer machines as replacements as those women retired. The added costs in retaining the slower, inefficient process of thread snipping was recognized as a rehabilitation expense; it could not be added to the cost of the garments or Altro would have lost business competitively. In contrast, when subsequently the industry introduced a thread snipping device for the sewing machine itself, thus dispensing with the entire finishing operation, Altro followed suit, transferring the few remaining finishing machine operators to other work.

What is of particular significance here is that the determination to retain work in the one instance and to eliminate it in the other was based upon both business as well as therapeutic considerations. The final balance had to be in favor of the "human product," but without both sets of facts the choice of retaining hand finishers might have thrown an added cost burden on the business operation to its detriment or the rush to automation would have left destitute a group of women who in a rehabilitative setting were largely self-supporting.

While, for the mentally ill, work tasks cannot be readily visualized as therapeutic in the sense that certain task motions can be treatment oriented for developing muscle strength or limb motion, a fairly wide range of kinds of work should be available through industrial therapy. If as is so often the case, contract work can provide but a limited range of tasks, the hospital or mental health center is turned to. The professional staff with business guidance can exercise some "therapeutic ingenuity." Landy and Raulet[105] describe the successful placement of a former stationery engineer in the boiler room of the hospital. What must be kept in mind is that the successful utilization of work settings is both a factor of the ingenuity of the therapist and of the work supervisor. The therapeutic manager must have a cooperative business "partner" for there to be a really successful endeavor. Otherwise, the program can have no lasting power, as was seen with the use of the hospital bakery in the project of Camarrilo State Hospital and the J.V.S. of Los Angeles, described in Chapter III.

THE CUSTOMER VERSUS THE PATIENT

One of the peculiarities of sheltered work and industrial therapy is that it must deal with two customers (consumers), the one who buys the product or service and the one who stands to gain in rehabilitation from participating in its production. Both customers may be expected to benefit from high levels of productivity, good quality and speedy delivery. The optimum is rarely achieved, however, and there will be constant necessity to balance the requirements of the business customer against the needs of the psychiatric ones. Even though the best of planning has taken place, the volume of work taken has been kept consonant with the expected productivity of the patients assigned, the contractor's time table is reasonable and the tested quality of patients' work is acceptable, complications do ensue.

Generally, the following problems most frequently face the industrial therapy director with balancing the needs of his two kinds of customers:

1. Business customer problems
   a. The customer's timetable for delivery must be altered or speeded up.
   b. New procedures in assembly or packaging are introduced while the job is ongoing.
   c. Quality deteriorates or standards rise.
   d. Unforeseen problems arise in storage, delivery, or protection of merchandise.
2. Therapeutic customer problems
   a. Changes in patient management cause sudden shifts in labor force.
   b. Unexpected deterioration in quality occurs with the loss of patient workers or the addition of others.
   c. Changes in therapeutic regimen alter productive capacity.

Changes in the customer's delivery timetable are not unusual in business and industry. A slowdown occasioned by conditions outside the industrial therapy operations need cause no alarm, unless it is accompanied either by the necessity to continue storage of finished goods because the customer does not want delivery as planned, or the slowdown is accompanied by delay in payment for work done. These two conditions are frequently seen in normal business and should be handled as business usually does. For example, the costs of unusually long storage may be negotiated with the customer or alternative storage provisions must be arranged if the added merchandise encroaches upon working space. The payment problem must be negotiated with the customer, or bank loan must be arranged to provide for payment to the working force. In no instance should there be deferral of paying wages earned to convenience a business customer.

The more complicating timetable problem occurs when the customer insists upon a speedup in delivery. The usual business approaches to meeting this condition are the use of overtime work, providing incentive pay for increased production or adding to the labor force. In most instances in industrial therapy the first two approaches are not available or else detrimental to the patient work force. Almost the only recourse is addition to the labor force. The usual alternatives are admitting larger numbers from the same referral sources, including another group of patients not now covered by industrial therapy (such as opening a ward-serving unit to day-hospital patients or vice versa), or hiring nonpatient personnel on a temporary basis. Unless provision is made for increasing the supervising force at least proportional to the increase in patients and for special attention to instruction in work process, the effect of increasing the number of patients can depress the entire productivity rate below that at the start.

The better, more certain, way of rapidly increasing production is by adding nonpatients. These people require less instruction and supervision for simple work. They tend to raise the total level of production in the shop. They can be dismissed when work slackens without confusion to the therapeutic aims. Of course, this approach presupposes a supply of manpower available in the community. Certain sheltered workshops serving the physically disabled keep a file of disabled people who can be asked to join the staff as part time or temporary workers at peak load times. In others, including some of the industrial therapy programs for the mentally ill, the nursing or occupational therapy supervisory staff is expected to "pitch in" on the production line when timetable pressure increases.

Sometimes while an assembly or packaging job is in process there are changes in materials or procedures introduced which may call for different ways of working. Occasionally, in subcontract assembly, changing processes somewhere else may call for suddenly changing the work steps in industrial therapy. For example, in a job assembling watch bands to inexpensive watches, the delivery from overseas of an inferior grade of spring rods required, in the middle of production, a higher order of finger dexterity for one operation than had formerly been the case. The choices available were to (1) cease further production and give up the job, (2) shift the operation to other patients, if available, who had the dexterity, (3) let supervisors do the task or (4) bring in nonpatients. In this instance nonpatients were added temporarily while a small jig was devised so that the less dextrous patients might return to the task. In another instance in this author's experience, such a change required the employment of non-patients to complete the job, whereupon future work of this kind was can-celled since patients could not handle it satisfactorily.

In addition to the problem of supplying more storage space because of a slow down in the customer's desired delivery schedule, other problems of storage arise which pose problems to the industrial therapy program. At times, even though apparently adequate provision has been made for storage of parts, raw materials and packages, work will be offered in which the quantity or bulk requires additional space. Some compromise in use may be called for between space planned for other therapeutic purposes and the needs of industrial therapy. This calls for a real understanding of the business requirements and the alternatives available as well as clarity as to the needs of patients. While the final decision should be protective of the "therapeutic" customers, it is frequently possible to find a solution that can provide satisfaction for the "business" customer as well. An illus-tration is a situation requiring secure locked space for storing expensive parts and completed units. The only readily available space seemed to be a room reserved for patients in disturbed states. The psychiatrist-in-charge was loathe to give up this emergency space and the industrial therapy supervisor did not want to lose a very good contract job. Resolution in-volved remodeling a closet that could be spared and a fiscal plan that made funding available out of reduced insurance rates and more adequate storage fees from the customer to meet the remodeling costs.

The problems arising from changes in the patient labor force, because of shifts in therapeutic management or because of changes in behavior of individual patients, cause greater complications in industrial therapy-business customer relations than do any of the business problems just men-tioned. Decisions on the ward, in the day hospital and in the outpatient clinic often determine what the working force will look like at any given time. Even though there may be specific procedures for admission to in-dustrial therapy, and there be set working conditions and expectations of behavior, turnover may be speeded up or slowed down by purely clinical considerations. There may result a working force of greater or lesser pro-ductivity than existed when a particular job began. While this is a condi-tion of life that the industrial therapy unit must be expected to live with, all too frequently jobs are "built around" particular work forces without planning for possible change.

A high-grade assembly job in which soldering is required is accepted with patient X in mind. Halfway through the job patient X leaves, moves out on discharge to a job or becomes disturbed and his work deteriorates, and there is no patient in industrial therapy capable of the required grade of soldering. It can be highly embarrassing and can mean the loss of future work to turn back an incomplete job. Planning for alternatives in production, with the requirements of both "customers" in mind is a necessary part of the industrial therapy job.

It was pointed out in Chapter V that while the top level business officer of the firm supplying work should be aware of and sympathetic to the aims of industrial therapy, it should not be assumed that the business contact from whom the work actually is assigned (production manager, supplies or contract officer, etc.) can express any viewpoint other than a strictly business one. The contract firm's reaction to problems of slow delivery, lessened quality and the like is the businessman's, and he will expect that their resolution will be in terms of familiar business solutions. Explanations in terms of therapeutic necessity, the psychiatric syndrome or the hospital management problems are likely to be misunderstood and misinterpreted.

In this author's experience the conclusion often reached by the businessman after such explanations is that the industrial therapy unit has no business interest nor competence and is no more reliable than its individual crazy patients. Many firms then withdraw their work; a few act upon the business naiveté and take advantage by setting a lower price against willingness to absorb a possible repetition of the problem. Open contact with a senior officer of the customer firm offers a means of clarifying such misunderstandings, but there must actually be a willingness on the part of industrial therapy to better the business practice. The fact that resolution for the future may require modification of patient management procedures or the instituting of steps within industrial therapy that are unusual or costly businesswise presents the challenge of balancing industry and therapy.

PERSONNEL RELATIONS VERSUS THERAPEUTIC MILIEU

One of the goals toward which industrial therapy strives is to supply settings apart from the ward, day hospital or clinic so that patients may actually experience leaving home and treatment center to "go to work." A principle is that the industrial therapy provide real work in a real work setting. This much return to or preservation of reality for the patient is expected to be therapeutic. Illustrations were given in Chapters II and III of settings in which supervisors from the trades in industry and business emphasize this reality, and others in which professional supervision allows for varieties of groupings from isolated working to group tasks for testing out and developing socialization.

It should be recognized that the combination of physical setting and type of supervision has an effect upon the roles and status of patients placed in industrial therapy. In a program in which supervision is by nursing staff, occupational therapists, psychologists or vocational rehabilitation personnel, it is to be expected that the psychiatrically ill persons admitted will continue to be referred to as patients or at least as "clients." Even in a more generalized sheltered workshop such as Altro, the strong involvement of psychiatrists, social workers and nurses in patient management leads to description as patients and clients by the professional staff and as "workers" by the industrial supervisors. The import of the distinction in title and its consequent role definition is that patients and clients can be expected to exercise their concerns for working conditions through therapeutic techniques of participation, including use of a "therapeutic community," while workers or employees are expected to express their concerns through personnel practice committees and labor unions.

Role confusion in these terms seems to be not much of a problem for industrial therapy units dealing with inpatients or day-hospital patients of mental hospitals or community mental health centers. It will become a complicated issue as the numbers of outpatients increase and as industrial therapy provides "extended care" to persons in mental health center catchment areas. As was indicated in Chapter V, some of the larger sheltered workshops are already facing the issue of client representation in setting personnel practices and working conditions. Questions are already coming to the sheltered workshops from the Federal Rehabilitation Services Administration as to the methods employed to insure that clients have the opportunity to participate in policy affecting their life in the sheltered workshop.

Three approaches show some promise in balancing the needs of patient-workers as employees and as patients in therapy. These are the use of what has come to be called the "therapeutic community," the use of group counseling techniques and modifications of the "patient management" process.

The therapeutic community is a treatment device first developed by Dr. Maxwell Jones at Belmont Hospital in London, England.[95] In essence it requires that all staff and patients meet regularly and frequently in a form of "town meeting" to share openly and frankly their immediate past behavior and their future plans. In group, with each person having an equal vote, decisions are made on all but a very few management policy matters affecting the patient's lives, and assignments and punishments for rule infractions are meted out. The professional members of the therapeutic community can and do supply on-the-spot interpretations of behavior and attitudes as part of the discussion. They must be willing to be bound by the community decisions as much as the patients. The openness and frankness are intended to lead to trust in one another, and the force of social interaction and group pressure has been shown to lead to positive changes in patient behavior and even, in the case of psychopathic personalities, to character development.

Where a therapeutic community exists on a ward or in a day hospital from which patients are assigned to industrial therapy, the questions and issues about wages and holidays, assignments and types of work, physical working conditions and the like, can be introduced into the community discussions. If the staff members of the industrial therapy unit participate in the therapeutic community there can be direct confrontation and hopefully direct resolution of problems. If the industrial therapy staff be not included, the therapeutic community can either recommend its conclusions to the work unit or transmit its orders via the senior professional who does participate.

While the utilization of a therapeutic community to solve personnel practices problems has intriguing possibilities, it has some fundamental dangers that must not be overlooked. First of all it is unusual for industrial therapy supervisors to participate in the therapeutic community. The patients in industrial therapy rarely come all from one unit, so that the work supervisors would have to divide their time between two or more community meetings. Not all the discussion would have to do with work matters and these community meetings tend to be quite lengthy, causing undue use of scarce supervisory time away from industrial therapy. While work supervisors from the treatment disciplines might be expected to learn the techniques of the therapeutic community, it is unlikely that supervisors whose backgrounds are in business or industry would put up with the shocks to the ego, insults, strains of self-analysis, etc., required of the staff in a well functioning therapeutic community. In addition, if the psychiatrist-in-charge or other professional supervisor of industrial therapy attends the therapeutic community at which personnel policy conditions are discussed and settled he may be placed in the awkward position of making decisions in favor of his therapeutic customers without considering the needs of his business customers.

It is fair to say that the therapeutic community serves well as a medium for allowing the patients participation in their industrial therapy working conditions when most or all of the patients come from one treatment service, when most of the patients are still fairly ill or in early phases of treatment and when the work supervision is by professional staff who will participate in at least those community meetings when work issues are discussed. Since these conditions are rarely present, some modifications of approach have been tried. One is to treat all of the patient-workers and the staff as a "personnel committee-of-the-whole." This is possible only in smaller shops, and it is not very effective other than in supplying a method of communicating decisions already reached by management. Of course, a skillful professional discussion leader who has real concern for the conditions of work will be positive that the patients have had every opportunity to express their feelings and to participate in decision making. Any good trade unionist would point out that at its best this is a benign form of "company union" and at its worst a farce.

Altro Health and Rehabilitation Services has developed an approach that should lend itself to settings in which an active treatment regimen accompanies industrial therapy. In this procedure small groups of patients are formed from amongst those in Altro Workshops. The primary focus of each group, under the guidance of a social worker trained in group dynamics, is on a matter of consequence to its members, such as process of job finding, control of aggressivity, the common problems of a group of unmarried mothers, recreational needs of young men in the machine shop, proper grooming for the women. The social work leader carries no work supervisory responsibilities; the patients know that he does not set personnel policy, but they also understand that he can be an influential advocate for their point of view. In addition to group therapy or counseling about the issues of primary focus, the group does offer a medium, often a safety valve, for discussion of gripes and desires as to the conditions of work. A series of communication channels, to be discussed in the next section, insure that the feelings of patient-workers are imparted to the policy makers and that adequate interpretation of policies funnels back to the people most directly concerned. The uses of the small group approach are many. The limitations are mostly in the availability of trained group leaders.

The traditional format for providing employee participation in the decision making that affects their employment and working conditions is through a representative body of their own choosing. In nonunionized industry and in many professional service agencies this takes the form of a personnel practices committee or a management-labor committee. Such a committee may have rights and responsibilities ranging from those only advisory to management to those in performing as a bargaining committee with management. Since a number of the more progressive mental hospitals and mental health centers have developed "patient management" programs as rehabilitative devices, it would seem to be but a simple extension of these programs to provide for patient-worker representation committees in the workshops.

As in the case of the therapeutic community, the determination as to where along the spectrum from advisory to self-determination such a labor-management committee can be is in part a factor of the kinds of patients served. For sicker patients or for those with a rapid turnover the advisory form seems to work, though not, in this author's opinion, as well as the group therapeutic approaches just described. Where the patients have longer stay, there is more of an extended form of sheltered workshop and less surrounding hospital or clinical structure, some form of self-determined representation more nearly fits the goals of a real work setting with dignity for the working man.

The rub for the industrial therapy director is how much representation and how much self-determination there should be. He quickly discovers, for example, that the representative committee of industrial therapy patient-workers is a far cry from the democratically elected patient-management committee on the ward. The issues that the latter body might deal with and the modifications in conditions their decisions might call for usually require but minor changes in the hospital's administrative practices. The industrial therapy committee, on the other hand, even with seemingly minor demands, can effect major changes in productivity, costs of production, delivery schedules and other matters that affect the business operation. Suddenly even the most sympathetic industrial therapist finds himself re-acting to employee organization as the average employer reacts to labor organizing. Again the problem of balance between the objectives of busi-ness and therapy is joined. The answer, easier to enunciate than to prac-tice, is that the apparent requirements of therapy for patients are not always pre-eminent over the rights of workers. People cannot really be always treated as both by industrial therapy.

In recent discussion, the medical director of the Glostrup State Hospital in Denmark told this author of his industrial therapy program's use of a labor union format. Not only do the patient-workers there choose their representatives, but these are also accepted in the councils of the local labor union. The trade union allows for special conditions affecting in-dustrial therapy workers, affording them temporary union membership through a reduced dues system and thereby certain union protections that do not interfere with the treatment responsibilities of the hospital. Such an arrangement is intriguing but would be difficult to achieve in this country. Few unions are involved in most areas of the simple work done by most industrial therapy programs. Furthermore, two of the primary principles of trade union organization cannot be supplied by most of industrial therapy: seniority of employment and job security. Movement of a patient to higher levels and better pay is most often therapeutically determined, and is not available because of length of service. Decision for "firing" is a re-habilitation determination, and union protection of job could not apply.

A contradiction does exist between handling those in industrial therapy as patients and as employees. When considered as patients, the relationship between the workers and their supervisors takes on the configuration of dependency and supportiveness. In the terminology of professional rehabilitation counseling that relationship might be construed as between teacher and pupil, as implied for example in the concept "personal adjustment training." If the workers in industrial therapy are considered as employees, then the relationship between worker and supervisor is from the world of employment and has no parallels in the therapeutic situation and few in the educational one. The industrial therapy supervisor or director must not then be surprised to find his employees reacting to their working conditions in very much the same way as do normal factory workers. The director should not belong to that group of sheltered workshop managers for whom, as described by Terence E. Carroll "It is obvious that if workshop employees are being given a key to the pearly gates, a legup on the ladder to salvation, they are ingrates if they want an adequate wage in addition."[43]

Nevertheless, the industrial therapy leader who has had a positive experience with unions or believes firmly in the protection of working rights can do much to insure the morale level that makes both for good business and for good rehabilitation.

Conflict and Decision-Making

It should be obvious that there is really no optimum formula for balance between industry and therapy that will fit all situations. Though there can be no compromise with the therapeutic intent and goals of industrial therapy, in individual instances choices have to be made between what seem to be, and may really be, conflicting principles. Sheltered workshops and industrial therapy units have evolved some interesting structures and techniques to help preserve the balance and to minimize conflict.

In its simplest form, the side by side working together of therapy and industry has the effect of forcing solutions and compromises. In a small shop, for instance, the work supervisor and the therapist can collaborate on resolving issues that might otherwise wreck the enterprise. For example, the bringing in of additional patients to complete a task when the patient-worker assigned becomes ill may mean that the therapist has registered understanding of the importance of quality and delivery while the work manager has learned something about the nature of the illness of his workers. Together they may plan a backup system for the next time such an episode occurs. Another example that may develop because of therapeutic requirements is the willingness of the work supervisor to arrange a special configuration of work tasks to make use of or test out the abilities of a patient presenting special treatment needs. Again, the act of working together fosters resolution of possible areas of conflict.

Dependence upon such informal channels of communication becomes less productive as the industrial therapy unit grows in size. Even in the smallest unit, the lack of a formal process of conflict resolution can become disastrous if both work supervisor and therapist are not thoroughly competent each in his own field. If either one is not competent the solution of problems often becomes biased in favor of the customer with the strongest advocate and the result is either no therapy or no industry, and in the long run neither. Unfortunately, the newer and smaller industrial therapy programs often depend upon less well-trained personnel at the daily management level. They command better qualified people only as they grow larger and more complicated. If the unit director is not prepared to train his staff for their duties, then he must be sufficiently competent to make the choice necessary in each instance of conflict.

As the industrial therapy program grows larger it becomes more difficult to depend upon informal channels of communication or the autocracy (benign though it be) of the director making each decision as problems arise. Three more formal techniques have been shown to be valuable for insuring the "eternal balance" between therapy and industry. The first of these is formal training. The Dutch use state supported training schools for converting industrial supervisors into sheltered workshop supervisors (see Chapter II). There is just the beginning of such training programs in the United States at a few university locations with support from the Federal Rehabilitation Services Administration. However, the American emphasis is on the teaching of potential sheltered workshop directors; the European emphasis is upon the work managers.

The other side of the coin is the training of therapeutic staff in the processes of industrial production. Little of this is done through educational institutions. More is accomplished through forms of on-the-job training. It is sometimes helpful to provide for periods of observation in normal industry for rehabilitation counselors, occupational therapists, social workers or others from the professional disciplines who will have to work closely with patients placed in industrial therapy.

The second technique for avoiding and resolving conflict is the use of teamwork. Teamwork is a much used, often abused, basic principle of rehabilitation practice. It predicates that industrial and therapeutic staffs must evaluate and plan together to serve the best interests of the patients. Teamwork does not just happen because it is wished for, or even because the two staffs meet together. It has to be worked at, guided and nurtured to achieve the kind of working together that spells mutual regard, understanding and trust. Regular team meetings concerned with intake or progress evaluation or discharge planning or a combination of these, set the stage for communicating, sharing and solving problems.

The third technique is all too infrequently utilized. It is the use of studies, experiments and research to challenge the staffs, open their eyes and reshape their goals. If used wisely and constructively, the effect of seeing the operations through the eyes of a project can be to raise morale, close ranks in joint effort. Management studies and professional surveys in which the staffs participate together can be effective media for starting teamwork that can carry over to patient services. Closely related to the survey technique is the use of staff committees to advise management on methods of meeting problems.

Altro Workshops is a good example of an industrial therapy program which has successfully employed a variety of these techniques. Informal contacts between work management staff and therapeutic personnel occur all the time on visits of social workers or doctors to the workshops, at lunch and in the corridors, etc. On the formal level are a number of communication channels. Certain social workers have been trained to understand the work processes and serve assignments to the work stations as "industrial duty social workers." Team progress evaluation meetings take place weekly, involving both sets of staffs. Special projects, such as research into rehabilitation of adolescent schizophrenics or special attention to high-level mental retardates, demand self-scrutiny and sharing in planning approaches to meet the special needs of patient-workers. In addition, staff committees have addressed themselves to problems such as the need for restructuring a work setting for severely disabled mental patients and the educational content of training programs.

Notwithstanding all of the structure and techniques for achieving balance between industry and therapy the best that can be hoped for in the finest of settings is that kind of balance symbolized by a pendulum. A swing occurs from more of therapy to more of industry and back again. Within well defined limits the optimum is ever shifting, depending upon all the factors of patient-worker characteristics, staffing changes and business conditions already described. Every so often the pendulum swings too wide—one customer is being too greatly favored over the other. The normal techniques and methods for resolving imbalance fail to work and the problem clearly is in the lap of the top management.

In the final analysis, then, it is the director of industrial therapy who must exercise ultimate control of the program. Should this direction be by a therapeutic agent, a business manager or by some combination of both? It would appear, at least in theory, that since, as was stated at the beginning of this chapter, "the services to client comes first," the director should be from one of the professional therapeutic disciplines. In industrial therapy for the mentally ill this is usually the case. Good directors come from a wide variety of backgrounds. The programs described in this book are led by psychiatrists, psychologists, nurses, social workers, occupational therapists and rehabilitation counselors. Some sheltered workshops are managed by educators, social scientitsts or by persons from the business world. There are no hard and fast rules. The personality of the director, his goals and values and his leadership qualities are the determinants rather than his professional discipline. It may be that in time college-training programs for sheltered workshop directors will establish educational and experiential criteria for the position, as educational programs for hospital administrators have done for the hospital field.

A distinction should be made between the role of industrial therapy director, in terms of the overall program, and that of workshop manager. In this author's opinion the two positions should complement one another in supplying knowledge and experience from both the world of therapy and the world of industrial and commercial work. Ideally the director might be the therapist and the shop manager the business man. It is possible to reverse the roles; in fact, in a few excellent sheltered workshops this reversal is the case. However, it takes an unusual person from the business world who can work so smoothly with the therapeutic professional.

In their recent study of Altro Work Shops, Etzioni and Lehman[58] suggest that a theory from the sociology of organizations explains the balancing feature just discussed. They point to the needs of any unit as requiring "instrumental" and "expressive" resources. The instrumental needs grow from the need to supply the resources required by the unit's activities and to allocate these resources among its components. The expressive needs are described as "the commitment of its members to one another as members of the group (i.e., their loyalty or solidarity) and their commitment to the shared values and norms the group supports." In Altro they point to the role of workshop managers as "instrumental," while the role of the social workers is the "expressive." Of course this is an oversimplification of the variety of roles and structures that actually operate in a complex social unit, but it does go far to substantiate the thesis that only through some such dyadic leadership relationship can there be assurance that both "customers" of industrial therapy for the mentally ill will be served.

THE FUTURE FOR INDUSTRIAL THERAPY

Since the early part of the 1950's the growth of industrial therapy programs for the mentally ill has been great. In England and Wales, where but two or three such units existed in 1953, a study in 1967 revealed that 100 out of 122 mental hospitals having over 100 beds had developed industrial therapy programs.[173] In the United States the numbers of sheltered workshops serving the emotionally ill increased from less than a handful in 1955 to nearly 500 by 1965.[65] As has been indicated, a good deal of this growth, both here and abroad, has been assisted by the increased governmental funding for programs serving the handicapped. In the mental health field it has also been influenced by the trend towards more community psychiatric care. The industrial therapy and sheltered workshops have also been aided in most of the Western world by a shortage of manpower supply accompanying a very low rate of unemployment.

While some economic changes are occurring that might upset this picture, a slight increase in unemployment and a slowing of governmental funding have not as yet influenced the industrial therapy growth rate. In fact, it appears as though the impetus to develop rehabilitation services as part of modern mental hospitals and in connection with comprehensive community mental health centers will carry the growth curve upwards during the decade to come.

While it is difficult to predict what the future will bring, two trends do appear to have significance for industrial therapy for the mentally ill in the years ahead. One set of developments, from the world of therapy, has to do with successful efforts to reduce psychiatric chronicity. As prehosptial care, better community care, shorter hospitalization occur, along with newer and more potent medications, a greater number of people who suffer psychiatric breakdowns will be able to maintain their community living arrangements and their jobs. The population of patients who will remain available for industrial therapy will contain an increasing proportion of the very ill, who have also been raised to better than former functioning levels by the newer treatment efforts. Such patients will remain in the workshops a much longer time, they will require greater supporting services and a significant proportion of them will need "extended" sheltered work for the remainder of their working lives.

The other trend affecting industrial therapy is common to business and industry. Increasing automation and productive efficiency continuously reduces the number of man hours necessary to supply the world's goods. Fewer people are needed on the production lines. However, automation itself requires man hours in its "softgoods" tasks, much paperwork and programming and planning functions, many of which demand a higher order of educational preparation and skills than are likely to be supplied by the handicapped. The longer training periods required by "normal" people to fill these jobs has the effect of reducing the manpower available for the lower tasks, lower remunerative work still required. Also, the rising level of living increases the demand for service activities—the many occupations that supply the recreation, leisure time pursuits, artistic and cultural opportunities made possible by the economic changes in society.

Both of these trends bear watching for they may call for changes both in the methods of industrial therapy as well as in its work content. The small group businesses proposed by Fairweather and his associates, described in Chapter III, offer one possible approach to meeting both the change in patient population and the trend to the service trades. But one would have to protect such groups against the high rate of small business failures.

It is too early, after only a decade of real experience with industrial therapy for the mentally ill to cast the lot for any one or any few of the variations which have been described in these pages. The best that can be said at this juncture is that industrial therapy for the mentally ill is here to stay. It will become more highly professionalized as training programs for staff become better established. It lends itself to research studies and to evaluation of methods and techniques as its social structure has become more stabilized. It will become more central to treatment programs for the mentally ill and will be more clearly recognized in the public health and mental health programs of the future for its role in tertiary prevention of mental illness and the stabilization of recovery states of patients in the community.

1. Allerton, W. S.: Work Therapy Programs in Army Psychiatric Treatment Centers. Unpublished paper, 1964.

2. ——: *Ibid.,* p. 5.

3. ——: *Ibid.,* pp. 6–8.

4. ——: *Ibid.,* pp. 8–9.

5. Altro-Montefiore workshop. Tempo, May 1964. Bronx, N. Y., Montefiore Hospital.

6. Andersen, B.: Work or Support: An Economic and Social Analysis of Substitute Permanent Employment. Employment of Special Groups, No. 2. Paris, Organisation for Economic Co-operation and Development, 1966.

7. ——: *Ibid.,* pp. 20–21.

8. Babayan, E. A.: The organization of psychiatric services in the U.S.S.R. Int. J. Psychiat. Vol. 1, No. 1, January 1965.

9. Baker, A. A.: Factory in a hospital. Lancet, February 11, 1956, pp. 278–279.

10. Barton, E. H. and Barton, E. F.: The Requirements of Effective Sheltered Workshop Supervision. San Jose, California, Goodwill Industries of Santa Clara County, Inc., March 1965, p. 97.

11. Bashina, V. M.: The work capacity and social adaptation of schizophrenic patients who became ill in childhood and adolescence. Int. J. Psychiat. Vol. 1, No. 2, April 1965, pp. 248–257.

12. Beard, J. H., Schmidt, J. R. and Smith, M. M.: The use of transitional employment in the rehabilitation of the psychiatric patient. J. Nerv. Ment. Dis. Vol. 136, No. 5, May 1963.

13. Bellak, L., Black, B. J., Lurie, A. and Miller, J. S. A.: Rehabilitation of the mentally ill through controlled transitional employment. Amer. J. Orthopsychiat. Vol. XXVI, No. 2, April 1956, pp. 291–292.

14. ——: *Ibid.,* pp. 286–287.

15. ——: *Ibid.,* p. 292.

16. Benedetti, G. and Müller, C., Contemporary European Psychiatry, New York, Grove Press, pp. 329–330; 346.

17. Bennett, Freudenberg and Catterson: A survey of long-stay schizophrenic patients. Brit. J. Psychiat. Vol. 109, November 1963.

18. Benney, C.: Factors affecting motivation for rehabilitation. Psychiat. Quart. Suppl. Vol. 38, Pt. 2, 1964, p. 5.

19. Benney, C., Lawentman, L. and Vern, H.: Cardiac rehabilitation: Comprehensive service to cardiac patients in work oriented rehabilitation center. N. Y. State J. Med. Vol. 64, No. 15, August 1, 1964, pp. 1966–1970.

20. "beschützende" Werkstaatt (sheltering workshop) in contrast to "geschützte" Werkstaatt (sheltered workshop).

21. Black, B. J. (Ed.): Guides to Psychiatric Rehabilitation, A Cooperative Program With a State Mental Hospital. New York, Altro Health and Rehabilitation Services, Inc., 1963.

22. ——: *Ibid.,* p. 28.

23. ——: *Ibid.,* p. 29.

24. ——: *Ibid.,* pp. 30–31.

25. ——: *Ibid.,* pp. 69–70.

26. Black, B. J.: Industrial Therapy for the Mentally Ill in Western Europe. Bronx, N. Y., Altro Work Shops, December, 1966, p. 11.

27. ——: *Ibid.,* pp. 32–36.

28. ——: The sheltered workshop—A challenge to social welfare. New Outlook for the Blind Vol. 51, No. 7, September 1957, pp. 293–298.

29. ——: The protected workshop. Rehabilitation of the Mentally Ill. Washington, D. C., American Association for the Advancement of Science, 1959, p. 209.

30. ——: Sheltered workshops in community mental health: Partnerships in industrial therapy for the mentally ill. Rehabilitation and Health, Vol. VI, No. 8, August 1968.

31. ——: The Workshop in a Changing World. Rehabilitation Literature Vol. XXVI, No. 8. August 1965, p. 235.

32. ——: The workaday world: Some problems in return of mental patients to the community. The Patient and the Mental Hospital, Glencoe, Ill., Free Press, 1957, pp. 577–584.

33. ——: Unpublished report of visit and correspondence with Dr. Malcolm L. Meltzer, Chief Psychologist, April 1966.

34. ——: Vocational rehabilitation. In: Harry L. Lurie, (Ed.): Encyclopedia of Social Work, 15th issue, 1965, New York, National Association of Social Workers, pp. 816–823.

35. Blanco, A. and Akabas, S. H.: The factory: Site for community mental health practice. Amer. J. Orthopsychiat. Vol. 38, No. 3, April 1968, pp. 543–552.

36. Brooks, G. W. and Weaver, Jr., L.A.: Psychomotility, drugs, and schizophrenic rehabilitation. U. S. Public Health Service Reports (MY-1752), 1962.

37. Burke, J. L. and Lafave, H. G.: Rehabilitation: comprehensive and inexpensive. Dis. Nerv. Sys. Vol. 24, No. 10, October 1968.

38. Burstein, A. G., Soloff, A., Gillespie, H. and Haase, M.: Prediction of hospital discharge of mental patients by psychomotor performance: Partial replication of Brooks and Weaver. Perceptual and Motor Skills No. 24, 1967, pp. 127–134.

39. Brennan, J. J.: Standard pay or token pay for rehabilitation of mental patients. J. Rehabilitation, March–April 1968, pp. 26–27.

40. British Information Services: Rehabilitation and Care of the Disabled in Britain, RF. P. 4972, Revised, May 1965.

41. ——: *Ibid.* For a most interesting critique of Remploy's rehabilitation problems, see: Remploy workshops in England: Paradox and Dilemma, J. Rehabilitation, January–February 1964, by William Usdane.

42. Centre de Postcure et de Readaptation Sociale Agricole de l'Ouest: Inauguration 13 Mai 1963, Sous la Présidence de M. Edgard Pizani, Ministre de l'Agriculture, Domaine de Prières, Commune de Billiers—Près de Muzillac—(Morbihan).

43. Carroll, T. E.: Sin, sloth and sheltered employment. The New Outlook, March 1966, pp. 8–12.

44. Carstairs, G. M., O'Connor, N. and Rawnsley, K.: Organization of a hospital workshop for chronic psychotic patients. Brit. J. Preventive Soc. Med. Vol. 10, 1956, p. 137.

45. Cowper, William: Retirement. 1.681. In: John Bartlett, Familiar Quotations. New York, Harleyon House, 1919.

46. Cumming, J.: A memorandum on the psychiatrically impaired unemployed. Privately circulated memorandum, May 2, 1963, 7 pp. mimeo.

47. Denber, H. C. B. and Rajotte, P.: Problems and theoretical considerations of work therapy for psychiatric patients. Canad. Psychiat. Assoc. J. Vol. 7, No. 1, February 1962, p. 31.

48. ———: Ibid., p. 30.

49. ———: Ibid., pp. 25–33.

50. ———: Mental Hygiene October 1964, pp. 539–543.

51. Dolnick, M. M.: Contract Procurement Practices of Sheltered Workshops. Chicago, Ill., National Society for Crippled Children and Adults, 1963.

52. ———: Ibid., p. 48.

53. ———: Ibid., pp. 37–38.

54. Eldred, D. M.: Background and progress report. The Vermont State Hospital Project for the Rehabilitation of Chronic Schizophrenic Patients September 1957, Mimeo., pp. 2–4.

55. ———: Vermont's program for psychoneurotics. J. Rehabilitation September 1945.

56. Elton, F. G.: Work Therapy: A Medical-Vocational Rehabilitation Service, New York, American Rehabilitation Committee, Inc., 1948.

57. Esterowitz, R.: The social worker in a labour rehabilitation programme. Basic Services and Equipment for Rehabilitation Centres, Part IV of Social Work in Rehabilitation Programmes for the Disabled. United Nations, Department of Economic and Social Affiairs, 1967.

58. Etzioni, A. and Lehman, E.: Dual leadership in a therpeutic organization. Int. Rev. Appl. Psych. Vol. 17, No. 1, 1968.

59. Fairweather, G. W. (Ed.): Social Psychology in Treating Mental Illness: An Experimental Approach. New York, John Wiley and Sons, Inc., 1964.

60. Federal Office for Social Insurance: Rehabilitation in Switzerland. Berne, Switzerland, 1963.

61. Field, M. G. and Aronson, J.: Soviet community mental health services and work therapy: A report of two visits. Comm. Men. Health J. Vol. 1, No. 1, Spring 1965.

62. ———: Ibid., p. 84.

63. Frost, E. S. (Ed.): A Workshop: Industry in the Mental Hospital. Hotel New Yorker, April 22, 1965, Proceedings printed by Brockton Veterans Administration Hospital, 1965.

64. ———: Viewpoint on mental health. Verbatim transcript of television interview, Channel 31, WNYC-TV, UHF, Wednesday, March 31, 1965.

65. Gadlin, W. (Ed.): Directory of Sheltered Workshops Serving the Emotionally Disturbed 1965. VRA Project No. R.D. 1471-P, New York, Altro Service Bureau, March 1966.

66. Gellman, W.: Job adjustment of "apparent unemployables" through a vocational adjustment workshop. Workshops for the Disabled. Rehabilitation Services Series No. 371, Office of Vocational Rehabilitation, U.S. Department of Health, Education, and Welfare. Washington D. C., U.S. Government Printing Office, 1956, pp. 113–128.

67. Gellman, W., Gendel, H., Glaser, N. M., Friedman, S. B. and Neff, W. S.: Adjusting People to Work. Chicago, Ill., Jewish Vocational Service and Employment Center, Monograph No. 1, 1955.

68. Glaser, W. A.: An International Survey of Sheltered Employment. New York, Bureau of Applied Social Research, Columbia University, December 1964, multilith.

69. Gordon, N.: Unpublished report on visit in 1967 at author's request.
70. Goertzel, V., Grumer, M., Hiroto, D. S. and Moes, J. H.: Coordinating Hospital and Community Work Adjustment Services. Final Report of a Joint Study by Camarillo State Hospital and the Jewish Vocational Service of Los Angeles, July 1, 1963–June 30, 1966, VRA Project No. RD-1156, January 1967, mimeo., 67 pp.
71. ——: *Ibid.*, p. 61.
72. Goldberg, J.: Industrial (hospital) therapy in a veterans administration hospital (chest center). Dis. Chest Vol. 44, No. 5, November 1963, pp. 524–527.
73. Goldin, G. J., Margolin, R. J. and Stotsky, B. A.: Motivational factors in the rehabilitation facility. Rehabilitation Literature Vol. 29, No. 3, March 1968, pp. 66–72; 83.
74. Greenblatt, M., Levinson, D. J. and Williams, R. (Eds.): The Patient and the Mental Hospital. Glencoe, Ill., The Free Press, 1957.
75. Griffith, W. D.: An exploratory study of the establishment of a sheltered workshop at the Boston State Hospital in cooperation with a private non-profit organization. pp. 25 dittoed, May 9, 1964.
76. ——: *Ibid.*, p. 21.
77. Guide for evaluating employability after psychiatric illness. Reprinted from J. Amer. Med. Assoc. Vol. 181, September 22, 1962.
78. Guyton, P. and Griggs, F.: Coordinated program for chronic mental patients. Rehabilitation Record July–August, 1962.
79. Heering, A. H.: The Organisation of Sheltered Employment for the Mentally Defective. Mimeo Sheet #7047 63 ms. London, First Congress of the European League of Societies for the Mentally Handicapped, October 2, 1961.
80. Hollingshead, A. and Redlich, F.: Social Class and Mental Illness. New York, John Wiley and Sons, 1958.
81. How to Bring Industrial Projects into the Hospital . . . and How to Get Them Done. SK&F Psychiatric Reporter September–October, 1962.
82. Hunt, R. C.: Rehabilitation potential of the mentally ill. In Greenblatt, M. and Simon, B. (Eds.): Rehabilitation of the Mentally Ill, Social and Economic Aspects, Publication No. 58. Washington, D. C., American Association for the Advancement of Science, 1959, p. 26.
83. Hyde, R. Bockhoven, Pfautz and York: Milieu Rehabilitation for Physically and Mentally Handicapped. Providence, R. I., Butler Hospital Center, April 19, 1962.
84. Isaac, D. M. and Lafave, H. G.: An evaluation-incentive system for chronic psychotics. The Psychiat. Quart. Suppl. P. 1, 1964, pp. 1–15.
85. Industrial Rehabilitation Report for 1962. Ministry of Labour Gazette December 1963.
86. Jewish Employment and Vocational Service: A work adjustment center for disabled persons with emotional problems. Final Report, OVR Project No. 355. Philadelphia, Pa. July 2, 1962, Mimeo, 39 pp.
87. Jewish Vocational Service of Cincinnati: Project Report of the Vocacational Adjustment Center. Psychiatric disability and work adjustment, OVR Project 306. September, 1963, Mimeo, spiral bound, 70 pp.
88. Jewish Vocational Service of Essex County: Final Report, Project No. R.D. 334–359, New Jersey, Office of Vocational Rehabilitation, Mimeo.
89. Jewish Vocational Service, Milwaukee, Wisconsin: Project Report of the Employment Adjustment Center for the Emotionally Disturbed. December

31, 1960, Mimeo, spiral bound, 114 pp.

90. ——: *Ibid.*, p. 13.

91. Jezer, A.: The workshop in the coronary spectrum. J. Rehabilitation, March–April, 1966.

92. —— and Hochhauser, E.: Rehabilitation of the cardiac. Brit. J. Phy. Med. Vol. 17, No. 1, 1954.

93. Johnson, R. F., Haughton, E. and Lafave, H. G.: Behavior therapy— Use in a sheltered workshop. Dis. Nerv. Sys. Vol. 26, No. 6, June 1965, pp. 350–354.

94. Jones, M.: Social rehabilitation with emphasis on work therapy as a form of group therapy. Brit. J. Med. Psych. No. 33, 1960, pp. 67–71.

95. ——: The Therapeutic Community. New York, Basic Books, 1953.

96. —— and Stoller, A.: Rehabilitation in Psychiatry. World Health Organization, United Nations, monograph (in English only), WHO/Ment/30, July 7, 1952, Mimeo.

97. Katz, A. H.: Poland's self-help rehabilitation program. Rehabilitation Record Vol. 5, No. 3, May–June 1964, pp. 30–32.

98. Kimberly, J. R.: The Financial Structure of Sheltered Workshops. Organization and Administration of Sheltered Workshops: Research Report Series, No. 3. Cornell University Rehabilitation Research Institute, June 1968.

99. Kovener, R. R.: Budgeting and accounting bookkeeping practices. Workshops at the Crossroads. Proceedings, NASWHP Annual Meeting, November 1964. Washington, D. C., National Association of Sheltered Workshops and Homebound Programs, Inc., 1965, p. 55.

100. Knudson, A. B. C.: Rehabilitation of the mentally ill in the veterans administration. In: Greenblatt, M. and Simon, B. (Eds.): Rehabilitation of the Mentally Ill, Social and Economic Aspects. Washington, D. C., American Association for the Advancement of Sciences, Publication No. 58, 1959, pp. 141–146.

101. ——: *Ibid.*, p. 142.

102. ——: *Ibid.*, pp. 144–145.

103. Koltuv, M. and Neff, W. S.: The comprehensive rehabilitation center: Its role and realm in psychiatric rehabilitation. Comm. Men. Health J. Vol. 4, No. 3, June 1968, pp. 251–259.

104. Kuder, G. F.: Kuder Preference Record, Occupational, Form D. Chicago, Ill., Science Research Associates, 1956; Strong, Jr., E. K.: Vocational Interests of Men and Women, Stanford, Calif., Stanford University Press, 1943.

105. Landy, D. and Raulet, H.: The hospital work program. Rehabilitation of the Mentally Ill, Publication No. 58, Washington, D. C., American Association for the Advancement of Science, 1959, pp. 85–86.

106. Langfeldt, G.: Contemporary European Psychiatry, New York, Grove Press, pp. 229; 254–256.

107. Lee, Harold: Two rehabilitation programs for the chronic services. Second Progress Report, NIMH Grant OM-547-2, Medfield Foundation, Inc., 1963, 23 pp. dittoed.

108. ——: *Ibid.*, pp. 5–6.

109. Meriwether, James B. and Millgate, Michael (Eds.): Lion in the Garden, New York, Random House, 1968.

110. Macmillan, Duncan: Mimeographed Memorandum, dated June 26, 1964, 4 pp.

111. Mallas, A.: The place of the workshop in our economy. Workshop at the Crossroads. Proceedings of the NASWHP Annual Meeting, Philadelphia, Pennsylvania, November 1964. Washington, D. C., National Association of Sheltered Workshops and Homebound Programs, 1965, p. 71.

112. Margolin, R. J.: Impact of social systems upon rehabilitation of the disabled. A.C.T.J., Vol. 21, No. 6, November–December 1967, pp. 189–192.

113. Marx, Karl: Preface to a contribution to the critique of political economy. In: Fromm Erich: Marx's Concept of Man. New York, Frederick Ungar Publishing Co., 1961, pp. 217–218.

114. McLean, A. A. (Eds.): To Work Is Human: Mental Health and the Business Community. New York, The Macmillan Company, 1967.

115. Melehov, D. E.: Development and results of social psychiatry in the U.S.S.R. Soc. Psychiat. Vol. 3, No. 1, January 1968, p. 15.

116. Meyer, H. J. and Borgatta, E. F.: An Experiment in Mental Patient Rehabilitation. New York, Russell Sage Foundation, 1959.

117. Miller, D. H.: Report to Northern Region BSW Employment Services Committee: Dealing With Patient's Employment and Source of Support. California, Department of Mental Hygiene, 1963, Mimeo, 12 pp., p. 6.

118. ———: Worlds That Fail, Part I: Retrospective Analysis of Mental Patients' Careers. Research Monograph No. 6, and Dorothy Miller and William Dawson: Worlds That Fail, Part II: Disbanded Worlds: A Study of Returns to the Mental Hospital. Research Monograph No. 7. California, Department of Mental Hygiene, 1964 and 1965.

119. Ministere de la Sainte Publique et de la Population: Recueil des Textes Officials Intéressant la Santé Publique et la Population. Organisation du travail thérapeutique dans les Hôpitaux psychiatrique. Fascicule Special No. 58-7, January 15, 1958.

120. Ministere de la Sainte Publique et de la Population: Recueil des Textes Officials Intéressant la Santé Publique et la Population. Lutte Contre les Maladies Mentales (Organisation Départmentale Modernisation des Hôpitaux Psychiatriques Anciens). Fascicule Special No. 60-12, March 15, 1960.

121. Ministry of Social Affairs and Public Health: Sheltered Employment in The Netherlands. Head Department for Complementary Social Provisions. The Netherlands, The Hague, 1963.

122. Ministry of Social Affairs and Public Health: Overzicht Van De Sociale Werkplaatsen in Nederland. waarop dd. 30 June 1962, personen in G.S.W.— verbard werkzaam waren. Mimeo release.

123. Nederlanse Vereniging voor Sociaal Pedagogische Zorg: de Geestelijk Gendicapte Mens op de Werkplatts. Verslag van de Studiedag, March 21, 1963, The Netherlands, Arnham.

124. Neff, W. S.: Problems of work evaluation. Personnel and Guidance Journal, March 1966, pp. 682–688.

125. ———: Ibid., p. 684.

126. ———: Ibid., p. 686.

127. ———: Psychoanalytic conceptions of the meaning of work. Psychiatry Vol. 28, No. 4, November 1965, pp. 324–333.

128. New York State Department of Mental Hygiene: The sheltered workshop—A study in progress. Men. Hyg. News Vol. XXXV, No. 7, March 1965, and from report of personal visit.

129. Organized Labor and Sheltered Employment, Platform for Partnership. Guidelines Developed from Conferences Conducted by the National Institutes on Rehabilitation and Health Services, Washington, D. C., July 1967.

130. Oseas, L.: Work requirements and ego defects. Psychiat. Quart. Vol. 37, No. 1, January 1963, p. 115.

131. ———: *Ibid.*, p. 121.

132. Padula, H.: Approaches to the Care of Long-Term Mental Patients. Washington, D.C., Joint Information Service of the American Psychiatric Association and the National Association for Mental Health, 1968, p. 8.

133. ———: *Ibid.*, p. 16.

134. Paquette, A. and Lafave, H.: Halfway house. The Amer. J. Nurs. Vol. 64, No. 3, March 1964.

135. Pichot, Pierre: France, In: Bellak, Leopold (Ed.): Contemporay European Psychiatry. New York, Grove Press, 1961, p. 19.

136. Pope, Alexander: Essay on Man. Epistle ii, 1. 101. In: Sherburn, George (Ed.): The Best of Pope. New York, The Ronald Press Co., 1929, p. 128.

137. *Public Law 113*. Vocational Rehabilitation Act amendments of July 6, 1943, 78th Cong.; 57 stat. 374; 29 U.S.C. 31-31.

138. *Public Law 89-601*. 80 Stat. 830, Section 14(d) (1).

139. Readaptation. Numero Special, No. 105, Decembre, 1963, pp. 21–30.

140. Road to reality—visit to Fountain House. SK&F Psychiatric Reporter, No. 31, March–April 1967, pp. 21–23.

141. Roberts, N.: Cheadle Royal Hospital: A Bicentenary History, Altringcham, John Sherratt & Son, 1967.

142. Rush, Benjamin: Medical inquiries and observations upon the disease of the mind. Philadelphia, 1812; reprinted In: Lich, Sidney (Ed.): Occupational Therapy Source Book. Baltimore, Williams and Wilkins Co., 1948.

143. Sanders, D. H.: The effect of group membership on community adjustment: Maintaining productive groups in the community. Unpublished, 1964, Mimeo, 6 pp.

144. Santé Mentale et Lutte Contre L'Alcoolisme. L'Experiénce de Santé Mentale du 13e Arrondissement. Paris, 1964.

145. Schmidt, P., Arnholter, E., and Warner, M.: Work Adjustment Program for Disabled Persons with Emotional Problems. OVR Project No. 275, Indianapolis Goodwill Industries, August 15, 1962, Multilith, spiral binding, 104 pp.

146. Schriver, W. R.: The prediction of worker productivity. Human Organization Vol. 25, No. 4, Winter 1966, pp. 339–343.

147. Selections from Jewish literature. The Union Prayerbook for Jewish Worship, Part II, New York, The Central Conference of American Rabbis, 1957.

148. Sheltered Workshops: A Handbook; ed. 2. Washington, D.C., National Association of Sheltered Workshops and Homebound Programs, 1966, p. 33.

149. ———: *Ibid.*, p. 34.

150. ———: *Ibid.*, pp. 36–37.

151. ———: *Ibid.*, p. 37.

152. Siméon, J. D.: L'Evolution des Therapeutiques de Readaptation à l'Hôpital Psychiatrique de Lannemezan. Edité sur les Presses de l'Atelier d' Ergothérapie de l'Hôpital Psychiatrique de Lannemezan, 1962.

153. Sletten, I. W., Hughes, D. D., Lamont, J. and Ognjanov, V.: Work performance in psychiatric patients. Dis. Nerv. Sys. Vol. 29, No. 4, April 1968, pp. 261–264.

154, Smith, A., Smith, R., Sanders, R., Weinman, B., Kenny, J. and Fitzgerald, B.: Predicting the outcome of social therapy with chronic psychotics. J. Abn.

Soc. Psych. Vol. 66, No. 4, 1963, pp. 351–357.

155. (Soc. Sec. Act Amend. 1968 Incentive Wage)

156. Soloff, A.: A Work Therapy Research Center, Monograph No. 7, Chicago, Ill., Jewish Vocational Service, November 1967, Offset, spiral binding, 93 pp.

156. ——: A work therapy research center. Summary. Chicago, Ill., Jewish Vocational Service, January 11, 1968, Mimeo, 8 pp.

157. Speijer, N.: Some views on sheltered workshops for the mentally handicapped. Int. J. Soc. Psychiat. Vol. V, No. 2, Autumn 1959.

158. ——: The mentally handicapped in the sheltered workshop. Release of the Ministry of Sociale Affairs and Public Health, The Hague, November 20, 1961.

160. Standards and Accreditation Program for Rehabilitation Facilities. Flier by Commission on Accreditation of Rehabilitation Facilities, Chicago, Ill., 1968.

161. Street, D. R.: The place of work therapy in the treatment of the mentally ill. Psychiatric Studies and Projects Vol. 2, No. 12, September 1964, Washington, D. C., Mental Hospital Service of the American Psychiatric Association.

162. Therapeutic Business on Long Island. SK&F Psychiatric Reporter, No. 32, May–June 1967, pp. 19–20; also, personal visit and department documents, unpublished.

163. TOWER: Testing, Orientation and Work Evaluation in Rehabilitation. New York, Institute for the Crippled and Disabled, Rev. ed. 1967.

164. ——: Ibid., p. 35.

165. Turley, J. P.: Industrial Therapy Organisation (Bristol), Ltd. Unpublished brochure, Mimeo, 4 pp., 1966.

166. U.S. Department of Labor. Sheltered Workshops under the Fair Labor Standards Act and the Walsh-Healy Public Contracts Act. Questions and Answers Pertain to Sheltered Workshops, Wage and Hour and Public Contracts Division. QA-IND-12, WH 64-305, Mimeo., 37 pp. See also, references 51 and 147.

167. U.S. Department of Labor. Special Minimum Wages for Handicapped Workers in Sheltered Workshops. Title 29, Part 525 of the Code of Federal Regulations, Wage and Hour and Public Contracts Divisions, WHPC Publication 1249, Reprint from Federal Register July 23, 1968.

168. Vocational Rehabilitation Act as Amended Through 1965. 29 U.S.C. Ch. 4, (Sec. 31 et seq.) U.S. Department of Health, Education, and Welfare, Vocational Rehabilitation Administration, January 1966. Also Public Law 90-391, 90th Congress, H.R. 16819, July 7, 1968.

169. Wadsworth, W. V., Wells, B. W. P. and Scott, R. F.: The employability of chronic schizophrenics; A comparative study of fatiguability of a group of chronic schizophrenics and a group of hospitalized non-psychotic depressives; A comparative study of chronic schizophrenics and normal subjects on a work task involving sequential operations. J. Men. Sci. Vol. 108, No. 454, May 1962, London, pp. 300–316. Also, An experimental investigation of the qualitative differences beween the work performance of normals and chronic schizophrenics. Psychiat. Quart. Suppl. Vol. 37, Pt. 2, 1963, pp. 325–335.

170. Wadsworth, W. V., Wells, B. W. P. and Scott, R. F.: The organization of a sheltered workshop. J. Men. Sci. Vol. 108, No. 457, November 1962, pp. 780–781.

171. ——: Ibid., p. 781.

172. ———: *Ibid.*, p. 783.

173. Wansbrough, N. and Miles, A.: Industrial Therapy in Psychiatric Hospitals. King Edward's Hospital Fund for London, 1968, pp. 5 and 14.

174. Weiner, H. J.: A group approach to link community mental health with labor. Social Work Practice, 1967. New York, Columbia University Press, 1967, pp. 178–188.

175. Wilder, J.: A case for a sheltered workshop for long-term psychiatric patients. Proceedings of a Workshop: Industry in the Mental Hospital. April 22–23, 1965, New York.

176. Williams, R. H., (Ed.): The Prevention of Disability in Mental Disorders. Mental Health Monograph 1, Public Health Service, U.S. Department of Health, Education, and Welfare, Public Health Service Publication No. 924. U.S. Government Printing Office, 1962, p. 16.

177. Williams, R. H.: Vocational Rehabilitation in a State Mental Hospital, Analysis of a Program. Staff Memorandum for Administrative Use, U.S. Department of Health, Education, and Welfare, Public Health Service, NIH-NIMH-10/14:300, November, 1953.

178. Wing, J. K., Bennett, D. H. and Denham, J.: The Industrial Rehabilitation of Long-Stay Schizophrenic Patients. Medical Research Council Memorandum No. 42. London, H.M.S.O., 1964.

179. ———: *Ibid.*, p. 3.

180. Winick, W.: Rationale and present status of CHIRP. Industry in the Mental Hospital. Proceedings of a Workshop, April 22, New York, Hotel New Yorker, 1965.

181. Wittkower, E. D., and Azima, H.: Dynamic aspects and occupational therapy. In: Greenblatt, M. and Simon, B. (Eds.): Rehabilitation of the Mentally Ill: Social and Economic Aspects. Washington, D.C., A.A.A.S. Publication No. 58, 1959, pp. 103–111.

182. World Commission and Vocational Rehabilitation. Rehabilitation of the Disabled in Poland. Prepared from information collected by Kazimierz Zakrzewski, New York, International Society for Rehabilitation of the Disabled, May 1962, Mimeo., 5 pp.

183. World Federation for Mental Health. Industrial rehabilitation of the physically and mentally disabled. A Special Report from the United Kingdom, (WFMH/IC/10/64/456).

184. World Veterans Federation. International Seminar on Employment of the Disabled. Paris (Ed.). Printed for the International Labour Office in Yugoslavia, 1960.

185. Wortis, J. and Freundlich, D.: Psychiatric work therapy in the Soviet Union. Amer. J. Psychiat. Vol. 121, No. 2, August 1964.

186. ———: *Ibid.*, p. 124.

187. ———: *Ibid.*, pp. 125–126.

INDEX